Time Travels
Exploration of Lives Remembered

Copyright © 2018 by Barbara Becker

All rights reserved. No part of this book may be reproduced in any form on by an electronic or mechanical means, including information storage and retrieval systems, without permission in writing from the publisher, except by a reviewer who may quote brief passages in a review.

Typesetting and Cover Design by FormattingExperts.com

First Edition 2018
ISBN 978-0-9787700-0-6

Published by Barbara Becker Books
United States

CONTENTS

Dedication ix
Foreword xi
Acknowledgments xiii
Introduction xv
1. The Legacy of Dolores Cannon 1
2. My Two QHHT® Sessions 5
    September 2013, First Session 5
    My Second QHHT® Session: Choosing to Incarnate . 11
3. Becoming a QHHT® Practitioner 15
4. The Portal 23
5. Multi-Planetary Ambassador and Parallel Life as a Reptilian . . 31
6. The Noxious Odor 37
7. Punished for Saving Jesus 41
8. Multiple Sclerosis For Protection 45
9. Indigo Client, Crystal & Rainbow Children 51
10. Communicating Styles of the Higher Self 61
    The Lunar Technician at Machu Picchu 61
    Seeing the Universe at the End of Her Nose 75
    First a Guide, Then the Higher Self 80
11. The Concept of Imprints & Dragons 91
    Star Being Downloads 92
    I'm a Dragon! 105
12. Guardian of the Knowledge 111

13. Creator Beings	119
He Got the Giggles	119
Flying Creator Being	127
14. Extraterrestrial Lives and Alien Abductions	135
Clink Clink	136
Unity Consciousness	154
ET Past Life and ET Encounter in This Lifetime	167
15. Where a Soul Goes After Life on Earth	173
16. Sacred Souls	187
Talking with God About Backdrop People	190
The Human Suit	195
17. The Eternal Question: What is my Life Purpose?	201
Becoming a Healer	201
Being an Advocate for Women	204
Disperse the Knowledge	207
18. The Healing Part of QHHT®	225
Gastric Reflux and Inguinal Pain	225
Healing Heartache of Loved One Who Crossed Over	233
Insomnia	241
Knee Pain Healed	249
Breast Cancer	255
Severe Healing of Migraines and Tinnitus	257
Urinary Incontinence	258
19. Entities & Emotional Attachments	261
The Overlay of Darkness	262
Unwanted Anger	266
Many Entities	272
Encounters with Reptilians	278

20. Surrogate Healing 289
    Potty Training Accomplished 290
    Positive Change in Situation at Home 290
    Golfer Husband's Shoulder Pain 290
    Husband's Hip Pain and Smoking 290
21. Living Multiple Simultaneous Lives,
    Plus Ascension Timeline Revealed 291
22. Dolores Appears 313
    Dolores Speaks 313
    Feeling Dolores' Presence 314
    Client Sees Dolores the Night Before Her Session . . 314
    I Walked with Dolores 314
    I Saw Dolores 314
    Dolores Sits on the Bed 315
    Photos of Dolores' Signs 315
23. Beyond Quantum Healing 317
Conclusion 323
About the Author 325

Time Travels

Exploration of Lives Remembered

Barbara Becker, QHHT® practitioner of the Quantum Healing Hypnosis Technique℠ modality created by Dolores Cannon, shares session stories from her client practice. These are the stories of other lives, other worlds, and other concepts.

DEDICATION

I dedicate this book to Dolores Cannon, the creator of the Quantum Healing Hypnosis Technique^{SM}. It was Dolores who made this book possible. If it weren't for her, I would not have received my first QHHT® session in 2013, and the healing of my thyroid in that session. It was Dolores who came to me in her energy form in my bedroom on the day of her memorial service in Arkansas, and expressed her gratitude for me becoming a QHHT® practitioner.

I also dedicate this book to all QHHT® practitioners around the world. These fellow dedicated souls, continuing Dolores' work in past life regression through hypnosis, are exploring concepts and experiences from ancient history to the far reaches of the Universe, beyond space and time.

Antigravity, teleportation, time travel,
energetic DNA evolution and consciousness transformation
could create a world few of us ever even dreamed of.

—David Wilcock

FOREWORD

There are a few extraordinary Quantum Healers who have come to this work *since* the passing of Dolores Cannon whom I consider to be extraordinarily powerful and effective healers, and Barbara is certainly at the top of that list. I am certain that Dolores herself shares that opinion as well, and yes, from beyond the veil!

The first time I met Barbara Becker in person was the summer of 2015 during our fourth annual QHHT® Practitioner Reunion, the first since Dolores' passing. Exuding a strong and confident yet caring energy, Barbara met my eyes with her own. Our warm embrace felt like I was reuniting with a member of my own extended family, because, of course, this is exactly what was occurring.

One of the most powerful and extraordinary QHHT® sessions I ever facilitated was one in which Dolores herself participated, offering specific and detailed advice for the client. The jaw-dropping, miraculous, and undeniable physical manifestation of healing was, however, somewhat puzzling. So, after my jubilant client left my office, I clearly heard Dolores instruct me, "Call Barbara Becker," and so I did. Soon it became clear why. As a former surgical intensive care nurse, Barbara was able to solve the mystery of the physical manifestation I had just observed, for she had observed the identical thing in a surgical suite after she had offered some of her own Star Energy Healing to that patient!

Barbara's collection of session stories, healings, and the information brought forth in *Time Travels* allows the reader a peek into the world of a talented and connected Quantum Healer who not only brings a precise focus, but the whole of her heart energy to each of her clients. I thoroughly enjoyed reliving the magic, surprises, and discoveries Barbara and her clients experience in this book, and I am certain you will, as well.

Candace Craw-Goldman

ACKNOWLEDGMENTS

I am grateful for my editor, Kari Redfield, whose editing expertise and wise suggestions prepared my manuscript for publishing. The cover designers and interior formatters at Formatting Experts exceeded my expectations for the execution and timely delivery of their services and talents. Their professionalism and quality of work is truly amazing.

I am deeply grateful for Candace Craw-Goldman and her love and support over the years. The original QHHT® practitioner support forum that Candace created provided a means for me to learn more from other practitioners in this sacred service to humanity.

My heartfelt gratitude is extended to Dolores' daughter, Julia Cannon, for continuing her mother's legacy. I thank my QHHT® Academy instructors, Susan Spooner and Marilyn Dyke, for sharing their knowledge and skills in this modality.

I give my unending deep gratitude to Virginia, the QHHT® practitioner who facilitated my personal QHHT® sessions. She is the one who asked me to become a QHHT® practitioner, became my mentor, and encouraged me as I learned the nuances of past life regression hypnosis.

I am grateful for my QHHT® clients and their written permission to share universal information that is beneficial to humanity.

My Higher Self, known as The White One, has my love and gratitude for verifying my becoming a QHHT® practitioner is in alignment with my soul path, before I took the Level 1 course.

INTRODUCTION

In her modality, Quantum Healing Hypnosis Technique^{SM}, Dolores Cannon developed a comprehensive method where the client heals himself/herself in the deepest level of hypnosis, known as theta. The theta level of consciousness is just above the delta level of sleep. Facilitating sessions for thousands of people all over the world spanning over four decades, Dolores encountered the bigger part of us, the part she dubbed the Subconscious. This is not the subconscious we know of in psychological terms. Rather, this is the part known as the Higher Self, Inner Self, Oversoul, Higher Consciousness, Super Consciousness and so forth. We humans have given it many names; yet, it has no name. It's the part that knows everything about us—past, present, future, and much more. It's the part that has access to the book of life known as the Akashic records, and beyond.

In addition to the singular perspective of the Subconscious, it also comprises a group of beings that are responsible for us. Much like our angels and guides, the Subconscious (the abbreviated form is SC), has an infinite amount of love, compassion, and concern for us. They help us stay on our spiritual path, complete our missions and contracts, and guide us on our journey to become self realized. I know this group of beings exist, because I see them during QHHT® sessions with my clients.

This book is a collection of QHHT® session stories of my clients who found answers to their perplexing situations and life experiences. All received healing in their sessions. Healing is imparted upon the client, no matter how the session is experienced. I've had clients who couldn't relax enough to allow the Higher Self to show them what they needed to see. It didn't matter, because in the QHHT® modality, healing is occurring behind the scenes, beyond our conscious mind. For all my clients, I help them to create a unique healing experience that they will have for the rest of their lives, by listening to the recorded session over and over. This is one of the most important parts of the modality, according to Dolores. Why? Because the client receives more, each and every time they listen to their session. More healing. More downloads of information. More insights. It's a gift that keeps on giving!

In the session stories, wherever I have found universal benefit, I have included the Subconscious' parting message. I base universal benefit on what I've been hearing from my channeled healing and angel reading clients, social media comments, and people I've met sharing their common challenges such as forgiveness, worthiness, not meditating, and not understanding what's really going on in their daily experiences. Even if the Higher Self's message helps one person on the planet, then it would not be in vain. I consider a QHHT® session an investment in one's self, a form of self love.

I wrote the session dialogue differently than Dolores. Dolores used the client's first initial when the client was describing the past life scene, and when the subconscious (Higher Self) was talking with her. I made a further delineation by separating the past life part from the subconscious part (Higher Self). I have facilitated sessions where the client's guides show up in the past life portion of the session. I recognize that I can start asking questions since they are the ones that are part of the Higher Self. When this happens it can be very subtle.

For purposes of clarity, I use the term Higher Self (HS) in the session stories. The Higher Self has no name, and they don't care what identification we use. They understand we humans use words to convey acknowledgement and understanding. Also, please understand that the Higher Self doesn't always have the proper language term when describing or identifying an object, person's name, planet, etc. The Higher Self doesn't always use correct sentence structure when speaking. For this reason, unless otherwise noted, I transcribed exactly how they spoke during the session.

As you read the session stories and the information contained within them, it is up to you to decide what you believe, as with anything you read, hear, or see.

In the beginning of my QHHT® practice, I followed up to hear about the amazing results, out of curiosity. This is an individual choice for QHHT® practitioners, as they don't have to follow up with clients because the healing is either done during the session, or set up for completion. It's up to the client to follow through, listen to their session recording repeatedly, integrate the recommendations, and allow the downloads and insights to come into their minds and reality, when they are ready.

Please keep in mind that any medical or health advice from the Higher Self is for that particular client. The reader must discern and consult with their healthcare provider if the information is applicable to them. This information is not to be considered medical advice. All my clients sign a client responsibility and liability release form, outlining the nuances of the QHHT® session, such as listening to their session recording, and that all healing is self healing. Each client in this book has given me their expressed written consent to share their session story as long as I keep their name and personal identifying information confidential. I changed the names of my clients to respect their privacy.

I invite you, the reader, to come sit with me in these session stories. Experience for yourself how the Higher Self imparts wisdom, insights, and healing in the most loving and caring way. If you can glean information that may apply in your life, as most readers do, then consider this a gift for you.

1
THE LEGACY OF DOLORES CANNON

Dolores Cannon's amazing method of past life regression hypnosis, Quantum Healing Hypnosis Technique℠ (QHHT®), involves inducing an individual into the deepest level of trance hypnosis through visualization. This is the state of theta level consciousness, just above delta, also known as sleep. This type of hypnosis is natural, because we all enter the theta level twice a day. We experience it as we go to sleep, and we pass through it when we wake up in the morning or from a nap. As we go to bed at night, we start from beta, being awake, then when we turn off the light and close our eyes and lay down, we enter the alpha level of consciousness. When we drift off to sleep, we pass through the theta level, onward to the delta level. In the morning, we reverse the process back to our beta awake state. During the QHHT® session, the practitioner gently guides the client down to the theta level, through the induction script written by Dolores. It is a relaxation script filled with comfort, compassion, and love.

Dolores began hypnosis work back in the 1960s with her husband, Johnny Cannon. Johnny was in the Navy and provided hypnosis sessions to enlisted members for weight loss, smoking cessation, and other behavior modification purposes. In her first book, *Five Lives Remembered*[1], Dolores shares the amazing story of a woman who underwent hypnosis for several physical ailments. With permission of her medical doctor, she underwent several sessions with the Cannons. What surprised Dolores and Johnny was when the client's previous lives came through and shared experiences. The Cannons and the client explored five lives. This was a first, and it sparked the flame of curiosity in Dolores.

As Dolores continued to explore hypnosis with clients, she found herself talking to extraterrestrials and a group of beings that she dubbed the

---

1   *Five Lives Remembered*, Ozark Mountain Publishing, 2009

Subconscious or SC for short. Dolores considered herself the researcher, reporter, and investigator of lost knowledge. Dolores found that the SC is the part of us that can give us information to help us navigate through our lives by giving us greater insights so we can grow and learn our lessons. She stumbled upon an infinitely knowledgeable and powerful aspect of each individual that can be contacted and communicated with. This part of ourselves, as Dolores had learned, is always present with us and exists just below the surface of our conscious mind. It was during these deep level hypnosis sessions that Dolores also found that any individual can gain access to experiences of past lives they have lived.

Over her more than forty five year career, her technique has proven to be effective on thousands of people all over the world, regardless of their age, gender, physical symptoms, religious beliefs, or culture. During the last ten or so years of her life, Dolores taught people all over the world her amazing technique, with her daughter, Julia Cannon, and other wonderful practitioners by her side. Students of Dolores have experienced amazing sessions even from the very first one they facilitate.

After Dolores' passing in October of 2014, her daughter Julia took the helm to ensure the continuation and purity of the Quantum Healing Hypnosis Technique[SM]. For a historical note, prior to late 2015, QHHT® was known as Quantum Healing Hypnosis Therapy. From my understanding, to align the verbiage throughout the world and in accordance with various disciplines and legal concerns, Julia enacted the slight name change. I noticed Dolores used the term "technique" in her videos too.

Prior to the QHHT® Academy formation, a private forum for QHHT® practitioners around the world was created in 2008 to provide continuing education, a world wide support community, and a directory listing of practitioners so clients could find one in their local communities. The woman who initiated the practitioner support forum, with Dolores' blessings, is Candace Craw-Goldman, of Augusta, Kansas. Candace, a Reiki master, met Dolores in 2008. She became a QHHT® practitioner and went on to assist Dolores in events, classes, and programs.

Candace is an amazing catalyst for the expansion of the fifth dimensional experience we are all evolving into. Through her radio programs, social media platforms, film creations, and her own QHHT® practice and other healing modalities, Candace is a shining star among us. She is a workshop leader, writer, speaker, and teacher. Candace and her family-run business work hard promoting light workers and those in service to humanity through her blog, practitioner interviews, and video features. Through Candace's *QuantumHealers.com* listing resource, people are discovering QHHT® and other modalities all over the world.

In addition to the many books Dolores has written and published through her family's company, Ozark Mountain Publishing, a QHHT® Academy[2] was established to provide an academic foundation for the continuation of Dolores' work and other modalities.

In late 2015, Julia Cannon and her family's company created a new website and support forum for the Quantum Healing Hypnosis Academy. This platform also provides a method of receiving the latest news and updates from Julia, as well as a global directory listing that includes contact information for potential clients to access practitioners.

Julia Cannon continues the legacy her mother created. People who are guided to become a practitioner enroll in the courses offered at the QHHT® Academy, and begin facilitating QHHT® sessions for clients for free during the training period. With thousands of practitioners worldwide, Dolores' QHHT® legacy continues.

2
MY TWO QHHT® SESSIONS

SEPTEMBER 2013, FIRST SESSION

I drive to the camping spot I went to the previous year, where it's not publicly known that extraterrestrial beings can be contacted. There, I find the best place to park my SUV and set up my zero gravity lounge chair. It's a beautiful place deep in the woods of Northern Arizona.

I had been reading several books about the highly intelligent beings from Arcturus, known as the Arcturians. Arcturus is the brightest star in the constellation of Boötes. I've read that Arcturians contact humans through the higher dimensions, through channeling, and most notably during a person's sleep time. Through a telepathic communication, the Arcturians told me they would contact me during my sleep while deep in the woods. Although I was open to any form of the experience, I intuitively felt I would most likely have a lucid dream and remember it. This was not to be the case. They surpassed my expectation!

All alone, I set up camp and eat a late lunch, reading David Wilcock's book, *The Synchronicity Key*[3]. Feeling the bliss of being deep in nature among the tall pine trees, I feel happy and at peace. The sound of the wind blowing through the leaves feels sublime. I thank God for everything. I communicate my love and gratitude to the trees.

Sensing someone watching me, I get up and walk around the area, finding four heart-shaped rocks on the ground, three partially buried and the fourth one on top of the ground. Telepathically they tell me to take the one on top, as it is their gift for me. They must have remembered that I left two moon stones and a rose quartz stone on the large rock, shaped like an extraterrestrial being's head, as my parting gift of my brief visit here last year.

---

3 *The Synchronicity Key: The Hidden Intelligence Guiding the Universe and You*, July, 2014

It starts to rain just after I settle down for the evening. I practice my yoga meditation with the soothing pinging sound of the gentle rain on the ceiling of my tent. Afterwards, I lie down in my sleeping bag. It feels so good to be on the ground, in the woods, this close to Mother Earth. I feel like a baby at my mother's bosom, cradled in her arms, very loved, very safe. I drift off to sleep.

During the night, I wake up and look at the stars twinkling in the night sky like diamonds on black velvet. Marveling at the infinite number of sparkles, I attempt to grasp the multitude of life on distant planets. It's impossible with my human brain. I return to sleep, then wake up to the harp tones on my alarm clock in order to take my thyroid supplement, which I faithfully did at the same time each day. I have no recollection of a ship or star beings. No lucid dreams. *Nada*.

I dress, eat breakfast, and break camp, then drive the 100-plus miles back home to Wickenburg, Arizona.

NOT WHAT IT SEEMED

Later, sharing my disappointment with the psychically gifted Shaman Lance Heard[4], on the phone, I told him I didn't have an experience with the Arcturians or any other extraterrestrial for that matter.

However, I noticed a red raised area on my left outer thigh, the size of a pistachio. It didn't itch or feel uncomfortable when I touched it. I felt it meant something, but what?

I took a couple of photos of the skin anomaly for my personal documentation. Lance commented that it could be another implant. I agreed, with inner knowing.

Implants are given to humans to assist the health of the human body. We are exposed to all sorts of chemicals and substances in our environment, food, and water that can adversely affect the functioning of our cellular processes. Who gives us these implants? The Higher Self. That part of us that is merged with God/Creator Source, and at the same time, comprise a group of beings who are with us 24/7. They maintain the human form and energy systems necessary for us to occupy these vessels.

I was guided to call my friend and award-winning drummer, Devara Thunderbeat. I told her about my experience and how I had wanted to

---

4 www.lanceheard.com

meet the Arcturians. In her book, *Look Up*[5], Devara shared her story of Dolores Cannon regressing her in a Quantum Healing Hypnosis Technique^{SM} (QHHT®) session. It was revealed to Devara that she is a Sirian ambassador and has been on space ships her entire life. She recommended I find a QHHT® practitioner near me and have a session to find out if anything happened during my sleep time in the woods. It could be that I experienced missing time and I just didn't know it.

As soon as I hung up the phone, I found a practitioner in Gilbert, Arizona, on the original Dolores Cannon website. The practitioner was located about eleven miles from the house I was renting in Tempe, Arizona, which served as the office/center for my healing practice. Perfect synchronicity! I wrote the practitioner's name and phone number on a piece of paper, then I walked into the living room and sat on the floor for my yoga meditation.

During my meditation, my third eye opened and I saw the whole movie of the previous night in the woods! I saw myself egressing from my tent, as a large vertical pyramid-shaped space ship landed in the clearing near my campsite. Two large Arcturians came out of the ship to greet me. They were luminescent human-shape forms.

I walked up the ramp of the ship on my own accord. I saw myself on a table, with Arcturians around me, looking over me as procedures were being done. There was no pain or discomfort, even when a long metal probe was inserted into my left outer upper thigh, the exact spot where the red area on my skin is located. I asked the Arcturians what was being done to me with the probe. They said they are upgrading my light codes and preparing me for trance channeling. I felt immense love. I didn't feel threatened or un-welcomed. It was as if this is a regular thing I did.

I saw myself leaving the ship and returning to my tent. At the end of my yoga, a vibrant blue colored light entered my third eye vision. Slowly, I returned to beta level consciousness—the awake state.

I called Lance and shared the information I received in meditation. He agreed I did indeed go on the ship. He said more is going to come to the surface for me. Now I was intrigued!

That afternoon, I realized the scar on my left anterior thigh that I've had since age four was from an implant that was removed from

---

5   *Look Up: My Encounters with ETs & Angels*, 2013

me. Although it appeared as a cyst to the doctor, it was an implant. I remember waking and sitting up looking at the implant in my leg during the surgery. The female nurse said for me to lay back down. They didn't want me looking at this procedure.

A couple days later, I returned to the house in Tempe where I was giving angel readings and private channeled healing sessions for clients and called the QHHT® practitioner Virginia.

I didn't do any research about Dolores Cannon and her work. The practitioner told me that sessions were private and lasted about four to six hours, followed by a de-briefing of the session and an audio recording of the hypnosis to take home. We scheduled my session, and she sent me the preparation information via email.

Virginia arrived at the house in Tempe. We sat in the living room, as I told her my life story. Afterwards, I laid down on my Reiki table in the healing room, and Virginia began the induction. I felt comfortable and at ease. At the time of my session, Virginia was a Level 1 practitioner. It was very easy for me to trust Virginia and the technique because I've done the inner work to learn to trust myself. When we trust ourselves, we trust others, using our discernment.

PAST LIFE: I WALKED WITH JESUS

I am shown a past life, where I see myself at the foot of the cross where Jesus had just died. My name is Jeremiah, and I was taught by Jesus. The purpose of this past life is to love and support Jesus by talking with people, sharing how to love, how to forgive, and how to live a wholesome life. People come to me.

As we progress through this life, I see scenes where I am a much older man. People look up to me because I'm compassionate and have an understanding that people who do bad things don't understand why they are doing it. There is a reason for this bad behavior, and it's to help the other person learn more about loving himself or herself. The ones I talk to are thirsting for this information, because Jesus is not among them anymore. This past life is a good life, with family. I die peacefully with my loved ones around me.

Virginia calls forth my Subconscious, which say that the purpose of showing me this lifetime of Jeremiah is to remind me of Jesus' teachings and to help others in this current lifetime. The teachings of Jesus are important in my current mission.

The following is part of the session transcript:

Virginia: *How should she spend most of her time?*

Higher Self: The channeling, awakening of people, teaching of love, forgiveness, teaching others to understand that the world is changing now. She feels a deep passion in helping people understand in the most tender, loving, and positive way. This is her dilemma right now. She continues to feel that people are not to accept her. The information that she knows. This is her dilemma.[6]

V: *They are thirsting for this knowledge?*

HS: Yes, indeed. They just don't realize it.

V: *So she should clear this dilemma?*

HS: Yes, my dear.

V: *Barbara has some questions about her health. Right now she has problems with hypothyroidism. Why has this situation manifested?*

HS: The throat chakra. She has been suppressed in many lifetimes about speaking her truth. Finding her voice and this is all connected.

V: *And yet in this lifetime, her life purpose is to teach. She will need her voice.*

HS: Yes.

V: *What types of ET experiences has she had?*

HS: She's been on spaceships. She teaches on ships, and she flies ships.

---

[6] The Higher Self doesn't always use correct sentence structure when speaking, nor always has the English language equivalent for a word or concept from another planet or realm. For this reason, I transcribed exactly how they spoke during the session.

V: *Are there any lessons, takeaways, messages she needs to have from these ET interactions?*

HS: When they occur, they are beneficial for her.

V: *And when the information is to be conscious, it will be made conscious?*

HS: Yes, anytime, we can explore anything here, she would like to know.

Virginia shared with me after the session that she could see my body turn into waveforms when I received the healing for my thyroid. After this session, I no longer felt the need to supplement my body with the homeopathic remedy, Thyrodinium. I received a complete thyroid healing.

V: *Can we make it very clear to Barbara what her purpose is in this life?*

HS: Barbara has come here to help with the many and Mother Earth. She is helping Mother Earth and Mother Earth's Ascension. Her purpose is to help in the transition. That is why she is having a very long life here. She has agreed to stay to help.

V: *And what is her main life lesson in this incarnation?*

HS: To become realized.

V: *Is she coming into her enlightenment?*

HS: Yes, she is stepping into it.

PARTING MESSAGE FOR BARBARA

HS: Dear Barbara, it is true, all your karma is gone. It is done. You will continue to do this work, my dear, to help people, to help them understand. And you will be working with the animals too. You will find new directions in that. We are not going to spell it all out for you. We honor you, and we respect you. Barbara, you are loved very much and you do have a great amount of love for yourself.

A couple of days after this session, Virginia called me and said, "I've never met a Subconscious like yours. I'd like to meet them again. Would you be willing to have another QHHT® session?" Since the first session was a very pleasant experience for me, of course I said, "Yes!"

MY SECOND QHHT® SESSION: CHOOSING TO INCARNATE

During meditation and energy healing sessions, people can experience and remember the time before their birth. Another way is through a Quantum Healing Hypnosis Technique^{SM} session with a trained facilitator. This second session reveals the healing gift I brought with me into my current life.

We had just explored one of my parallel lives as a researcher and data collector of other planets, a life shared in detail in Chapter 14.

At this point of the session, I find myself in a new scene looking at a ball of light, at an egg-shaped object that's milky white and translucent.

Virginia: *Are you small or large compared to this light?*

Barbara: I'm part of it. I'm on the outside looking in. Like it's right before me.

V: *Are you getting ready to step into this egg-shaped light?*

B: Yeah, it's like I'm going to go inside, like I'm going to come into it being born. Oh, this is how they do it!

V: *Do you have a sense of yourself? Can you look down and see your feet?*

B: I'm consciousness, getting ready to go into this form and become human!

V: *Did you make the decision to do this or did someone tell you to do this?*

B: It's like a collective decision. I'm all prepared. I'm ready to go. Everything is all set.

V: *Is there anything you are bringing with you?*

B: All my gifts, all my skills.

V: *And what are those gifts and skills?*

At this point I begin speaking the healing mathematical star language that I channel as my Higher Self speaks during the monthly Star Energy Healing Tele-Conferences I facilitate for groups of people.

V: *So you're bringing language with you? (yes) Are you being prepared to be Barbara?*

B: Yes, very much so.

Virginia asks the Higher Self to come forward.

V: *She wants to know more about you. Who are you and how she can bring more of you into her daily consciousness?*

HS: We are a collection of love, frequency, of consciousness, of beings, entities, planets, stars, all, the power that emanates from the Great Central Sun, all knowing, all loving, all correcting, all being. To incorporate us into Barbara's being is for Barbara to just be herself. We are here. We are not separate from Barbara. She is not separate from us. That is what she needs to know. As you know in our incarnation as humans, we forget. Yes, and more and more of this is being peeled away.

V: *Is there a name or visual image you could attach to yourself so Barbara can make requests and have conversations with you on a daily basis?*

HS: The White One.

V: *Can you help to reveal the specifics of her ET experiences?*

HS: Yes, all she needs to do is to go into meditation, request it, and we will provide. Visuals, sensations, information—all she needs, all she desires.

V: *She feels she was a commander of a star ship. What was her role as a star commander?*

HS: To explore. Her ship is what you would see as pyramid shape; however it's not vertical, it's horizontal. Very much this is an exploration ship with lots of other star beings on board performing tasks and gathering information, teaching, learning. Many schools are on this ship. She determines where to go next. Receives information from the Command. All based in love. This is all based in love. Very, very much so.

V: *Is there anything else she needs to know about being a star commander that would help her in this incarnation?*

HS: She can draw strength upon this, that she knows exactly what she is doing.

V: *I imagine there is a lot of leadership in that role.*

HS: Yes. This is why people on Earth look to her for guidance, as she sits there befuddled, "Why are they staring at me? Why are they looking to me?" Because she has this leadership and they know it, because they are on the ship too. This will be helpful for her, to put closure to that questioning.

V: *So these people are recognizing Barbara subconsciously as their leader?*

HS: Yes.

When a QHHT® client listens to the audio recording of the session, downloads of insight come through into the conscious mind. For instance, when I realized, "This is how they do it!" I came to understand that there is a group of beings guiding the process of consciousness embodying into a human. I further understand we have the ability to place our consciousness into an energy form (here on Earth as humans as the egg-shaped light), and this is done with thought. "It's a collective decision," means I have met with my guides, council of elders, beings of light, angels, etc., to draw up the game plan, so to speak, preparing me for my missions on Earth.

This part of the session answered my questions about trance channeling my Higher Self and the star language that is not indigenous on planet Earth. Also, the information affirmed for me that the language indeed is a gift. The opening of the mathematical star language is presented in my book, *Enclosure: A Spiritual Autobiography*[7]. An audio sample of the

---

7 *Enclosure: A Spiritual Autobiography*, Barbara Becker, 2012

language with healing can be heard on the StreamingForTheSoul.tv[8] *SuperPowers* show interview with host Karl Fink, on YouTube.

Over the years, through my conversations with Dr. Peebles, a grand spirit of love and compassion, who is trance channeled by the great channel, Summer Bacon[9], I learned of my past life regression work that is automatically done by the client's and my Higher Self, unconsciously on my part. I share the stories of healings and miracles in my autobiography. Knowing this information, Virginia decided to contact me about becoming a QHHT® practitioner a year later.

---

8 www.streamingforthesoul.com
9 www.summerbacon.com

3
BECOMING A QHHT® PRACTITIONER

In the fall of 2014, Virginia received a QHHT® session from a fellow QHHT® practitioner in Colorado. Her question as to whom would be the best person to pair up with for a QHHT® office practice yielded the answer, "Barbara Becker."

Virginia called me and asked if I would consider becoming a QHHT® practitioner. She told me that my healing work would be a good match for QHHT®, as it would give the client tangible evidence that the client is doing the healing.

I told Virginia I would put myself under hypnosis and speak with my Higher Self that afternoon. Synchronicity showed up here, as I had already planned to hypnotize myself to get guidance on where to take my healing career next. Some people call this coincidence.

I laid down on my bed and relaxed myself into the deep trance level of hypnosis. Then I was taken off the planet, up into outer space, and swooshed down rapidly into the ancient town of Pompeii, Italy.

This experience felt much like doing a "find location" in Google Earth. I saw myself and Virginia as two men working as partners laying the metal pipes for the city's water supply. In 1995, I had toured Pompeii and Ercolano, Italy. Now I understood why I had instantly recognized the exposed pipes under the cobblestones of the street, pointed out by our private tour guide. In my past life, Virginia, as a man, fabricated the pipes.

In the trance state regression, I served as negotiator and architect for the system. I also saw that Virginia and me in that life were very successful in business together. At this point, I asked my Higher Self if QHHT® is in alignment with my soul path and agreements.

"Yes, very much so," they replied.

***

After my Higher Self's valuable guidance, I took the Level 1 course in late October, completing it on November 3, 2014 after passing the exam. During the recorded course, when I saw Dolores demonstrating a live QHHT® session, I received an instant download epiphany, "This is sacred work!"

During the entire course, I continued to receive healing energies and insights of just how powerful this form of deep trance hypnosis really is.

Dolores Cannon had just passed away on October 18, 2014. At the time of her memorial service in Arkansas, on November 9, 2014, I went into deep meditation in my bedroom on my boyfriend's ranch in Wickenburg, Arizona. Even though I had not asked for Dolores to communicate with me, she appeared in the middle of my bedroom, in the form of a violet ball of light. Dolores spoke:

"Barbara, I am glad you decided to facilitate Quantum Healing Hypnosis Technique^{SM} sessions. I will be with you in every session you facilitate."

Then, she blasted me with love. The loving energy was so powerful I could hardly contain it in my energy fields and human body. My heart chakra exploded wide open and tears rolled down my cheeks profusely. Dolores knows how to "flip the light switch on" when it comes to doling out the love!

I asked my dear friend, amazing angel communicator, mystic, author Ann Albers, to help me get the word out there on social media and through her popular worldwide newsletter that I was accepting clients for QHHT® sessions.

I offered these initial sessions for free, with just a little help with the fuel expense for my vehicle, as I traveled between thirty to fifty miles one way to the client's home or hotel. Within two weeks, I was booked up from December to April of the following year. It became apparent to me that QHHT® is a popular modality in Arizona!

I instantly fell in love with QHHT® and see it as very comprehensive and client centered. Dolores thought of everything to provide comfort, love, and compassion during a hypnosis session, and she placed it in her hypnotic script and technique.

I had facilitated sixty-three sessions by the time I attended the Level 2 QHHT® training in Springdale, Arkansas, in the summer of

2015, with Virginia. We traveled together, with Virginia picking me up at the Carefree Highway and I-17 freeway, north of Phoenix. Off we went, catching up on each other's news and activities, as we drove across country to Arkansas.

We stopped in Amarillo, Texas, and spent the night in a hotel. After breakfast, we drove to Rogers, Arkansas, and checked into our hotel.

In our three-day Level 2 course, we students learned additional techniques to help our clients relax in their hypnosis sessions and how best to help clients with challenging perceptions, and to experience their sessions with a broader perspective that yields positive outcomes. We worked on perfecting our voice to help the client go deeper and deeper into the theta level of hypnosis. We practiced our voice rhythm and tone and shared our experiences so that other practitioners could take away more knowledge and skills. Those were the highlights, but I can't go into the course details because that information is for QHHT practitioners only.

At the end of the three-day course, we received our certificates from Julia Cannon and expressed our gratitude to the course teachers. It was fun meeting other practitioners and sharing our experiences.

After the course, Virginia and I attended the annual QHHT® Practitioner's Reunion in Springdale. Of special honor for me was listening to a practitioner's healing. She was the client of Dolores that was healed of her Stage IV cancer and lung disease. This provided inspiration not only to me, but also to the many people who read about her and decide for themselves whether to have a QHHT® session.

The morning following the practitioner reunion, Virginia and I headed back toward Arizona, stopping along the way at a hotel we had stayed at five days before in route to the training. I prepared myself for my first time facilitating a QHHT® session with Virginia, who had facilitated my first session and introduced me to this amazing hypnosis work.

I placed myself in the mind frame of an experienced practitioner and set forth on Virginia's journey into the quantum field of discovery. After her past life scene was shown as a fruit bat, I got the surprise of my life. I found myself speaking with God! At first I was like a deer caught in the headlights. I managed to get my wits together quickly by sinking back and allowing the questions to come forth. It felt as though my Higher Self were guiding the questions.

Barbara: *Where would you like to go now?*

Virginia: Darkness, floating in a void. No sense of a body. She can be anything, but actually nothing.

B: *Where would you like to be?*

V: In the void.

B: *What does it feel like?*

V: Peaceful.

B: *Anyone with you?*

V: Everyone and no one. Oh, I am the Universe. The entire Universe. Everything that is, is here! [She went back to Source!]

B: *From that perspective, can you help us to understand the purpose of the New Earth forming from the Old Earth, and its relationship to the Universe?*

God Source: The Earth is so small. It's so tiny. A little, beautiful speck, and there's no molecule more important than the other. The absence of any molecule affects all other molecules and changes what it is. Everything that is in me is dynamic! I am not static. I'm not unchanging. And I'm moving. I'm not a rock. I am not stone. I am a living thing. All of the parts of me are living things. Living things grow! That is the definition of life. It changes and it grows. If it weren't changing and growing, we would call it dead, and therefore not life. So, the Earth has many, many sisters. As a part of living, she evolves, she changes, she grows. And this is just part of her natural, normal growth. Some day, she will, as like to you in a human body, she will die like a dead skin cell. But at this point she is growing, that is the shift and the change. Every planet, every star, every piece, every aspect of the Universe is always changing and growing and dying and being born, and growing and changing and dying, and living. And this is her life.

B: *You said the old Earth will eventually die. Does this mean that everyone on the planet will eventually leave?*

GS: Oh, yeah. The people on the planet will be long gone by then. Long, long, long gone.

B: *Will the people remaining on the old Earth have a difficult time?*

GS: Eventually, but it happens gradually. There's nothing sudden. It's a natural change. Over the generations, it's a gradual thing. This is what happened to Mars. If you want to know what will happen to Earth, look to Mars, her neighbor. It's the same. It's okay.

B: *I heard there are inhabitants on Mars at this time, in contained communities.*

GS: There are some. There are, it is more common to have non-third dimensional beings. Few third dimensional. No natural inhabitants. Those generations have died out. So, the entities are visitors. And some day that will be the Earth. This is so long from when you speak.

B: *What about Mother Earth's moon? How is the moon? I know she is a sentient being.*

GS: The moon is like a little sister to the Earth. She learns from the Earth. She observes the Earth. She, in some ways, envies the Earth as a big sister, and because she does not have natural inhabitants anyway, when the natural inhabitants leave Earth, the moon and the Earth will still be together. They are partners. When the Earth dies, the Moon will die. The Earth will stop spinning. In the process of the end, the Moon will fall into the Earth or be pulled into the Earth, and they will die as one entity. And then after that, their mass will be pulled in additional directions. Their mass, therefore energy, will combine with other planets. And these entities will eventually get pulled into stars. Not into the sun. Their energies will relive again as new planets, as the explosions that come from the stars.

B: *We only see one side of the moon from our Earth. On the back side of the moon, are there people on the other side of the moon?*

GS: There are visitors.

B: *Is there a purpose for that?*

GS: There are, from the moon's perspective, these are nuisances. Trivial irritants. Like Mars, there are visitors, both inter-dimensional and human visitors on that part of the moon. There are times when they are on both sides of the moon. From my perspective, it is silly what they do, because what they seek is of marginal benefit to the humans. It's a futile exercise.

B: *We humans launched a rocket with astronauts to the moon, landed a vehicle on the moon. Did that happen?*

GS: Yes. And today there are vehicles both third dimensional and fifth dimensional and twelfth dimensional vehicles that travel to and from, to and from, to and from. Such an enormous effort for such little benefit. But humans are like many of their sentient brothers and sisters, in that they have been created to be explorers. This is inherent in their DNA.

The father of disclosure of the existence of extraterrestrial life on Earth and exposing the rogue government cover-up of this information, Steven M. Greer, M.D., stated in his book, *Unacknowledged*[10], that the moon landing did occur; however, the flag planting segment of the video was filmed on a sound stage in New York. NASA (National Aeronautical Space Administration) knew from previous lunar mission flybys around the moon, that there were advanced extraterrestrial structures on the back side of the moon. We know the video imaging is delayed, so they were able to cut out the reactions of the astronauts to the presence of the extraterrestrials. I recommend reading Dr. Greer's books and viewing the video testimonials of the people he interviewed who worked in covert projects and have bravely come forth to reveal the truth for the rest of us. Your exploration can start at www.siriusdisclosure.com.

* * *

Virginia and I got up the next morning, and headed toward Albuquerque, New Mexico. She dropped me off at the Albuquerque

---

10 *Unacknowledged*, Steven M. Greer, M.D., 2017, A&M Publishing

International Sunport at about ten thirty in the morning. Virginia offered to hang out with me for a while, but I told her it would be best for her to get a head start on returning to her home in Colorado. We hugged goodbye.

I ate a nice lunch at a Mexican restaurant as I began reading Dolores' book, *Jesus and the Essenes*[11]. After lunch, I stretched my legs by walking around the terminal. Knowing my flight would leave after supper time, I purchased a veggie sandwich and a cup of coffee at the one of the coffee bistros. Walking down the corridor to an empty gate, I sat down and picked up my book. After several paragraphs, I was intuitively guided to look up. At the precise moment, my gaze locked eyes with a blonde-haired woman. She was walking in a robotic manner, with a long stride, at a fast pace, swinging her arms wide from front to back. She walked from my right field of vision to the left, with her head cocked toward me. She stared directly at me with a silly grin. I got the feeling this was happening just for me. "Who was that?" I asked my Higher Self. They responded, "Dolores." Chills ran through my body in confirmation. Smiling, I said, "Hello Dolores!" in my mind.

I knew this trip would be something special. As luck would have it, a storm named Hurricane Dolores was brewing, heading toward the airport. How apropos! The lightning and thunderstorm delayed my flight by four hours. Boarding didn't start until midnight, and during the delay, a new client's mother called me asking for a session for her daughter, and I made arrangements to call her daughter the next day.

With everything that had happened—the training, meeting some of my mentors, learning from fellow students, working with Virginia, and now all these small but powerful synchronicities at the airport—I had to say: this wasn't just a special trip. It was a magical trip!

***

I facilitated QHHT® sessions all over the Greater Phoenix area. Clients were asking for sessions from all over Arizona. As word spread, I facilitated sessions for people from Portland, Los Angeles, San Francisco, Palm Springs, Tennessee, Seattle, Santa Fe, Taos, Kansas City, Hawaii, Minneapolis, Las Vegas, and Calgary, Canada.

---

11 *Jesus and the Essenes*, Dolores Cannon, Ozark Mountain Publishing, 1985

During the QHHT® sessions I facilitate, I see a white light traveling through the client's body and they, the Higher Self, express themselves to me as ancient beings. The client's face and head disappears, and I see the Higher Self's face. In some sessions, they show me several faces, alternating in place. It's not unusual during sessions for the entire room to be filled with white light radiating with the feeling of immense infinite love. And that intense love envelops me. There is only one thing more exciting than facilitating a QHHT® session. That's having one!

4
THE PORTAL

I had a very unusual experience on September 30, 2013, and I wanted to know what really happened. At that time, although I lived with my boyfriend, Peter, at his home on a twenty-acre ranch fifty miles northwest of Phoenix, I also rented a home in Tempe, Arizona, where I had a healing room and gave angel tarot card readings.

At the Tempe house, during a discussion with Carol, an energy worker, I began to feel strange as if in two places at the same time in two different dimensions. My energy felt weak, and I felt like I might pass out. Carol, who was familiar with my Higher Self and had seen them in group healing sessions facilitated by me, saw them standing behind me. With me leaning on her, we were able to walk over to the living room sofa so I could lay down.

I went into an altered state of consciousness. Carol intuitively stood up and walked to the other side of the sofa, behind my head and began toning. I was out of my body, just above and staring back at it; my body was in respiratory arrest. After some time (we both felt it was at least five minutes), I came back into my body, began breathing again, sat up, feeling perfectly normal, and said, "Where do you want to go for lunch?" Carol looked like a deer in headlights, shocked at what she had just witnessed and experienced.

I had to return to the ranch because I could no longer afford the rent for the house in Tempe. Note: During the year leading up to my return to the ranch, all of my finances dried up, even though I applied various manifesting prosperity and abundance techniques, including Feng Shui and affirmations. This doesn't mean I don't believe in manifesting techniques. This experience showed me that no matter what we do in the physical realm, if there is a higher calling or project that we agreed to perform, then we need to trust that all will be provided. We must remember that we showed up for the mission, and the

Higher Self does have an obligation to take care of the details behind the scenes to support us. This is not to express an entitlement; rather, it is considered a mutual agreement. What I have found is that the Higher Self provides above and beyond our wildest imaginations.

Virginia facilitated my third session in our hotel room the night of the first day of our Level 2 class on July 13, 2015. Although a person only needs one QHHT® session for the remainder of their life, for some people, it's a challenge to relax down into the deep level hypnosis, as Dolores found and I've found too. For those people, having another session convinces the ego that this modality is safe and informative. A session benefits the ego because its job is easier when the client knows his/her direction, life purpose, and answers to pressing questions.

It was in this session that Virginia and I learned more about me. We decided not to go into a past life and instead focus exclusively on speaking with my Higher Self to get answers to important questions. My Subconscious was accessed immediately in deep level trance hypnosis from the code word I had given Virginia two and half years earlier.

> Virginia: *Barbara had an unusual experience in the home she was renting at the time. An energy worker named Carol visiting with her saw Barbara's guides standing behind Barbara, as Barbara shared that she felt a strange sensation of being weak and disoriented. She would like to know what happened.*
>
> Higher Self: Well, dear Carol saw us standing behind Barbara. We were calling her back for the moment. We needed to see her in council, because there was some indication that she did not want to continue her mission. So it was very important that we have a little chat, so to speak.
>
> V: *What was the indication that Barb gave? Was that in the physical realm or in the spirit realm that the indication was given?*
>
> HS: It was in the spiritual realm. Barbara was not consciously aware of this, of course, because she did not understand what was transpiring in her body. We gently guided her to a higher realm, and we had to make adjustments in her body, which she did see that she was in, what we call a partial suspension. And this was

done because we had to make adjustments in her, and we had a very constructive and productive talk.

V: *Can you share with Barb, in this realm what was her hesitancy for not continuing her mission?*

HS: She didn't really want to go back to the ranch. And that we had to remind her that there was important construction, if you will, that had to continue there, and we needed her there. And that is why we were the ones that changed all the finances, and the situation that she was in, in Tempe. She had finished construction of the portals, the gateways, if you will, in the Tempe area of the Valley. That was done. She agreed to do that, and now we asked her to please go to a special area in the desert, an area where it is conducive for transportation of souls to go to different points, wherever they are needed; different places of the solar system, the galaxies, if you will, other planets and star systems.

Virginia: *This new construction project at the ranch, she was hesitant to go and do that. Can you tell me more about this construction project at the ranch?*

HS: She's very much an instrument, if you will, the unconditional love that is required to construct this portal. It's all constructed with unconditional love. She is doing this with others. There's a great number of others, participating in this. It's a group effort, if you will, and we will say that it is about 90 percent complete! We think she will be pleased with that number. It's going to be a little bit more for her. And then she will be moving to Durango, Colorado!

V: *Will there be construction projects in Durango, or will she be focused on different types of work?*

HS: Oh yes, in addition to her sessions in the Durango area, and there are more portals to be constructed there, she's going to be changing energies up there. She will be working with others, of course. And this is all part of the assistance for the Earth.

V: *The construction of the portals are done with unconditional love. Why does her physical body need to be there? Why can't they be built from a distance? We know energies can travel great distances. Love can travel great distances. Can you help us to understand the mechanisms of why the physical body needs to be there?*

HS: Yes, yes, my dear. Well, she holds a frequency. And the human body holds a frequency, and that is the requirement. She holds that. It's part of the matrix of the construction of the mechanics and the energetics—the mechanisms that allow entrance and exit. Of course, this is not in the physical realm. This is through dimensions, intergalactic travels. It's a very beautiful place.

V: *You mentioned more than just Barb is involved in the construction project. [Interrupted]*

HS: There are thousands!

V: *How many of these portals are on the planet?*

HS: Goodness gracious! Let us see here, two thousand to three thousand. We can't make an exact number there, because they are in different stages of development. Sometimes there's interference.

V: *You mentioned after the construction project, and going to Colorado? What is the timeline for her?*

HS: Still not yet. We know she's wanting. There's part of her that says, "Okay, I'll go along, and I know this will come about in the perfect timing." She has come to terms with that. And we are very appreciative of her being there, in the Arizona. She has more work there to do. She will be given the information. It will come and it will be very obvious to her: "It is now time."

Another interesting event occurred, and I wanted to know more about it…

On February 12, 2015, between four and four-thirty in the morning, I was awoken from deep sleep by loud sounds, as if a spacecraft crashed onto the tile roof above my bedroom. Then something boomed, sounding like tiles crashing on the flagstone walkway outside of my bedroom. My heart raced. Since I didn't hear anything else, I told myself I would look at the damage later in the morning when I woke up. Later, when I looked outside, I found nothing out of place or disturbed in any way.

The answers to what happened that day came during the thirty-fifth QHHT® session I facilitated. A psychically gifted oriental medicine practitioner's Subconscious revealed this:

> HS: There was a sacred geometry being put over your house, and what you were hearing was the shutting of this shape from one dimension to the other. Your house is being worked on, as well, so that you can continue your work at this house. It was being surrounded by sacred geometry. It needs work before you are to leave it. The physical house and land needs work. It needs sacred geometry around it, so you can leave it and move forward.
>
> Barbara: *Is this being done when I'm asleep?*
>
> HS: Yes.
>
> B: *Will this be done by May?*
>
> HS: Yes. You can't do all the work yourself. This geometry, we are re-setting the house so that you can leave it. But the slamming was the geometry opening the portal and then shutting.

More sounds occurred during my sleep on many occasions that spring. One time, I heard a loud bang through the dimensions that sounded like a slamming closure of the lid of a steel trashcan. I listened further. Not hearing anything else, I fell back to sleep.

On March 25, 2015, my forty-third client, who is also very psychic, mentioned claircognizantly that the portal was about sixty percent complete. This was discussed during the debriefing part of the session. As Dolores found in her sessions, the same information keeps coming through different people.

On May 30, 2015, my Indigo client from the Pleiades (whom I write about in Chapter 10 of this book) encouraged me to ask a couple of my own questions. I was intrigued to discover what her Subconscious would say about the portal. The SC checked on the portal and said they have a hard time translating into a percentage range regarding completion.

> HS: The portal above the ranch is now more than sixty five percent. Just know it's more. It's almost completed. It's big. It's a place for certain people, depending where is your next mission. You

(meaning Barbara) will be moving in 2017. One and a half years. It's changing. The timelines can compress. If the light work is to be completed, then 2017 is the year. That is what they are saying. Continue the work in the Phoenix area.

Regarding the location of the ranch portal:

HS: Because of the ancestors, with this energy, it's virgin here. It's easy to work here. The energy flows very well. Other areas are very polluted. It used to be very powerful. No one paid attention to it. But, that's good for us, that's why we are here. The light work will be completed soon.

On July 17, 2015, in the Amarillo hotel, when I facilitated Virginia's session, I asked more questions of Virginia's Higher Self about the ranch portal.

Barbara: *In my recent session, my HS mentioned about the portals around the Earth and that there are two thousand to three thousand, depending on the stage of the construction and interference. What is that interference? How does that come about?*

HS: There are many beings from many places that have come to this place in the galaxy to help with the growth. The portals are a necessary part, and this takes a lot of effort. It's not magical. It takes time and commitment and ability and resources to bring these beings in. Many cannot stay in Earth's atmosphere for very long. As helpers are shuttled in and out, contributing to the amount of work that's completed, can ebb and flow. This is the source of the unpredictability of the building of these portals. There are many beings that have given their life for this work because they have stayed in the Earth's atmosphere and dimension too long and have sacrificed their life for this effort.

B: *Virginia's HS told me the ranch portal is very close to completion, more than seventy-five percent.*

HS: You've been away. This is an example of the unpredictability and, although, it's very close to completion, more than three-fourths completed.

B: *I wondered why there is a difference between two Higher Self's perception of the completion percentage of this particular portal?*

HS: The chef knows the ingredients and how much time it takes to prepare, mix and bake a cake, has this one perception. Someone who is just watching the chef, has a different perception, because they don't know all the steps, the components, and the procedures to make the cake.

B: *What is the most important time for me to be at the ranch for the construction?*

HS: The work goes on when you are in meditation, when you are in thoughtful, open heart space, in addition to sleeping. When you are walking with a loving, open heart with the flowers, birds, and trees around you. This is helping to build it.

My Higher Self was right when they said I will know when to leave for Durango. The message was loud and clear when my boyfriend came home from Switzerland in October of 2016 and announced unexpectedly that he was returning to Europe without me.

In addition, the Indigo client's guide, Sonar, said I would be moving in 2017, and Sonar was right. I moved from Durango, Colorado, back to Phoenix in May of 2017.

5
MULTI-PLANETARY AMBASSADOR AND PARALLEL LIFE AS A REPTILIAN

I facilitated a session for a lovely fifty-eight-year-old woman who helps people on their journeys in life as a healer. Susan had her first session with another practitioner two years prior, which revealed that Susan is an ambassador of worlds. She wanted to learn more of this, and also about a couple of puzzling experiences. Of special note, Susan felt she instantly recognized me, but couldn't remember from where. We agreed I would ask the HS about this familiarity during the hypnosis. I have found that many of my QHHT® clients instantly recognize me. Each time I ask, the HS shares that we are working together during the night or our paths are crossing in the other realms while we sleep.

Susan's first puzzling experience was waking up in the middle of the night in her bed and seeing a reptilian creature's head above her, staring at her with glowing red eyes. This occurred in 2009. Her second experience was waking up in the morning and seeing a beige-colored creature holding her stomach area. The third experience was when she and her husband saw a bright flash of light in their living room in the middle of the day.

Her physical symptoms included left shoulder pain and spasms, and interstitial cystitis causing frequent urination, all of which had been happening for several years. She also had claustrophobia, discoloration of the lower legs and ankles in a scaly pattern, and restricted breathing from the lungs.

PAST LIFE

In London, England, Susan is a wealthy man named John, who also serves as a judge in Parliament where he mediates decisions regarding land ownership disputes. At the time, business people were encroaching upon the common people's land. The HS shows Susan the birthday party of John's eight-year-old son, a happy event for the family.

In the next scene, John is elected as a very high-ranking judge in Parliament. He is involved in a lot of business meetings and not as close to his wife as before. He feels he has no choice, as his work keeps him away from home for long hours.

On the last day of John's life, he says, "I'm shot in the left shoulder because I agree to many things. I was in the way of those who wanted to pay me and control me. They were Frenchmen."

John reports that he feels a lot of pain in the shoulder and is losing blood. "I'm shot on the steps of the Parliament building. People are helping me, but they don't know what to do." He leaves the body as he dies. Susan experiences the death scene without discomfort, as if watching a movie.

HIGHER SELF

Barbara: *Why did you show her this life as John?*

The HS, in its infinite wisdom showed these scenes of this past life to Susan to help her understand the value of money, and what it can and cannot do for her. This life was also shown so Susan could see what a family means to her in terms of value. Also:

HS: Always stand up for your values. Not to let the majority sway you, be strong. She is a healer, her energy is very strong. Even when she doesn't realize it, she is healing. She doesn't realize her potential. She doesn't allow herself to broaden her perspective of her abilities. We have put many opportunities in front of her. It is for her to realize these opportunities, but she doesn't always pay attention. She needs to be released—to the restroom now!

In a commanding voice, this is the HS telling me the client must go urinate. After the toilet break, Susan is able to relax and go even deeper into trance, and the Higher Self continues:

HS: She is an ambassador of the worlds. She is always in contact with other ambassadors of other worlds. [Deep sighs.] Her main purpose is to keep the peace among the universe. Many worlds have what you would call contracts with each other in terms of peace among these worlds. When there is conflict, then her duty is to convene at a specific location so these matters can be worked out. This is why she is shown this past life. She is the mediator between worlds. She is highly regarded for her clear thinking, for she has been groomed for this, from the beginning.

B: *Why do I look familiar to her?*

HS: Many times during her trips you have interacted. Where you have almost the same mission, but on different levels, so your paths have crossed many times. It's no accident.

B: *Would you help Susan understand why she saw a reptilian face above her bed one night?*

HS: This was not a physical contact. What she saw was a hologram. She was taken to the ship and was greeted by the physical form. This was a mate of hers. This is a parallel lifetime, and he is her mate. He did not harm her. They have a good relationship in that life.[12]

Since her reptilian mate's name cannot be pronounced, Susan is able to produce a sound. It is fascinating for me to listen to her voice change dramatically. Also, during this time when the HS talks about the client's mate, the room fills with immense love. It is an honor to sit in this space of pure love and compassion. At this point, I also see the client morph into a reptilian creature. In other words, Susan's body disappears, and a reptilian being replaces it. This does not shock me. I consider my third eye skills a divine gift and am grateful for the ability to see into other realms.

B: *Would you help her understand her experience with the beige being standing over her one morning?*

HS: She saw a beige being. It's eyes popped open wider when she woke up. This is one that has been watching over her since she was a child. This was a physical healing being given that day. There are more planned encounters with this being.

---

12 Just as humans come in all shapes, sizes and temperaments, so do reptilians. Some do good, and some do otherwise. Please refer to Chapter 19 where a client is tormented by reptilians coming through a portal.

The HS shares the name of the beige being, so that Susan can directly express her gratitude and love to the being.

B: *Would you help her to understand what the flash of light in the living room was about?*

HS: It was her mate paying her a visit. This was missing time for Susan. Her husband was placed in "suspended animation," so no time was noticed [by him]. The purpose of the visit was because Susan has two children with this reptilian mate. She was needed to help the reptilian children. [This gives us another perspective about multi-tasking and is an example of bending time and memory affects.]

The HS interrupts me by saying Susan needs to use the restroom again. Since this was one of Susan's physical ailments, I ask the HS to heal her bladder.

HS: [Deep sighs.] It's physical and mental. She experiences anxiety. Partial root cause of interstitial cystitis is the mental causes the physical. The root cause is stress. The healing took a matter of seconds to complete.

HS: Can she go at this time?

I oblige immediately. When Susan returns to the bed, her HS comes back very nicely again…

HS: Additional root cause of her interstitial cystitis is her body is always in a state of worry from the beginning. Always fear. Always worry. After the session, she will receive a release of her anxieties. She will be a different person after the session. She will be merging with her other selves. It is time. This will bring peace and strength.

Her high blood pressure is due to the build up of pressure from the past that manifests in a physical way. Once she starts to let go of her past, this will release, explains the HS. The high blood pressure will no longer be an issue after the session, though it will be a slow process, until eventually she can discontinue her medications.

Her left shoulder spasms and pain are caused by cellular memories of the past life. Her body can now release the cell's memories—and the pain.

Her right shoulder pain comes from making up for the left shoulder, taking some of the pain. This too will be released, continues the HS.

The root cause of her claustrophobia came from being buried alive in a past life, which also causes her breathing problem in the lungs.

At this point in the session, the client coughs and coughs. The HS says her claustrophobia will be gone, but first she must believe that instant healing is possible. [Such as when my thyroid was healed instantly in my first QHHT® session.]

> HS: The discoloration of the skin on her ankles and legs are partially attributed to capillary fragility but, [sigh], she has reptilian DNA, and this is part of that. Nothing to be concerned about. Just a reminder of who she is. Subconsciously she understands, because she jokes about it.

ONE MONTH FOLLOW-UP

From the day of the QHHT® session, Susan's shoulder pain is gone and has not returned. She is very happy about this. Her anxiety is much less. She's breathing better. She has more clients. More people are asking for her guidance, and she has repeat clients now. She has noticed she doesn't worry about being near a restroom anymore, as the urge to go has lessened greatly.

6
THE NOXIOUS ODOR

A delightful woman of sixty-two who has had an amazing life so far came to see me for a session. She was born in the Southwest part of the United States. Cleo was always positive and living in the flow of life. Jobs came to her easily, and she was very adaptable.

Cleo shared with me that she smells a noxious chemical odor that no one else senses. This has been bothering her for years, and she wanted to know the root cause of it. She had rheumatic fever as a child. She had repeat strep throat infections—and wanted to learn their root causes too. Cleo was also wondering about the black spot on her chest X-ray that was discovered years ago by the medical doctors.

PAST LIFE

We are about halfway into the relaxation phase of the hypnosis script when suddenly all she sees is pink light. I know instantly that she is going into another life.

Swoosh! Cleo lands in Egypt as a young barefoot female child, of royalty. The child lives in several palaces with courtyards. Wearing a linen wrap, and a gold band high on the arm with a scarab jewel, she is an oracle that counsels people who come to her for answers. Her father is the king who killed her mother because the mother did not respect him.

Cleo leapfrogs into another life as a jovial man who is a traveling messenger, delivering the king's good news to people. He travels with an entourage of two other messengers. He wears a sword with his ornate garment.

[It's not unusual for the Higher Self to show several important scenes from various lives. All of the information shown is used to convey messages and answers for the client.]

Cleo goes into the death scene of yet another life as a five-year-old girl who is shot in the chest by two men, while she is standing between her parents, on a sidewalk. They are going out for a meal and the movies. Cleo goes into the death scene without my prompting. I ask her to go backwards, to a point earlier in this last day to help us figure out what happened. We go backward and learn that her father is a police officer. Two men target and kill her and her parents. I ask her if this is a revenge or gang type of event. She replies, "No."

The two men get out of their car, and grab and stuff Cleo into a gunny sack. She is thrown into the back seat of the vehicle. I ask her to listen to the men talk in the vehicle as they drive away. She hears one say joyfully, "We did it!"

She can feel her life slowly draining away as she dies in the back seat. The men stop the vehicle and get out. They throw her bagged body by the side of the road. One of the men kicks the sack and watches it roll down a ravine. She goes out of her body. She sees that no one finds her decomposing corpse in the woods.

HIGHER SELF

The HS wanted us to look at the little girl's death scene because it probably was the root cause of several of her ailments. The first reason this lifetime was chosen was for Cleo to release it. The black spot on her lung that was found on an X-ray was where she was shot in that previous life. The chemical smell that had been bothering her for four years was cellular memory from the death scene. The HS said it was from the burning flesh of the bullet entering her chest. Her body remembered the sensation and the memory. The HS healed this odor memory during the session.

This was also connected to the dark circles under her eyes. They healed that too. The throat issues of strep throat were also tied to this scene from the smoke inhalation when she was shot, along with cellular memory from a different lifetime where she lived in a cabin with a wood-burning stove. As the Higher Self healed her throat, she coughed twice and released the cellular memory with the breath, which the HS confirmed.

Even the rheumatic fever and the damaged valve were from the death scene cellular memory. However, the fever was also a positive way for her to remember her connection to the Divine. As the fever burned, it was a passion, according to the HS. The valves were fine, though the HS saw a little bit of scar tissue. I asked for them to repair it. "Seeing it healed" is the way the HS healed it.

The man who shot her in that lifetime was her first ex-husband in this lifetime. The reason she was shot was for karmic balancing because she took his life in the first lifetime shown, when she was the child in Egypt.

The karmic balancing could very well be a reason why in our current times there are innocent people who are shot and killed "randomly" by a stray bullet, or run over by a vehicle with no malicious intent by the driver. We often call this "being in the wrong place at the wrong time." Is it really wrong when it is meant to balance karma?

This is the beauty of a QHHT® session. Imagine if people who are riddled with guilt from causing unintentional harm to another discover under hypnosis it was pre-planned before birth? Could the Higher Self remove the guilt program running in the mind, thus freeing the person to live a happier, fruitful life, rather than drowning in alcohol or escaping the emotions through drugs? Imagine a different outcome!

Even good deeds can have dire consequences in the human experience. The next client session gives us an example of a soul who suffered for helping a man considered, by most, to be the greatest man incarnated on Earth.

7

PUNISHED FOR SAVING JESUS

I facilitated this session for Gloria, a middle-aged woman who had been married and divorced three times, with the last one ending in domestic violence.

She sustained a severe auto collision many months prior to this session that fractured her lower cervical vertebrae, and fractured and broke her first two ribs. Gloria left her body and returned, without a memory of what happened. She was dependent on prescribed pain medications and wanted to be free of the constant pain in her neck and back.

Also, of note: Gloria was very psychic.

PAST LIVES

Gloria comes into not only one past life scene, but five different scenes, all at the same time. This is a bit overwhelming for her. I ask her to describe each scene, one at a time. This works nicely.

In front of her, she can see an Asian woman, wearing a coolie hat, picking rice in a field in the rain. To the right, she sees an Asian woman hanging clothes on the clothesline and the green rice fields in the distance. Gloria feels she is standing in a puddle of water, wearing dirty ragged clothes, barefoot. She feels she's a man with a beard and long hair in his mid-forties, and he has time traveled. He wanders the streets in the rain. He has a silver metal pocket watch in his coat pocket. He feels like he is dead or stuck there.

To her left, Gloria also sees a wife, two kids, and a different man, while looking in the window of a speakeasy (an illicit liquor bar during the Prohibition era of 1920-1933). Gloria also sees Auschwitz, the Nazi death camp in Poland.

Since Gloria is seeing all of these "movies" at the same time, I ask her to move back to an important day and time.

The HS is in charge of the session and knows exactly what to do. I am amazed at what happens next.

Gloria finds herself as a woman, dressed as a man looking at people riding camels in the sand. She has long silky black hair, dark skin, sandals, and a long garment with money bags hidden in the fabric, fashioned on her body with a rope at the waist. Her name sounds like Sue. She carries a golden staff encrusted with jewels. She is on a secret mission, in disguise, and feels nervous about something. She is to meet someone at a location near the marketplace. This could take some time, so I move her forward to when she meets the person.

She walks up to a wooden door of a building, looks both ways, and hurries in. The room has dirt floors and a wooden table. She takes her outer garments off and sees she is indeed a small-framed woman. Several people occupy the room. She sees something move under the kitchen table, which turns out to be a trap door to a staircase, leading to a tunnel.

She goes downstairs into what looks like a dungeon. There, she helps free a man from a cell by opening a lock with keys she has in her hands. She recognizes him as a male prophet. He has brown hair, a long brown beard, and light brown eyes; his garment is white and tied with a rope. Upon my request, she asks him his name, and he says, "Jesus."

I ask her what is it like being with Jesus. She says it's "nerve racking" and good at the same time. I ask, "Who put Jesus in this dungeon?" She replies, "The king's men."

Jesus is twenty-two years-old. He kisses her on the forehead and says, "Thank you; don't worry. I'll see you again." She gives him the bag of money from her garment, and he leaves by walking away down one of many corridors in an underground tunnel system. She goes back up to the kitchen.

I ask her, "How do you know you were to go there to free Jesus?" She replies she received a note, by carrier pigeon: "Come at once." (Carrier pigeons were used for sport as early as three-thousand years ago, according to Wikipedia.[13])

Suddenly, Gloria begins experiencing excruciating physical pain in her lower neck. I tell Gloria she will not have any discomfort mentally or physically. I ask her to leave the scene and move to an important day.

---

13   https://en.wikipedia.org/wiki/Homing_pigeon

Gloria sees the gallows set up with a guillotine. The woman who had opened the door to the place above the dungeon area that day was already hanging from a rope. Now it is her turn. She senses it will be the guillotine for her, for helping Jesus to escape.

A sack is placed over her head. She kneels down, the blade drops, her head rolls, and she goes out of her body before I even have a chance to say she will not feel any physical sensations of discomfort during this procedure. Gloria's neck pain increases.

I repeat several times that she does not feel any physical sensations as she moves her head back and forth in discomfort. She reports that her body and head are thrown into a wagon to be discarded and probably burned.

The physical sharp pain in her neck persists. I help her to breathe and relax. I feel we got to the root cause of her neck pain. As she is out of the body, I ask her if she'd like to go into the light for a while. Archangel Michael assists to take her into the light. She says she feels she is having difficulty trusting this. I ask her to repeat, "I trust, I trust, I trust." It works. She relaxes and goes into the light.

HIGHER SELF

When I ask the Higher Self why they showed her the various scenes, this is what they say:

> HS: The man standing in the puddle was not in Asia. He was in Chicago. He was a time traveler. This lifetime as the man was to show about being lost between worlds. The life as the woman who saved Jesus was a lesson to trust God that no matter what happens, she will be okay. Her soul will be okay. She needs to learn to trust her intuition and to do what she feels is right.

I ask why Gloria sustained a neck injury in the auto collision.

> HS: She's quite "hard headed", and her life was out of sorts. We had to shatter the illusions. She was spinning out of control. But, we were the ones who held her in [the vehicle]. She had minimal damage. She did leave her body. She did go down a tunnel, and she met us. She can now refer to us as the "Light Beings." She doubts that we are there. Some of the feelings should make a dif-

ference. She's been afraid to be in her body. Safety issues have been in several lifetimes. This current life is about experiencing joy and love, and having fun with grandchildren. She's got to let go, or we can't do our job. Let go of control. It's an illusion. More happiness comes much quicker. She knows when she's off. She gets stuck in a loop of fear.

The HS begins working with her to heal her; however, a trust issue comes up, and she begins feeling hot and uncomfortable. I ask the HS to help her to not feel so much discomfort. They say she feels the need to punish herself, because she makes wrong decisions and judges herself. The HS adjusts her star codes, and she feels much better. When this happens, the HS takes over my body, and the mathematical healing star language comes out of my vocal cords. I have no control over this.

HS: All discomforts and physical issues are taken care of and healed.

AFTERMATH

Gloria wrote to me the next day. In her email message she said the car drive home the next day was a little uncomfortable, that's all. Other than that, she feels really great!

As for evidence of Gloria's healing, the social media images and posts I see of Gloria are enough for me to know that she healed herself through her QHHT® session and her follow-through. She is smiling, very active in physical projects, and exuding happiness and joy with her grandchildren. Gloria is a living testament to the power of self healing through Quantum Healing Hypnosis Technique^{SM}.

In the next session, a medical condition is used for the purposes of helping the client to help herself.

8

MULTIPLE SCLEROSIS FOR PROTECTION

Carol, a delightful middle-aged woman with multiple sclerosis (MS), pain and numbness in her body, a burning sensation on her right side with the left arm pulled upward, back spasticity, fatigue, cognitive impairment, forgetfulness, and the inability to focus, scheduled a session with me. Her other physical complaints included taking an antidepressant every other day, in addition to costly monthly immune system suppressant infusions for the MS.

During our session, Carol relates a very normal happy childhood. She reveals that she craves wine. She has a technical job. Amicably divorced five years ago, she describes her ex-husband as negative, judgmental, belittling, and domineering during their long marriage. She wonders if she has unresolved hidden anger toward him. If so, she'd like to clear this issue. Carol knows her biggest challenge in her current life is patience. She wants to know what the MS is teaching her. She also wants to stop craving wine.

PAST LIFE

Carol is standing outdoors looking at a Native American tipi, located on the prairie. She is a young barefoot woman with long dark hair, wearing a leather dress, without jewelry or beading. She sees camp fires and women walking around, dressed in leather clothing. This is her village. She walks into the largest tipi because I ask her to go into the tipi where she sleeps, where men gather in a circle with a fire in the middle, smoking, and talking. Her husband is the chief of the tribe. She's not sure what she does in the community. She has no children. Her husband is giving her an angry look, and she doesn't know why.

We move to an important day. She's marrying the chief. It's obvious Carol has moved backward in time. The chief is standing there with his head feathers, getting ready for the ceremony. She's afraid because she was forced to marry him. Her family lives in a different place, and is not part of this community.

The next important day is the birth of a baby girl. Her husband is with her, and she is feeling unhappy. Life in this relationship is rough, and she's afraid of him. He doesn't talk to her. He rapes her. He raped her on the wedding day. There was no romance.

I ask her to look at the skin on her arm and tell me the color of the skin tone, so we can learn if she had been captured from a village or town. She has a hard time looking at her arm, but she manages to see it is light and the same color as the chief. They are of the same tribe.

On the last day of that life, soldiers attack the village. She is shot in the back, falls down, and dies. Out of the body, she tells me the purpose of that life was to be killed and that she does not know that life's lessons.

HIGHER SELF

I ask the Higher Self why they showed that past life.

> HS: The lessons in that life were painful and that life can be cruel. The purpose of her current life is to find peace and accept herself. She needs to learn to love herself. It is recommended she put herself first, before others, including her [present] family. She worries too much about other people. It's time to pay attention and care for herself.

I ask the HS what was the root cause of her symptoms.

> HS: The diagnosis of multiple sclerosis regarding her symptoms is accurate. She manifested the disease to protect herself from herself, to teach her to take better care of her body, and to listen to her body. She can pay attention better by relaxing, calming it, and not getting worked up about things. The recommended method is to just be still, relaxing and listening to her body. Her body talks to her, and she listens part of the time.

> The lessons of multiple sclerosis for her is to not take everything into her body and for her to express her emotions. She needs to use her words and not be angry and internalize the anger. She needs to tell people they are upsetting her, and she needs to not tell people it's okay when they upset her. She needs to address

the situation with kindness and love, not with anger. She's already learned this; she just needs to practice it. The symptoms of the MS came from the prior life she was shown in this session. The chief in that lifetime is her ex-husband in this [current] life.

When she relaxes in meditation, she needs to envision a healing taking place in her body, the spine, along the spine, and the brain. She needs to picture the healing with love. She can she heal herself. Meditate everyday, in the morning, ten minutes first, work up to thirty minutes. If she follows the recommendations, she will be cured of the MS.

She's not sure if she wants to be cured. She uses it for protection. She would like it to be manageable. The symptoms are part of a contract in this lifetime, and it's teaching her to love herself within. When she loves herself, she will be cured. She will learn that when she says no, she won't have to use the disease to say no.

B: *She would like to know what is the root cause of her impatience?*

HS: She has no concept of time, and this is why she is impatient. She enjoys the instant pleasure, so waiting is not what she likes to do. She needs to meditate, relax, ask for patience, and learn patience. The best method to learn patience is when she becomes impatient, she needs to stop and breathe and let it go. Whatever she is wanting, needing, asking for—to just release it. With practice she can let it go.

B: *What is the root cause of her craving for wine and the need to take an antidepressant?*

HS: Meditation will take place of the wine. She won't want the wine after that. The wine relaxes her. The meditation will do the same thing. She doesn't need the antidepressant anymore. She's cleansed a lot of her anger, sadness, and jealousy, through the energy healing and learning and becoming aware of what is making her angry. She wasn't enjoying her life. She wanted the lives of others. She can wean off the antidepressant every two days, then every three days. She will run out of the medication and won't need to refill the prescription.

Immune suppressant infusions should continue until she learns to relax through the meditation. She will know when to stop. She will go once every five weeks, then once every six weeks, etc. She will stretch it out because she won't feel the need for it. She will determine weaning off from this drug.

B: *What is the root cause of her fatigue?*

HS: The root cause of her fatigue is she prefers to check out of life and not be burdened. She wants to escape for a while, and the fatigue serves a positive purpose in this. It relaxes her. She needs it to heal too. The fatigue will help her to not be so active. Rather, she should meditate and be quiet and peaceful. The fatigue will diminish as she meditates more. Her cognitive impairment, forgetfulness, getting lost driving a car, and losing focus when working on problems, are messages to get her to relax and meditate. She is doing too many things for too many people. She needs to do for herself. She needs to stop, and breathe into these symptoms and situations, and relax.

During the body scan, the Higher Self shares this about her body:

HS: Very healthy, apart from the MS. There are no other issues for her to be concerned about. Healing will occur during the night too.

While the HS is scanning the client, my body is undulating in my chair. I have no control over the movement. I can feel waves moving through my entire body. I know the HS is doing something important. I ask the HS about this.

HS: That was to show you how Carol feels sometimes. She's in motion while she's standing still. Show her what it looks like. There was no ill effect on you while this occurred.

PARTING MESSAGE

HS: The strongest message is to really love who she is and where she's at in this life. She needs to take better care of her heart and her soul. She's learning that. She's making a lot of progress. She's happy because she's accepted things now. She's no longer swimming upstream anymore, fighting the current.

A month after her QHHT® session, Carol said she felt more relaxed. Her neck felt better, and she had no craving for wine, whatsoever. She went six weeks between MS drug infusions.

At three months post session, Carol reported she was off all medications and feeling very positive. "Life just keeps getting better and better!"

Carol healed herself from MS and depression. Do you see why I love QHHT®?

In the next session story, the client learns about her life purpose and missions.

9
INDIGO CLIENT, CRYSTAL & RAINBOW CHILDREN

When I was a legal nurse consultant in an insurance company, I taught a course in soft tissue bodily injury, medical terminology, physical anatomy, and pathophysiology. In my preparation for the class, I discovered the concept of the Indigo[14] children during my spiritual studies. I did the math and realized I had Indigos in my class!

To tailor the course presentation, I threw out most of what I was taught about adult education techniques and incorporated a different style for the best method to teach people who have Indigo traits, such as they already know the answers and have a wealth of knowledge they can tap into, and they came as fierce brave souls to shake up the old programs and make it easier for the newer children coming to the planet, earning them the nickname "system busters." These people shine with a deep blue aura around them, giving us an indication of their intuitive skills and activated third eye, which explains their name.

Knowing this, I added in metaphysical and potential future information they may consider down the road to apply in their work and/or in their life in general. What adjustments did I make in the course delivery? I told them I understand they are busy multitasking at their desk and may not be able to arrive to class on time. Not a problem. Just come into the class when it's feasible and pick up a handout. If they could not make it to class, call me and I'll give them a one-on-one presentation at their desk. I told them I didn't even care if they fell asleep in class because I know they are still with us.

The Higher Self never sleeps! This was proven to me on the last day of the course when a student fell asleep during my presentation. I couldn't remember the name of a new surgical procedure[15] that just

---

14 *The Care and Feeding of Indigo Children*, Doreen Virtue, 2001

15 https://www.spine.org/KnowYourBack/Treatments/SurgicalOptions/ArtificialDiscReplacement.aspx

received FDA (Food & Drug Administration) approval in the United States for spinal disc replacement. This student woke up, raised his hand and said, "I know the name, Barbara." He went on to describe the procedure, the name of it, and the fact his father will be undergoing the procedure for his spinal condition. I smiled and thanked the student.

It was a distinct pleasure and honor for me to teach these beautiful souls and present information in a way that was not demanding, limiting, or restrictive. The paradigm-busting Indigos play an integral role in preparing the entire planet for ascension. Without the old programs and restrictions, current souls on Mother Earth are free to express their divine nature as creative beings, with love and light in many forms. For instance, success and wealth can be perceived as service to humanity by helping one another, not as how many toys one has accumulated in the course of a lifetime, or how productive one must be on the hamster wheel to achieve money.

This session story could fit into several different chapters, but I chose to put it here with the name Indigo as a chapter title because there are people who don't know they are Indigo and can resonate with this client's session. For our dear Indigos, this chapter is dedicated to you.

* * *

I had the pleasure of facilitating a session in 2016 for a tall thirty-five year-old business woman from Phoenix. Phoebe recognized me instantly and knew right away that we were doing work in the other realms of existence. She knew she was an Indigo. She had an advanced degree in her field.

As I sat down in the hotel room, Phoebe pushed her phone in my face, to show me a blue aura around her image in the photo. This behavior was confirmation of her Indigo trait. This is what I love about Indigos! Indigo people are brave, strong, and powerful. They are here to shake up the old programs and tear down the unnecessary and somewhat harmful paradigms, in order to lay a foundation of love for the new children coming into the planet, known as the Rainbow children[16] and the Crystal children[17]. Depending on whom you talk to or what you read, these children are described with various traits;

---

16 http://www.starchildren.info/rainbow.html

17 http://www.starchildren.info/crystal.html

even the date range of their incarnation on Earth varies. Whether you chose to place a label on these beautiful children, or not, just know their mere existence on Earth is proof that the human being is evolving, and the collective soul is ascending to a higher dimensional expression.

Phoebe was very comfortable with me and had absolutely no expectations, not even questions for her session! We came up with a short list of questions, and she said I could ask any questions of the universe that I wanted to ask.

I was impressed with her level of trust in me. All of her life she has healed herself and was in perfect health. Phoebe has never done drugs and didn't take any prescription medication. Her teeth were in perfect health with no cavities ever.

Her reasons for a QHHT® session were to release emotional trauma from being bullied at school in her childhood and from abandonment from her parents when she was young, and to find out her mission and purpose in this current life. She had become confused with all of her recent upheavals. After multiple employment changes in a row, divorce, and then homelessness, she finally landed a lucrative and fun job, which was a relief, but the challenging journey left her wondering what it all meant.

PAST LIFE

In the first scene, she is on a red planet, with a red sky, that has a jail facility for "people" from all over the universe that are not playing by the rules. The buildings are very tall and pointy on top. She sees flying space crafts that people use for transportation.

Wearing a long red robe like for graduation or a judge's gown with colorfully decorated chest, and a gold hat, she is considered the governor of this place. She is young (forty Earth years), and her body is humanoid and healthy. She does not have a gender or family. For clarity, I will still refer to her in the feminine.

Two beings are speaking with her, asking her to make a non-military determination about something that happened. They are warriors, and they want to make peace. People address her with a title in a foreign language meaning, "Your Honor." She is a judge who handles intergalactic disputes. She reports to a council. I ask her to go to her office. The wall in her large office is decorated with commendations and awards for her service and leadership. She is highly respected.

People are re-habilitated on this planet to be better cosmic citizens, then transported back to their worlds.

> Phoebe: We collect people from all areas of the universe. Unfortunately, not all can be changed. We look for the "bad guys." Most of the souls on Earth who have been causing trouble have been removed. We have already removed a great number of "bad guys" from Earth already.

She sees her picture in the office and notes her name: Zakraton. She comes from everywhere. Her mission is to take care of the bad people. Zakraton's new mission will be as a diplomat, and this is an advancement for her.

We leave this scene to another important day…

Someone very important is coming to visit the detention rehabilitation facility to see how it's maintained. They are pleased with her work. A celebration is underway for all the progress that has been made.

> Phoebe: The whole Universe is being improved by our work. No one wants to do this work, but I will do it. I'm proud to do it. It's hard work. This is why they respect me.

She gets a promotion. We leave this scene to another day…

Zakraton is older and "they" [the council] are talking about how different sections of the universe are divided and who is going to which part, as a representative, for the different life forms.

> Phoebe: There is no one from the Old Earth, because they can't come. Representatives from the New Earth are becoming part of the council. It's a new planet for all eyes.

I ask about the current state of the universe.

> P: We are getting along. We exist in the mind of God. The mind is getting along. It's getting a vast amount of information and experiences. The Ascended Masters create universes. They work with different experiences to bring to the mind of God.

After a long silence, we move to another important day. This time we go to a scene in her current life…

P: I'm on Earth, going to school, in the sixth grade. I feel lonely and sad. Celebrating the Day of the Virgin Mary. Each girl in the school room is given a ticket to be chosen to be the Virgin Mary in the procession.

Phoebe is chosen, and has tears and laughter at the same time.

She can't pay attention in class. School subjects and information are boring. She knows it all. She looks out the window. She wonders why she is here on Earth. Her dad left the family, and she misses him. Crying with a broken heart and no place to live, she is sent to live with her grandparents.

Phoebe releases a lot of sadness during this part of the session through her tears. I give her emotional support to allow the healing to take place.

We move to another important day. Another long silence and deep breathing…

On Earth, in Phoebe's current life, the HS shows her the college graduation scene for her bachelor's degree. Her grandmother passed three days prior. More tears of sadness are shed. *"She was my Keeper for this life."* I ask if she can see her grandmother. She replies in the affirmative.

While I sit in silence, Phoebe and her grandmother have a heartfelt private conversation in Spanish with laughing and joyful tears. It is beautiful to witness this private, loving encounter. After the conversation, Phoebe repeatedly sighs deeply and has moments of silence. It feels as if a very deep clearing was done by the breath work.

HIGHER SELF

I ask about why Phoebe was shown the life on the rehabilitation planet. This appears to be a parallel life she is living.

> HS: Zakraton is who she is in her multi-dimensionality. Her purpose is to maintain balance in the universe. She is learning to be a person with authority. She is in preparation, and her time will come. Her current life job changes occurred because she needed

to meet all those people. She will be in her current new job for the next five years. Eventually she will be working on the other side. Her new job has not been decided yet. She's on track with her missions. She needs to know herself and believe who she is. She needs to get rid of the fear. The bad people in her life have been trying to get rid of her, because of who she is. She is totally protected. She never needs to worry. We need her energy on Earth, and it's important. She's a healer. She can manifest and create from anything. There's nothing to worry about. Everything's covered.

The HS deletes the worry program, and downloads and installs a new program while we wait.

HS: She can heal with her hands and by thought. When she was younger, she healed her grandpa when he was in critical care and given a terminal prognosis by the medical doctors. She was taken to the bedside and he was instantly healed. The doctors were baffled when he walked out of the hospital completely healed. She is meant to be single. She signed up for a life without marriage or children. She is at peace with this.

She is from the Pleiades. She stares at the constellation Orion, because her star family is there. She communicates with them telepathically. Her star father's name is Xarba. Her star brothers are there too. This is why she is sad. This is the root cause of her sadness and feeling alone. She goes there at night; plus she is working with others during that time. There are conferences to attend. There is much discussion about the people with karma. Not everyone will pass to the other side. We are trying to make it smooth. Everyone goes to where they need to go, according to their consciousness.

At age four, Phoebe walked from school to her home, which was a long distance. To this day, Phoebe's mother is perplexed how her daughter made that journey so quickly and safely.

HS: We helped her by just moving her. There was a guy who tried to talk with her. We made her disappear from him and reappear at her house. We protected her because of her mission. There was another purpose to this. The parents were about to divorce, and we tried to prevent it, but it didn't work out. She became closer to her grandma.

THE HEALING PART OF THE SESSION

Phoebe said that she received the emotional healing she sought from this session. She also sought healing from a motorcycle accident in which she was attempting suicide at age fifteen that had caused a broken clavicle that had not healed correctly.

I inquire about any unseen brain injury. The HS says there was no injury, as an angel caught her so that Phoebe's head did not strike the pavement.

> HS: The root cause of chest pain is she is feeling the ill intentions of others who want to do her harm. It is because of her openness of her heart. She loves everyone. She feels scared to reject them. She needs to reject them and not be with them. This chest pain helps her to recognize them and be away from them. This is a positive communication tool she uses.

After the healing was complete and the HS answered the client's questions, I begin to ask my questions.

Barbara: *How does healing occur in these QHHT® sessions and how do you prepare the client?*

HS: The intuition will guide you [the client] to find the facilitator. The connection will occur. Everything will happen. There must be an intention, what needs to be done, to keep it in mind. When you do the session, the healing is already occurred; however, it must be communicated to the person, so they will know on this level of consciousness.

Barbara: *Whom have I been speaking with?*

HS: Sonar.

B: *Are you the representative of the HS?*

Sonar: No.

B: *Are you her guide?*

S: Yes.

B: *Do you communicate with her HS, then relay the information?*

S: Yes.

B: *Is she aware of you?*

S: No, there is a group of people here.

Then, Sonar directs his attention to me, relaying what the HS is telling him.

HS/S: You will be moving, 2017. One and a half years. It's changing. The timelines can compress. It's the light work is to be completed, then 2017 is the year. That is what they are saying. Continue the work in the Phoenix area.

We learned from Dolores that the Higher Self is a group of beings that are connected to us and are responsible for us. This is the group that Sonar is talking about. It is perfectly normal for a guide or angel to come through and relay the answers to the client's and practitioner's questions, as a bridge, so to speak, from the Higher Self.

PARTING MESSAGE FOR PHOEBE

Sonar: They are saying, "Don't be afraid. You're doing a good job. We admire you for what you are doing. You are really brave. Continue doing it and you will see the change that you make. Just be strong. Don't worry about it. Nothing is going to happen. Everything will be provided to you. Just continue the path. You will be okay, because you are a warrior. Don't worry. Your way is peace."

When I reviewed Phoebe's session, I realized a concept in the session that is very familiar to me. For many years, I've been saying to others, when I hear about crimes committed by people on Earth, "I wish all the people who can't play nice, be transported to another place off world, and let them figure it out, so we can live in peace!" Here in this session, we were given a possible reality that is occurring behind the scenes, perhaps in another realm of existence.

In the next chapter, I give a couple examples of the Higher Self's different communication styles.

10
COMMUNICATING STYLES OF THE HIGHER SELF

In this chapter I share a couple of stories that illustrate the various styles the Higher Self uses to communicate during a hypnosis session. Although in most QHHT® sessions, the HS will use the client's vocal cords to tell the story and answer questions, I've observed that there are exceptions. This is not to say the information is not valid. Rather, it shows the flexibility of the HS to convey messages and concepts.

THE LUNAR TECHNICIAN AT MACHU PICCHU

I facilitated this session for a delightful middle-aged man who was human immunodeficiency virus (HIV) positive, had breathing problems described as difficulty with air moving in and out of his lungs, digestive problems since he began HIV medications, foot pain, and low back discomfort. After reading Dolores' book *Three Waves of Volunteers*, he wanted to know if he was a volunteer, an Indigo or Rainbow warrior.

Robert was born in the US to a father who was unavailable emotionally and physically. The father worked and expected the mother to take care of everything else. The family moved to a large city. He felt devastated when he had to leave all of his friends in the previous neighborhood. He shared with me that he had abandonment issues from his parents divorcing when he was young. When Robert's father re-married and had more children, this caused even more abandonment issues, as the father's attention was focused on the new children.

When Robert was told he was HIV positive years ago, the doctor said he was a "slow-progressor," meaning his titers were elevated only a little. He went on medications, but they made him feel awful. For the past two months prior to the session, he quit taking the medications and wanted to be rid of HIV for good. Not taking his medications was his decision alone.

As you'll see in the session, Robert experienced going back and forth between allowing the HS to speak, then listening to them and telling me what they said.

PAST LIFE

Describing Machu Picchu in Peru, Robert sees the llamas, the green grass, the adjoining green luscious mountainsides, the large carved stones, and many other beautiful sights. We explore his sensing of the environment. He begins describing the doorway with hanging leaf garlands and the people cooking food, sitting on mats. I know he is in another life, before I even complete the relaxation script.

People are using a tool to crush the corn in a big flat bowl, adding water, crushing it into a paste material. People are making clothes with an instrument, weaving the cloth together. He describes the clothes as not colorful. The garments are brown with stripes, and with black and white zigzags.

Inside this structure, there are beams overhead. You can touch your hand on the low ceilings. The roofs are pointed and made of wood and tree branches. The walls are clay mud. The floors are dirt with lower areas and cut into for cooking.

>Barbara: *Are there a lot of people here?*
>
>Robert: Only four and myself.
>
>B: *Do you get the feeling you are related to these people?*
>
>Robert starts crying.
>
>B: *It's okay.*
>
>R: [Crying] There're my family.
>
>B: *How nice. Can you describe them to me?*
>
>R: One is my wife, one is my mother. Two daughters that are making the clothing.
>
>B: *What are you feeling now that you are looking at your family?*
>
>R: I don't know why, I feel sad.

B: *You feel sad. Is it about something you know or something that was said to you?*

R: [more crying] I feel very separate from them. Like I can't walk in. I can only stand by the door. I feel like there's a lot of separation from us. Maybe we are not allowed to be together.

I ask Robert to describe himself. His brown skinned feet are bare. Wearing a one-piece garment with short sleeves, the skirt part goes over his head. He is wearing a satchel on the waist made of wood or straw. His hair is black, fashioned in a short bob to just below the ears. In his hair he is wearing peacock feathers, brown on the outside and white in the middle. The left wrist has yellow beads from the seeds of a fruit. His necklace with large blue beads goes down the middle of his chest. His hat with feathers sticking out, is flat on top with a rounded backside. The front of the straw hat is pointed at a forty five-degree angle.

B: *What is the significance of your hat?*

R: Part of the job. Some kind of authority is given when wearing the hat. I watch and record the moon.

B: *How do you do your job?*

R: On the other mountain, away from my family, there's a moon temple. It's four or six of us watching the moon every night. We draw pictures and record it and watch the cycles.

B: *How do you record it?*

R: There's instruments there, and I don't know how they work.

B: *Describe one of the instruments.*

R: There's a stake in the middle, circle around the stake, something connected to the top coming down to the circle. It turns around the circle and measures how much the moon has shrunken, grown or changes. A lot of parchment paper.

B: *What is done with this information? Do you know?*

R: We share it with the shaman. It's for the community.

B: *What does the shaman do with the information about the moon?*

R: He talks about the moon's power, its energy and [how it] replenishes us and rejuvenates us. How the moon is one of our brothers. There's a lot of love. Everyone loves the moon. The shaman tells us the moon loves us back.

B: *Very nice. A lot of love. Are you standing there with your family?*

R: A campfire and the shaman is talking.

B: *The others that also record, are they allowed to be with their families?*

R: We can only visit.

B: *Is there a reason for that?*

R: They would distract us from our job. The temple is on a different mountain. We have to walk and climb. It's far away.

B: *Do you have to stay there for some time?*

R: Several weeks, sometimes it's months.

B: *Does your family recognize you?*

R: Affirmative mumble [crying].

B: *So what do you do now?*

R: We are all hugging—group hugging. [Robert is crying].

B: *Sounds like you have an important job that helps the whole community.*

R: Yes, I love my family. I love the moon. [more healing crying] It's so beautiful. I feel guilty; I love my job more than my family.

B: *Do they know you love them?*

R: They do.

B: *Is there anything you want to tell them at this time?*

R: I'm telling them I love them.

We move forward in that life… He leapfrogs to another life, another time.

B: *What is happening?*

R: It's a day party for one of my children. It's the forties or fifties. Old cars out the window. Everyone has really drab clothing, nothing colorful.

B: *What is the environment like?*

R: We're all happy, drinking, laughing in a big living room.

B: *Describe the people there.*

R: I think my mom was my wife. [She has] curly brown hair. Wearing a white dress with red patterns and polka dots on it. Big collars, button up shirts. Thirty people. It's my son's birthday.

B: *How is he?*

R: He's very happy. He's turning eight today.

B: *Is everybody happy at this party?*

R: Yeah.

I ask Robert to describe himself. Wearing shiny black shoes, cuffed brown trousers, and a white shirt, his body is healthy in his forties. His brownish red hair is short. He notices a wedding ring on his left ring finger, as he looks down at the martini in his left hand.

Walking outside to the backyard, he is watching the children playing. Another man is standing next to him.

B: *How are you feeling at this time?*

R: Ashamed.

B: *What about?*

R: I think this man is the one I'm having an affair with. It feels secretive, it seems wrong. We shouldn't be together in the back yard. We have to hide it.

B: *Have you been in this relationship with him for some time?*

R: A year. I think he's married to a woman too.

B: *Are you talking with him?*

R: No.

B: *What happens next?*

R: I don't feel right, so I'm going to go back inside.

B: *What do you see now?*

R: I'm back at the party making myself another drink. I'm trying to forget about him.

B: *Does the alcohol help you?*

R: [Affirmative mumble]

B: *How does the alcohol help you?*

R: Numbs down the feelings I have for him and to help me cope with this situation. I drink a lot in my office.

B: *What do you do for the majority of your time?*

R: I see myself in my office, as a banker or some business.

B: *Do you enjoy that work?*

R: No.

B: *What don't you like about it?*

R: Nothing creative about it. It's very bland and insignificant. Yet, at the same time I work more than I need to. It's a distraction.

B: *Does it keep you away from your home and family?*

R: I think I work at home, but I'm still separated from my family.

B: *How do you feel about that?*

R: Part of me feels guilty. I feel like a victim. It's not the reality I want to be in. It's not fair.

B: *Do you feel there are a lot of restrictions in your life?*

R: Yes.

B: *Tell me about them.*

R: I can't be free. I can't be singing and dancing. They will judge you, or you could end up in an insane asylum.

B: *Is that what they do to people?*

R: Some people. So many judgments. Everybody has to hide their secrets. Everybody has to hide.

Moving to another important day in that life…

R: It's my wife's funeral. I feel like I'm in my sixties.

B: *What happened to your wife?*

R: She got sick. Hard to breathe.

B: *Do you know the sickness?*

R: No. I have mixed emotions. Part of me is glad she's gone. I don't have to hide so much anymore.

B: *What is happening at the funeral?*

R: Everyone's left except me. I'm being very reflective thinking about our life together. I can't bring myself to cry. I'm stoic. I have glasses on.

B: *What happens next?*

R: I'm alone in the house, living alone. No more relationships. I'm very lonely. I don't talk to my children very much.

B: *Why?*

R: I don't think they want to hear from me.

B: *They don't want to hear from you?*

R: I was always working.

B: *What do you do now?*

R: I'm retired. I'm just sitting there doing nothing. Feeling miserable.

B: *Do you do that all day long?*

R: Every once in a while I go to the grocery store and make dinner. I listen to the radio.

Leaving that scene, we go to the last day of that life…

R: I'm in a hospital bed. My two kids and their spouses are with me, standing next to the bed.

B: *Did the body become ill?*

R: I feel like I'm eighty or eighty-one. Not sure what I died of. Maybe the heart.

I help him to be comfortable and look at what is happening to him.

B: *Are you out of the body?*

R: [Affirmative mumble]

B: *What happened?*

R: A heart attack.

B: *What did they do with the body?*

R: They buried it in a casket next to my wife. [long silence] I just seem so unhappy, maybe emotional pain.

After helping him to feel comfortable through emotional support, he was able to look back at that life…

B: *What were the lessons?*

R: I should have been there more for my children and my wife. [crying] Even though there were restrictions, I could or should have found time. I should have loved more.

B: *Should have loved more?*

R: [crying, affirmative head nod]

HIGHER SELF

Barbara: *Why did you show him the lifetime as the father?*

Higher Self: To show him that he's like his father in this lifetime. [Big sigh]

B: *And what are the lessons from that lifetime is he learning in this lifetime?*

HS: Whoever is your family, whoever is with you, you must love them. They need you.

B: *What was the purpose of that lifetime for him?*

HS: To get ready for this lifetime, to open up like a flower.

B: *Is he doing that?*

HS: [Affirmative head nod]

B: *Why did you show him the lifetime at Machu Picchu, as a moon observer?*

HS: It's one of his favorites. To show him why he loves the moon so much in this lifetime.

B: *What were the lessons of that lifetime?*

HS: Diligence, hard work, and to appreciate your family when they're gone. Magic!

B: *And what about the magic?*

HS: To appreciate the moon's magic and the magic of the shaman. To find beauty in nature.

B: *Would you tell us more about the magic of the moon?*

HS: It can be very similar to the light of God, the magic of Source. It replenishes you. It refills your battery. There's so much love for you to connect with it. Lots of creative energy too.

B: *Is this also the moon's importance in this lifetime?*

HS: Yes.

B: *What is so powerful about this full moon we have during the summer solstice. What significance does it hold for Robert?*

HS: [crying more] To fill him with more love and more courage, confidence, and healing. A lot of healing to take place.

B: *Are you able to go inside his body now?*

HS: Yes.

Silence for several minutes…

HS: Still scanning. There is fear, which he has been working on releasing. The digestive system has fear.

B: *What's the fear about?*

HS: About abandonment. So afraid to be alone. Lungs are being healed. We're going to teach him how to take big deep breaths. Bring in more air.

B: *What is the root cause of the lung problem?*

HS: His mother's smoking. He needs to exercise more.

B: *What type?*

HS: Cardio, easy on his feet, like biking.

B: *Are you able to heal his lungs at this time?*

HS: Yes.

B: *How are you doing it?*

HS: Thought, intention, healing energy.

B: *Healing energy in there?*

HS: Healing his wrists.

B: *What happened to his wrists?*

HS: Repetitive motion injury from his work. He needs more hydrotherapy on them. He knows this.

B: *Are you able to go in there and heal his wrists?*

HS: Yes.

B: *Very good. How are you doing that?*

HS: The same.

B: *The healing energy?*

HS: Don't even have to think about it, it's just happening.

B: *Yeah. Very nice. Will he notice an improvement in his wrists after this session?*

HS: Yes.

B: *Very good.*

HS: Now we're healing his back. It's not just me, there's others here. I see her, Aphrodite with her staff.

B: *What is the root cause of the back pain, back discomfort?*

HS: His kundalini is not fully awakened yet. Yet, he does this for his clients. There's blockages.

B: *Where did that [blockage] come from?*

HS: He doesn't take care of himself. He does so much for others, he doesn't do for himself.

B: *What do you recommend?*

HS: More meditating. He needs to do yoga. He knows this. To stretch out his spine. He needs to get away from his house at least once a month, somewhere in nature to recharge.

B: *Will he know where to go?*

HS: Yes, he'll know where to go. The feet we can only help a little.

B: *Why was he born with the club feet?*

HS: He chose this to pay off some karmic debt.

B: *Okay. Can you share with us what that karmic debt was about?*

HS: [silence] I cannot say at this time.

B: *Will you be able to give the information later when he listens to his recording?*

HS: I don't know; it's not up to me. I'm not sure.

B: *Are you speaking in council at this moment to determine this?*

HS: I am; I don't know what they are saying. He knows he needs to help the children. He's been shown to work with foster children age at eighteen, fifty percent become homeless. He knows he's supposed to work with them.

B: *Does he know how to do this?*

HS: Yes, he knows already.

B: *Is this one of his missions?*

HS: Yes. He's meant to do this. He's very good at this. He has to do something to help the whales. To honor them. He's spent a lifetime on a fishing boat killing them. He has to do something for them.

B: *And this will help balance the karma?*

HS: Yes.

B: *Is the scanning continuing?*

HS: I think we're done with the body.

B: *Well, what about the immune system?*

HS: He doesn't have to worry about that anymore. We're taking care of that.

B: *Wonderful! Is his immune system healthy?*

HS: Yes, plus he's eating the right things, the right fruits and vegetables, the juices. We're directing him to eat.

B: *So he doesn't need any medications for his immune system?*

HS: No.

B: *Is there any supplements you want him to take?*

HS: Yes, he's taking some of them already.

B: *You want him to continue those?*

HS: Yes.

B: *You shared you want him to dance more, and you want him to be comfortable when he dances.*

HS: He knows what to do. He tightens his shoes very tightly and puts on the ankle braces. He doesn't like wearing shoes. He loves to be barefoot.

B: *Is it healthy for him to be barefoot in Nature once a month?*

HS: Yes.

B: *Is he considered a volunteer?*

HS: Yes.

B: *Indigo?*

HS: No.

B: *Rainbow?*

HS: No, he's a Crystal child.

B: *What would he like to know about this?*

HS: He affects everyone that he's with. They are all changed for the better just by being around him.

B: *I've heard they are pure love.*

HS: He doesn't see how that could be. He looks back and sees how people fall in love with him. Even his clients.

B: *What is his purpose?*

HS: To affect the change for everyone that's around him with love.

B: *So he's completing his mission?*

HS: Yes, he's a healer.

B: *What missions need to be completed?*

HS: He's paid off karma by helping people in similar ways. He always gives money to charities, gives money to tip jars, he helps homeless people. He just needs to stay on his path. Love will come naturally. Random acts of kindness. He needs to do more of these things.

B: *He'd like to know does a person need to have a partner in order to ascend?*

HS: He does things differently. He doesn't need to follow anyone else's path. His path is beautiful.

B: *Will he ascend anyway, no matter who he is with?*

HS: We hope so.

B: *What is the ascension?*

HS: The ascension is when the Earth will transform into fifth dimension. There's many beings and healers that will be guided to rise and ascend, to heal, transform. She's shaking off the debris and energy. She's getting rid of it. A lot of people will ascend with her. She will still host them as their planet. The others will go to a different planet. They will go where they are supposed to go.

B: *Sounds like everyone is going to be okay.*

HS: Yes, they will.

B: *Is there more peace on Earth?*

HS: They tell me yes. It's very secretive. It's beautiful. Like all of sudden fireworks will all connect.

In a QHHT® session, the client will use any and all their extra senses to convey and describe what they are experiencing. In Robert's case, we see that he is using his clairaudience sense, by listening to the group of beings and telling us what they said, and allowing the HS to talk through his vocal chords. The HS references the client in the third person and uses the word "We" many times through the moist nasal speech.

He chose to have club feet in this life and go through the numerous surgeries for them, so he could balance karma. The HS obliged my request to decrease the discomfort in his feet because they want him to dance more for his health. His digestive issues were about abandonment. The low back discomfort was about his kundalini. Yoga and meditation were recommended.

PARTING MESSAGE FOR ROBERT

> HS: Remember who you are. Remember to love yourself. Stand in your power.

In his session, Robert discovered why he loves the moon so much. He learned about his missions and what direction his life is to go from here. Robert cried during most of his hypnosis, releasing toxins and pains he had kept bottled up inside.

Falling tears are very healthy for the human. Emotional release is one way the human body, mind, and spirit heals. The communication style presented in his session is a typical form of the Higher Self speaking in the third person, talking directly with the QHHT® practitioner.

In the next session story, the client alternates between allowing the Higher Self to use her vocal cords, and listening to what the HS tells her in her mind, then repeating out loud what they said.

SEEING THE UNIVERSE AT THE END OF HER NOSE

Sophia was a middle aged woman whose teenage son died in a motor vehicle accident in another country several years ago. He died in her arms. I couldn't begin to fathom the depth of her sorrow. Sophia couldn't focus on anything. No hobbies. No creative expression engagement whatsoever. She just celebrated the first wedding anniversary with her husband.

Self employed, Sophia was glued to her cell phone 24/7 and was extremely left brained, according to her. She told me her third eye is closed, so she did not see images at all.

Sophia's concerns included fear of her daughter dying prematurely, and she wanted her third eye open.

PAST LIFE

We begin the induction upstairs in her bedroom with her cell phone on the nightstand. At first she has a hard time seeing images, then her third eye opens very nicely, just like that.

She is taken to her son's death scene in her current life, hearing her daughter screaming at God to not take her brother. (Even a scene from earlier in our present life is considered the past.) The client tells me that she doesn't go back to this scene in her conscious state because she wants to move on in her life, for her daughter's sake. I give her emotional support, and we journey further.

She describes the last breath of her son and a woman placing a towel over her son's face. Sophia throws the towel off, and attempts cardiopulmonary resuscitation, to no avail. Although he dies, Sophia doesn't become overly emotional, nor ask to stop the movie.

We leave that scene and go forward to her wedding day, one year ago, on a California beach. She is happy.

HIGHER SELF

The HS comes in with a deep breath, and Sophia says she is hearing what they are saying, so she relays their messages. She starts doubting. I ask the HS how can she relax.

> Sophia: What I'm hearing is: "Put her phone away."
>
> I stand up from my bedside chair and put her phone in the adjoining bathroom across the room, and return to the bedside.
>
> B: *Why did you choose this lifetime for her to see?*
>
> Sophia: I'm confused. While you were talking, I saw myself in an armor suit. I'm not sure.
>
> B: *Why did you show her that lifetime and the suit of armor?*
>
> Sophia: I feel proud, I guess. I don't know.
>
> B: *What was the purpose of showing her this life?*

S: [long silence] I feel like I have no idea. I feel like I was some kind of warrior.

B: *Sophia would like to know how she can relax more. Can you help her?*

[Silence]

B: *Do you recommend some ways for her to relax?*

Sophia allows the Higher Self to speak, alternating between listening to them and letting me know what they say, as well as directly allowing them to use her vocal cords.

Sophia: All I'm hearing is "put her phone away".

B: *She feels she is worried about losing her daughter. What would you like to tell her about this? What are they saying to you?*

S: I'm being told I'm just being a protective mom, and it's natural because I lost my son.

B: *How do you feel she's doing in this respect, as far as being protective of her daughter?*

HS: Good.

B: *Does she need to change anything in that regard?*

HS: No.

B: *Her feeling anxious and nervous all the time, does this affect her health in any way?*

HS: No.

B: *Can you help us understand why this doesn't affect her health in a negative way?*

HS: Because it's natural, and these are imperative years for her, so I have to make sure that I watch over her closely.

B: *Do you feel she's doing a good job as a mother?*

HS: Yes.

B: *Can you share with us: Is she going to live a long life?*

HS: A decent one.

B: *Will she see her daughter grow up and become an adult?*

HS: Yes.

B: *Can you help adjust those anxieties that she has about being around for her daughter?*

HS: Yes.

B: *Does she know how to become more patient?*

HS: She needs to become more spiritual.

B: *How does she become more spiritual?*

HS: Take a class.

B: *What class?*

HS: Reiki.

B: *Could you go into her lower back and tell us about the root cause of her back discomfort?*

HS: She needs to stretch more.

B: *Where does the discomfort come from?*

HS: Stress.

B: *What is the stress about?*

HS: Probably her son.

B: *Can you help us understand what the stress is, about her son?*

HS: Holding grief inside her body.

B: *Are you able to help her release it at this time?*

HS: Yoga.

B: *Are you able to release some of this discomfort?*

HS: It feels like it is. She needs to be consistent.

B: *Help us understand about her need for abundance in her finances.*

Sophia: I'm hearing, "just let it be".

B: *Are you taking care of everything regarding her financial abundance?*

HS: She's doing good.

B: *What about her self-employment business?*

At one point Sofia says they are discussing something among themselves, then they tell her the answer.

Sophia: I'm hearing, "She's where she needs to be." It's sufficient.

B: *Will her work change in the future?*

HS: Yes, just give it time.

B: *She feels she is holding onto anger in regard to her son's passing. Can you go into her body and tell us where it's located?*

HS: It's a lot better.

B: *Can you help her now to release it?*

Sophia: I heard, once she works more spiritually, she'll have that connection and won't have that void.

B: *Would you please give Sophia a physical body sensation so she knows you're connected to her?*

Sophia: So, my eyes are closed, they're moving a lot (REM-rapid eye movement), where my nose is, I can see like a moon, it's round, a white circle, and it keeps moving. Then the stars and black sky.

B: *The third eye is open.*

PARTING MESSAGE

HS: Yoga, meditate, Reiki, relaxing, go to a school.

The SC gave the client what she wanted most: to see clairvoyantly with an activated pineal gland. She was looking at the cosmos with her third eye wide open.

When Sophia came out of hypnosis, she apologized for not allowing the Higher Self to talk all of the time. I told her this was unique for her. I thoroughly enjoyed how she alternated back and forth using her clairaudience, versus allowing them to speak. Her third eye was open because she was seeing words to convey the answers. It seems her Higher Self was being very gentle with her and showing her in a subtle way that she is clairvoyant. Then, the grand finale image was seeing the universe at the end of her nose.

FIRST A GUIDE, THEN THE HIGHER SELF

The following session story demonstrates how a client's guide can appear to answer questions and provide healing. It's possible that the Higher Self chose to have the guide handle the initial interface, so the client could adjust to the energy in a gentle, slower way. In these situations, as the practitioner, I ask the guide to summon a higher power for any questions it can't answer.

Carl was a twenty-seven-year-old honorably discharged Air Force specialist. He went on assignment in the Middle East, after which he acquired mild PTSD, manifesting as anxiety. He was very nervous that his third eye wouldn't open, even in hypnosis.

When I entered Carl's home, he said a sensation of calmness overcame him. During the three-hour interview, he also noticed energy moving around his body.

I reminded him that his Higher Self was already making adjustments for him and helped him to understand his third eye was already open. It's fun to watch the wave of realization appear on the client's face, and seeing them smile during the interview.

Carl's main concern for the QHHT® session was his impatience and anxiety. Also, he wanted confirmation about his current life decisions.

PAST LIFE

We begin the hypnosis. I barely start the first line of the script when Carl's eyes enter into rapid eye movement, confirming that the third eye is open and he's seeing images.

The first past life movie is in early America, as a young man with a small family, eating potatoes in his stew, in the log cabin style home.

The second past life is as a married man living a comfortable life as a couch potato. His wife works in the medical field, and he doesn't have to work because he had made enough money already, so he spends most of his time in his recliner watching the news on TV. Of particular note, he watches the moon exploration and the ET artifacts they found on the moon. (I realize that the Higher Self is showing him a scene from the 1960s Apollo moon program, and the information that will be coming forth during the Disclosure.)

After he leaves his body, dying from cancer, he goes into the light and meets his guide, who is very stern, extremely loving, and helping him to learn patience. "My guide grabs my hand and walks me to a chair. She sits next to me. She wants to explain what I just processed. She is so loving. She loves pink! She has a pink gown and blonde hair. She has light purple skin. She cares about me. She says I need to relax more. She says I'm too tense."

Barbara: *Does she have the ability to help you with being too tense?*

Carl: Yeah.

B: *How does she do that?*

C: I just feel the relaxation. She knows me very well. She's stern with me and patient! [big deep breaths repeated]

B: *Do you feel better?*

C: Yeah. She says she wished I trusted her more. I feel like I trust her, but she says, "It's not enough."

B: *Do you tell her you trust her now, that you can feel it?*

C: Yes, I will trust her now! I feel chills and tingles.

B: *What do the tingles represent?*

C: Comfort. I can relax now. Love. Compassion. She says I don't trust as much as I need to. [laughing]

B: *Is she helping you to change that now?*

C: She is. She is helping me to breathe deeper. She says there's too much tension in my lungs. [deep exhalations] She's helping me to process it out.

B: *Is that why you have tension in your chest when you get anxious?*

C: It's a light. She's helping me to get it out. The tension is from not trusting enough. Trust! She's tired of me not trusting people.

Without asking for permission or prompt on my part, I now speak directly to his pink angel guide.

B: *Is he running some old programs?*

Angel: Yeah.

B: *Are you able to go into his mind and remove those old programs?*

A: Yeah.

B: *While you're in his mind, could you download, install, and launch a new program where he feels at peace, calm, centered, balanced, love, harmony, and anything else you feel would benefit him?*

A: Yeah.

B: *How is he feeling now?*

A: He feels better.

B: *May I continue to ask questions while you're doing this healing?*

A: Yes.

B: *You showed him the life of the man who was a construction worker, with a small family. You could have shown him any lifetime. Why did you show him that one?*

A: He needs to learn patience. He's a very impatient person. I want him to be more patient. With that family, he needed to be more patient. That was the biggest lesson for him.

B: *What was the purpose of that life?*

A: To learn to love his family more. To prioritize and love his family.

B: *In that life, did the work come before the family?*

A: Yes.

B: *In the next life he was staying at home, not doing anything. It seems to be the exact opposite of the previous life. What can you tell us why you showed him that?*

A: I showed him that life because he needs to find balance. He can't over work himself, and he can't be lazy. Even though he was well off in the second life, he was really lazy. The lesson to be learned is balance. In the first life, he worked too hard, and his family paid the price for it. In the second life, he watched TV all day. He had to see both sides to learn balance. You can't be too lazy. You can't work too hard. You've got to find the middle ground, and still be productive, still be loving, showing yourself enough love, and for others around you.

B: *What happened to the son in that first life?*

A: The son looked up to the father. The son did everything the father did. The son felt neglected. He felt loved, but he wished the father was around more.

B: *The two contrasts you showed him about love and family, is he applying this into his current life?*

A: He's trying. He just needs to learn patience. He's going down a path he really loves and enjoys. He just needs to be patient with the process and not forget to take care of himself and not forget to love those around him. In this life, he just needs to find the sweet spot between the lives he's seen.

B: *Has he chosen the right path for his future employment?*

A: Yes. He can do whatever he wants to do. He likes to see people excel. He's concerned about finances.

B: *What would you like to tell him about this?*

A: He's made the right decision. He made the right move to Arizona, for his growth. The main reason he came here was to experience more growth in himself and guide himself down this path. That is why he met you. He's free here to be himself and to grow and experience. He will create his own family. He's right on track with his path.

B: *Besides patience, what else is he to learn in this current life?*

A: To take the time to love everyone. He has a feeling of being vulnerable.

B: *What is the root cause of that?*

A: He was hurt in the past. Betrayed by women earlier in his life. This has happened many times. Every time he opens himself up to love, he ends up getting hurt.

Now the angel talks directly to Carl.

Angel: Who cares what others think? You're going down your path, and they're doing down theirs. Who cares? He gets it. He totally understands. He doesn't give himself enough credit.

B: *Can you help him with that now?*

[deep breathing]

A: He really blocked off from this breakup.

B: *Where is that located in his body?*

A: In his legs. His neck. A lot of tension in his chest.

B: *Are you breaking down that armor he put around his heart?*

A: Yeah. [deep breathing]

B: *From all the rejection and the let-down.*

A: He likes people who keep their word. When they say they will do something, they do it. His girlfriend is very patient with him. She loves him very much. He needs to keep her. He's very intelligent, smart. He thinks too much. Sometimes he thinks himself into oblivion. He drives me crazy.

I'm trying hard not to laugh, but gosh, this is so endearing.

B: *Are you able to make adjustments in his brain? The parts where he uses his playfulness, his imagination, his creativity, so that he is able to have a greater awareness of who he is, his environment, and his interface with the environment?*

A: Yeah.

B: *Can he feel that?*

A: Yes, he feels tingling all over, especially in his hands.

B: *Thank you for that confirmation. Besides learning patience, and love and trust, what is his purpose here on Earth?*

A: He holds positivity and light. He is to share and spread that light and love. He has a tendency to hold back due to the rejections. He holds back his light too much.

B: *Is he completing his mission on Earth?*

A: Yes, but I'm not sure. I think so. I don't know the bigger picture of the whole. I don't know the whole thing.

B: *Are you able to ask someone who does know?*

Carl exhibited deep breathing for about twenty-five seconds. Then, someone came forward and identified themselves.

HS: I Am One. His purpose here is to love at his highest level.

B: *After today, will he be able to do this?*

HS: Yes.

B: *Thank you. In his current relationship, is this the best relationship with her?*

HS: She teaches him a lot. She's teaching him patience. Trust himself. Be gentle with himself. She's teaching him compassion.

B: *Does he have any karma to balance?*

HS: No. He's already went through his karma.

B: *Is there any trauma from this life or another that he needs to heal that is holding him back?*

HS: Slow down. Take a break. Just let things come. He already knows the lessons he's to learn.

B: *What can you share with us about his time overseas when he felt he was always on high alert? What did he learn from that experience?*

HS: He learned faith. He needed to learn that faith over fear. He needed to learn to have faith above fear. He has a tattoo of it, even though he ignores it. That lesson can also be spread across the theme of his life. Faith over fear. He's a lot more balanced now. He's not resisting me. Not as much as I thought he would.

B: *Good. With whom am I speaking?*

HS: I AM One. His Higher Self.

B: *Thank you so much.*

HS: He's very grateful to you.

B: *Thank you. How can he create more love, harmony, and peace in his life?*

HS: He must meditate more.

B: *What do you recommend?*

HS: Exercise, just don't over do it. Take the time to be in the present moment. Smell the roses. His mind is always racing. He needs to pull the reins, pump the brakes, and just be.

B: *Can you help him make that adjustment now?*

HS: [deep breathing] Must be gentle with this. It's done.

B: *What do you want to tell him about his third eye?*

HS: To not fear it. Be patient.

B: *You showed him quite a bit just a while ago. Does he now understand his third eye is open?*

HS: He has concerns about the calcification.

B: *Can you look at his pineal gland?*

HS: Hard, but functioning. He's not seeing everything clearly, but it's functioning. It needed to be cleaned up.

B: *What is the root cause of that hardening?*

HS: Diet. The fluoride. Toothpaste.

B: *What do you recommend he brush his teeth with?*

HS: Baking soda. He's so tense!

B: *Can you help him to relax?*

[Deep breathing]

B: *You're so good at this.* [I see Carl's body visibly relax.]

HS: Baking soda. More water. He doesn't need to decalcify it all the way.

B: *Can you decalcify it all the way? You've done it for others.*

HS: Not the time.

B: *Will you do it at night while he sleeps?*

HS: He doesn't need it to decalcify.

B: *Is it in proper order?*

HS: He has to let it flow on its own.

B: *Are you going to help him with that?*

HS: Yes.

B: *Thank you.*

HS: It will be slow and gentle.

B: *Can you help him to understand, by what we did earlier, by the visualization of the lemons and the dreams that it is a form of the third eye?*

HS: He understands.

B: *Would you please do a body scan?*

HS: He's in great shape. Pretty good health. He needs to take it easier at the gym. He needs to balance his rest with his exercise. Yoga. Active rest. He's very in tune with me. He has a sense of it all. Sometimes he overthinks the feeling. Most things he wanted to know I've already communicated with him. He just didn't know it was me. I communicate through feelings, subtle urges, the butterfly confirmation in regard to you [as his chosen QHHT® practitioner]. That was something that was strong enough to get his attention. He had been asking for a form of confirmation. That was the perfect solution. He just needs to believe it.

B: *Is the body scan done?*

HS: Yes.

B: *May I speak to the I AM One.*

HS: Yes.

B: *Does he have a role in the ascension?*

HS: He is to guide others. His family. He will be the voice for them in their time of need and time of not understanding. He's going to be their shepherd. Keep his vibration high. To remain living in times of fear, turmoil, stay centered and love. He's heard everything he needs to know about the ascension. He spends a lot of time researching on the web. He needs to be patient during these times. Stay secure and stay balanced. Remember to love unconditionally. Be patient with others. Patient with yourself. There will be rough times ahead; you are to guide others through.

B: *As he goes along developing his spirituality, how can he let go of the fear?*

HS: Give into faith. To trust there's more light than dark. There's more love than hate. Be patient with himself. He doesn't have to rush into these things. There's no race. Be gentle with himself. To remain loving the entire time. He puts too much pressure on himself. He needs to give himself a break.

B: *The most recent past life you showed him, he was watching the news on TV about finding the ruins on the moon. Why did you show him that?*

HS: I wanted him to know things will be revealed in a more public way. Currently he's looking for more confirmation of these UFO space topics. Soon all will be revealed. It will be enough to satisfy him. It will be a form of initation for him to know he's ushered in this new reality for him to begin to help usher those through the knowledge and information he's gathered.

B: *What will he notice after the session from the healing being done?*

HS: He will feel refreshed. He will feel lighter. His heart will be open.

B: *Thank you. Is there anything he needs to do in his conscious awake state to support the healing?*

HS: Continue to meditate. Continue to silence the mind. Continue to be in the present moment. Not think too far ahead. Not think too far behind. Be with himself. Be gentle with himself. All will be well.

B: *What do you think will surprise him the most from what was said here today?*

HS: How easy it was.

B: *When he contacted me for a session, what did you hope he would receive most from the session?*

HS: Someone to guide him through his awakening process. You are very attuned to his vibration. Your energy calms him. It was for you to serve as a guide through this process, as he doesn't have anyone to go to for this. You have done well.

B: *Thank you. Is there anything else you wish he would have asked about today?*

HS: Spirit guides.

B: *What would you like to tell him?*

HS: They love him very much. Often times he's too impatient and they want him to know to be more patient. They want him to be more patient.

B: *Thank you. What is the most important thing he didn't know about himself that you'd like to explain to him?*

HS: His light is very bright. He needs to embrace it, not fear it. He needs to let his love shine through.

PARTING MESSAGE FROM THE I AM ONE

HS: Continue to trust yourself. We have a strong connection. No need to worry. Continue to love. Don't be afraid to love. Spread your love. Be love. Your girlfriend is right for you. She loves you far more than you can imagine. Relax into her love as she relaxes into yours. Grow together. She is the right one for you.

During the debrief, I shared that his hypnosis experience is a testament to the inner work he has done, in regard to his impatience, fears, and anxieties.

The day after his session, he wrote this testimonial:

For starters, I want to thank you from the bottom of my heart for such a great session and for such a great EXPERIENCE! When I was on YouTube watching QHHT® sessions, I immediately felt like it was the next step for my spiritual development.

I ended up finding Barbara and immediately felt butterflies in my stomach, which I later found out was my Higher Self giving me confirmation on her...

Barbara guided me into my session very gently and lovingly and made me feel really at ease during the entire time. I learned so much about myself, as we went on an adventure to two past lives and had a great dialogue with my Higher Self. After the session, I woke up feeling AMAZING. My anxiety is gone, and I feel like I can love at my highest level again.

11
THE CONCEPT OF IMPRINTS & DRAGONS

Dolores reported in her book *Between Live and Death*[18] that we can imprint any past life that has ever been lived by anyone anywhere so we that have a base to work from while here in this incarnation. This means that if the person (soul) has not been a human before, or has had a limited number of lives, and therefore, doesn't have the experiences most humans have to draw upon, they can. The imprint serves as a reference. What is interesting is just how well the imprints work. You would not know a person is here for the first or third time because they behave in a humanly manner.

It's interesting how the Higher Self uses imprints to help the soul function in a human body on Earth, and to illustrate the qualities such as love, strength, power, and freedom, for the soul to draw from in the human experience. There are clients who experience their past life with Jesus, and others had past lives as Jesus. I understand this can be mind bending, but often it is imprinting—the Higher Self uses information from any life lived ever by another soul, and interfaces or imprints it with the client's soul memories. It's my understanding that everything in our reality is consciousness. Souls are consciousness, therefore, even a single cell is a soul. If our bodies are composed of billions of cells, our bodies are composed of souls. We can take this concept further as we remember we are all connected to one another and everything that is existing.

In the wise words of Colorado QHHT® practitioner MJ Olinger[19] "As you activate more of your DNA, you will remember more of who you are. The reason why you remember being Jesus or any other person

---

[18] *Between Life and Death*, Dolores Cannon, 2013, p. 246. Dolores wrote about imprints in her *Convoluted Universe* series too.

[19] mjolinger.com

is because as your true essence, you are everything. It is only your current programming that decides what aspect you bring forth in this body. Some people have only activated very specific aspects, while others have activated so many more. When every aspect of you is activated, you will embody your true essence, everything that you are."

STAR BEING DOWNLOADS

I facilitated this session for a delightful sixty-six-year-old woman from another town in Arizona. Susan was born in a wealthy family with four siblings. She had one older brother. Both she and this brother were different. They never fit in. They marched to the beat of a distant drum. The parents had definite plans and perceptions that they used to gauge the success of their children.

Susan never felt love from her father. He was neither there for her nor her siblings. He wasn't ready for children. The mother stayed at home and felt she never had enough money. One of her siblings told Susan that she manipulated the parents through their wallet because that was the only thing they understood.

At the age of five, Susan fell from a two-story bedroom window onto the top of her head, with no recollection of this, and her mother (who is now passed), would never talk about it.

There were no significant events in her childhood that she could remember. When she came to me, her body was healthy, although she was a little overweight. She had graduated from high school as the president of her class and then went to college for four years and took as many classes as possible, majoring in world religions and the sciences and attaining advanced degrees. Susan stated she had worthiness issues and had been working on this.

PAST LIFE

>Susan: It's just dark. The cloud went into a dark area. It's just dark.
>
>B: *Is it like you're in the sky or space?*
>
>S: It feels like it.
>
>B: *Do you get the sense you still have a body?*

S: Yeah.

B: *Can you describe what you're sensing about yourself?*

S: I may be part of the wind.

B: *Can you describe it to me?*

S: A sense of flowing. But I'm not on the ground. It's like it's part of the wind, and there are other parts that have personality.

B: *Are there others with you?*

S: There are other energies.

B: *Are you feeling you're moving, going somewhere?*

S: Yes, but then it just rolls back on itself.

B: *Like the wind swirls around?*

S: Yeah.

B: *How does that feel to you?*

S: It's interesting. It's a form of freedom, I guess. It's gentle. It must be part of a current because there are light parts and dark parts down below.

B: *Do you get a sense you're at the planet Earth or someplace else?*

S: It must be someplace else. It must be the atmosphere.

B: *Are you able to communicate with the other energies with you?*

S: They don't have a voice. They communicate that they are just a force.

B: *What's their purpose?*

S: They're clouds around Jupiter.

B: *Can you see Jupiter?*

S: I have a sense of it.

B: *What is the sense like?*

S: It feels like there's something underneath. Whatever it is, it's looking up.

B: *Does this feel like someplace you've been before?*

S: No, it's that I sense I've been in this atmosphere before. I'm part of it.

B: *Would you like to continue exploring this?*

S: I get the sense there's not much more. It's more of a journey to experience how it feels to be an energy matrix. It's not really attached to anything.

Leaving that scene…

S: There's a crack of light. I don't know what is on the other side. It sounds like there is a party.

B: *Do you want to explore this?*

S: Yeah, I'll take a look at it. I'll go in here. It looks like a party thing going on. A mix of all different eras and creatures. At first I thought it was the 1920s, but it's like animal figures. There are books of animals that look like people wearing clothes and stuff like that.

B: *Do you have a sense you have a body?*

S: Yes. Furry feet. Brown and hairy with nails, four to five toes, not sure. I'm wearing clothes, yellow robe with fur trim, like a cape. I have a belt and sword.

B: *What is the sword for?*

S: It just means power. I have a muzzle with an elongated snout, like a fox, but larger, brown eyes, fur on my head, a crown made of material of amalgam of gold and copper. There's a gem in the middle that is red.

B: *Was the crown given to you?*

S: Yeah.

B: *Who?*

S: My father.

B: *Ornamentation?*

S: A ring, left hand, third finger, silver metal with green stone. Not sure where I got it.

B: *Does it have significance for you?*

S: It does but I can't figure it out.

B: *Is your body male or female?*

S: Male, tending toward older, healthy. It's a large party, celebrating. All the creatures are happy to see me. I'm sitting on a special seat.

B: *What do you do for the majority of your time?*

S: I make sure things stay in order, head of society, keep peace.

B: *What kind of things?*

S: The individuals and what they're supposed to do—creatures.

B: *Are you an administrator of this community?*

S: Yeah. I have a relatively important position.

B: *Are you on a planet?*

S: Ortho-felis [phonetically spelled]. The star system starts with a P. A five-star pentagram symbol is shown. It's in a different dimension—fourth.

B: *What type of food do you eat?*

S: It's a vegetable matter. Things that grow from the Earth. The atmosphere is a different color than here on Earth. A reddish-greenish hue. The trees don't grow that high because the light from the sun doesn't come in like Earth.

B: *Do you have a family?*

S: Yeah. There was a sickness they got. They're not here. Some of the bad plants can be mistaken for the good ones. Not of lot of stuff is happening now.

Leaving that scene…

S: I think I'm on an island. There are buildings that are very white. Reminds me of Crete or Greece. There are boats in the water. They have oars. I'm standing on a porch watching the boats. The buildings have columns. The sky is blue, and there's a cloud on the horizon. I have sandals. I'm a young male wearing a short toga type of cloth covering and tied with a rope type belt. I'm watching the boats. I must be in school. My hair is brown, shoulder length with a piece of leather that wraps around my forehead. I have an instrument to play music. I don't know what to do with it. I'm just learning how to use it. It's made out of a reed material, but its shaped like a bowl with two sides and a hollow part in the middle. It has an opening on one end, five inches across, eight inches long, tapered at one end. I play it because they think I can do it.

B: *What do you do with the majority of your time?*

S: I play dice games, walking around.

B: *What do you do for a living?*

S: I don't have to do anything. It's a school I'm in. It seems there's a bunch of people my age that work on different things.

B: *Do you have a family?*

S: Not there, no.

B: *What happened to your family?*

S: They left. Something happened. The Earth opened up and people got swallowed up. An older couple took me in. I have some kind of wound that needed to heal on my right leg, on the inside thigh. It healed with herbs.

B: *Are you happy?*

S: Because of what happened years ago, we don't know what it is to be happy. But we're okay. Things are getting better. We've got boats in the harbor.

B: *How do you get your food?*

S: There are farms on the hillside. We don't have to do that. We have to work with the music. There's things that we do at the school. It's important. There's some information we've got to get across. It needs to come out, so we have to be there. I can't be bothered with the other things.

B: *What kind of information do you need to get out to the people?*

S: It has to do with star beings.

I look up at Susan from my note writing.

S: It's some information that we get out. It comes to our head and we don't know why. We tell them what it is. They write it down.

B: *It sounds like you're being downloaded information telepathically. Then you know it and share it. Is that how you do it?*

S: Yes. That's why we can't leave. Not everybody can do it. But they can tell if you can do it.

B: *These star beings, where are they located?*

S: I hear Andromeda, but I can stand on the porch at night and point to it. The galaxy. They are giving us information because it's going to be important in thousands of years from now when that cataclysm opens up again. But it's more than that. It also tells us of a spiritual nature, things like how to move from just being three-dimensional physical to the more energetic form.

B: *Are you able to share with us a couple of those?*

S: Some are diagrams. Some are formulae. Diagrams looks like the Kabala tree. Numbers that don't have existence in this dimension. We don't know what this is all about. We really can't interpret it.

B: *It's recorded. Is that right?*

S: Yeah.

B: *Where are these records located?*

S: They have a cave. They keep it down there. And the cave, they have stuff we don't have up here in the school, like technological stuff like light bulbs and things like that. So that's why the cave is kept hidden. I got to see it by accident. Nobody—I followed one of the old guys down there one day just to see where he was going. It's like it opened up in the side of the hill. You wouldn't even know it was there. Then he went in, and I could see lights and libraries and stuff like that.

B: *Is there a name of the town or community you live in?*

S: Puffila. It must be the Mediterranean. It's not the Atlantic or Pacific. No, it's not there. They're saying it's not there. I'm not sure where it is. Maybe more where Saudi Arabia is now. I'd have to check the history. I don't think you can get to the caves by land anymore. It doesn't matter because they're protected because of the technology they have.

B: *How many of you are given the information at any one time?*

S: There's just ten of us here now. I don't know if our language is the same as the people in the town. It's different.

B: *Do you get the feeling people understand you and your role in what you do?*

S: I think a lot of this is hidden from them. We don't go out. We stay there. I think the people talk only to the old ones. They may not even know we're there.

B: *Are you on a special mission?*

S: We didn't really choose it. It chose us.

B: *Do you know why and how that earthquake occurred?*

S: I see splitting. It could be the Earth flipped. It could have been something from outside hit it. I'm not sure. It looks like a crater when I see it.

B: *Do you ever see these star beings?*

S: They're not see-able. They are like ripples in the air. I can see the air ripple.

B: *Is it a cloaking device?*

S: Yeah.

HIGHER SELF

I ask about the last lifetime the Higher Self showed Susan, when Susan lived as a young man on the Greek Island.

Barbara: *Why did you show that lifetime?*

HS: Sometimes Susan doesn't realize what she knows. She needs to be more confident in what she knows. To realize even if it comes from the outside, it can be the truth. There's something on the horizon she knows about, and she needs to make sure it gets out. I can feel the energy of it going together, and it's time for her to bring forth the messages of what's coming together. She is not to be fearful, for she is protected, but she needs to know even though the environment she was raised in was limited, it was there for a reason.

B: *This information she's bringing forward, are you allowed to share with us at this time?*

HS: Let me see what I can do. It has to do with—there has been a darkness around things, and it's kept the light from coming out. Now there are many people who hold this light and their power. They need to get that light to the surface so that it can be seen and can illuminate because much of the hidden information needs to come out right now. But it's in a kind of code, and these people who have these bits of light, they are planted throughout the world. Need to set up a grid, like ley lines, to focus their energies so that this hidden knowledge can be seen again, can be known. It's very important now, because there's a huge shift going on and people need to know the direction to be safe as the shift continues.

B: *What does "safe" mean for the people holding this light?*

HS: Safe means that people learn of their own power and not give it away to others because every person is the same. And the light can see that.

B: *This lifetime you just discussed, is this a real past life or an imprint?*

HS: It was real for her.

B: *You also showed her a lifetime as the furry creature on another planet. Why did you pick that lifetime?*

HS: Because she needs to see what it means to have a good time. That was a place where all creatures had a good time. There was no judgment. Even though each one could find themselves different, they were all fine.

B: *What was the name of that planet?*

HS: Richland.

B: *You showed her the wind as a life form around the planet Jupiter? Why?*

HS: That was because when she did her shamanic journey, her spirit animal is the wind. I had to show her why.

B: *The furry creature lifetime, was that an imprint?*

HS: That was not real.

B: *So it was an imprint?*

HS: Yes.

B: *It has purpose, correct?*

HS: It's very important for her to know how to enjoy and to see that just because shapes are different, it doesn't mean that they can't enjoy things too.

B: *Thank you. She would like to know what is her purpose?*

HS: She knows. She has a star inside of her. Her purpose is to get it out. She needs to accept the star inside and that it is important now for it to shine.

B: *How can she best do that?*

HS: She has to let go of a lot of those hang-ups that she holds onto. She has to remove herself from judging herself in the light of how other people see her.

B: *Would it help her to do some forgiveness work?*

HS: She's working on it for other people, but she needs to do it more for herself. It's more than forgiveness; it's acceptance work. I think that's more important now.

B: *Is she running an old program in her mind of not being worthy and self loving?*

HS: Yes, she keeps going back to that because you know how sometimes it's easier to do the bad stuff because you're used to it—and to accept the good stuff, you must make such big changes. You have to see things differently. It's easier to fall back on that, so she needs to just realize that it's caca, she doesn't need that.

B: *Would it be possible to remove that old program and download a new one?*

HS: Let me see.

B: *You're really good at this.*

HS: Oh, yes. I can do some healing right now.

B: *Thank you so much.*

HS: There's stuff down. I have to pull it out. [HS chuckles]

B: *Thank you. How do you do that?*

HS: You know you have a spinal column. You also have a column of light. People can close off that column of light and fill it and code it will all sorts of stuff from the outside they believe, crap stuff. So you have to scrub that all off and just let it go. Yes, it's better now. It's going to take a while.

B: *Are you able to download, install, and launch a new program of self worth, self love, choosing the best for herself?*

HS: I can do that. We're embedding that into the column.

B: *I know she's going to appreciate that.*

HS: We hope so.

B: *Thank you for the tingles in my body of confirmation.*

HS: [laughing]

B: *I love how you work with people. It's very beautiful.*

HS: Thank you.

B: *She shared with us she has a problem with money and finances. Does she have blocks?*

HS: She has a lot from her past. It has to do with self-worth. Money is an outside kind of thing. People with low self-worth have money problems. We'll work on this.

B: *She shared that she feels she hasn't found home here. Can you help her to understand the root cause of that?*

HS: This is something she's lived with for many lifetimes. The concept of home. I think she needs to define it as community and it will come more easily. Community is beginning to form. If you can remove the concept of home from a place to a group, then it will be easier to find her home.

B: *Was this one of the reasons you showed her that lifetime helping the community because her family was gone?*

HS: Yes.

B: *Will she find home in a community where she is appreciated and respected?*

HS: Yes, these people with special gifts find home in community because they fit in. There are many, and they are finding each other. It's like the grid I talked about. It's all going to come together.

B: *She doesn't remember her childhood from age two to nine. What happened in that time?*

HS: I know people often talk about these things called walk-ins, but it's not a walk-in. It's as if though she had a placeholder. If she had lived through the experiences during those years, it would have been very negative for her development. So she needed to step back and let the placeholder come in, and do whatever the placeholder is going to do, and then, when she is strong enough to move into her own personality, then she could come back.

B: *Was this like she stepped out for a while and allowed one or multiple…*

HS: There was just one placeholder. She was there in the background, because she was like in a trance, asleep, because they were not nice to her. If she had to live through that she would have been a very different person.

B: *When you say "they," whom are you speaking of?*

HS: Her parents.

B: *The placeholder came in and endured what happened during that time?*

HS: These placeholders, they come into many different people. They don't hold onto the energies that are thrown at them. They're like a wall that you can throw things on and then wash it off. So they wash it off, and they're fine.

B: *Is there anything you'd like her to know about that time to give her resolution?*

HS: She already knows about the placeholder. She doesn't need to know about the other stuff.

B: *She shared with us at age five she fell out of a second story window onto her head. What was that about and what was the root cause of that?*

HS: It wasn't much of an accident that she thought it was. Her parents drank a lot. She was in the wrong place at the wrong time.

B: *Did someone push her out the window?*

HS: We seem to think that is what happened. She has some idea that is what happened. She was strong, and the placeholder could take some of the sting out of it. The placeholder helped her to get back in the house. So they knew she was hurt.

B: *Did she have any brain damage at the time?*

HS: She was in a place where she, if the placeholder wasn't there, she probably would have shut down. [meaning the body would die or severe brain damage would ensue]

B: *What does her brain look like now?*

HS: It looks... there is some extra scar tissue. She needs to work with her brain to open up. She feels it now: The pineal gland has got to become activated. We're not talking about damage. We're talking about how things are now. She needs to learn the importance of the empathetic brain. She relies often too much on the conscious brain. That brings information on a conscious level, but empathy brings relations not only on an emotional level, but also on a spiritual level, and it connects with the universal network of empaths.

B: *How do you want her to work with her brain in this manner?*

HS: She needs to work more in meditation, and she needs to realize she knows these things. When she takes her walks, she can do walking meditation. She has studied Zen. She knows. She needs to do this more and not try to get into the thinking mode when she's in the other mode.

B: *Can you activate her pineal gland now? You've done it for others.*

HS: It's actually active. She doesn't let it out. She just needs to trust more that what she is seeing is truly there.

When I began facilitating QHHT® sessions I used to ask if each lifetime was an imprint or not. After discussing with my colleagues, I've come to realize that it doesn't matter if a lifetime is an imprint. It's the story and the message in the story that the Higher Self conveys for the best interest of the client, much like when we read a book and discover a different point of view to embrace or reject. If the message helps us, then who cares where it comes from? You can have serendipitous experiences in the most unlikely places. Why not in a QHHT® session?

I'M A DRAGON!

I facilitated this session in a hotel room for a delightful woman of fifty-nine-years-old from California. Dorothy had worked in a stressful job and came for a session to help her decide where to move to best continue her work in the healing arts in service to community, as well as to resolve several health issues.

Dorothy grew up in the Northeast, in a family that argued and criticized each other on a daily basis. She was hyper-vigilant for what might happen next, and always felt she needed to defend herself against these mental and emotionally charged attacks. Dorothy never married, as she had witnessed the dismal marriages of her friends over the years. However, she desired a loving relationship with a man.

Dorothy's health concerns were a right sided temporomandibular joint (TMJ) malformation and dysfunction producing pain in her jaw when she moved it. This began as a teenager, when she was involved in a head-on automobile collision, sustaining a concussion, left sacroiliac joint pain, and cervical neck discomfort. Migraine headaches had plagued her for more than ten years. She woke up every two hours from her sleep apnea disturbance.

Dorothy shared with me that she had anger issues and had been doing liver detoxification through several modalities. She also shared that while working in her chosen field, she "flat-lined" her adrenals, from the tremendous amount of stress. As a testimony of the inner work she had engaged in over the years, her session went very well.

PAST LIFE

Dorothy sees herself as an iridescent glow of light in energetic form, seeing no color, just gray monolithic objects and prisms of light. Other energies are with her but are isolated and unable to communicate with each other. QHHT® practitioners know that there is a resting station between lives, and this is where Dorothy is while re-energizing. I move her ahead to where the regeneration is complete. Her light is full, and (whoosh) she takes off. She's in outer space, out among the stars with her guide. She sees planet Earth. The lesson she wants to learn in this current life is about belonging.

AN IMPORTANT DAY...

Dorothy experiences the sense of flying and sees a dragon with a human rider on its back. She isn't sure if she is the human or the dragon.

I ask her to look down at her feet. "I'm a dragon!" We both laugh. Her body is circular in the center and oblong in length, with big black claws and four toes on each foot. The wings are soft and can fold back. The head has an arched forehead, nostrils, and angular cheeks. She wears a collar made of gold with a ring attached to it [for the reins]. She eats vegetation, but is not well fed. Feeling "on-guard," standing in a slate gray colored quarry area, with surrounding hills, she waits for the big, burly red-headed Viking rider surveying the land. They perform long distance reconnaissance for more areas the Vikings can live in. They take off flying again.

ANOTHER IMPORTANT DAY...

Now she is a male dolphin named Flicker, jumping in the water and swimming really fast as dolphins do. She describes himself as a happy dolphin in his family pod, young, healthy, just playing. The ocean feels smooth as silk. Flicker is enjoying this lifetime because it feels free.

ANOTHER IMPORTANT DAY...

Dorothy finds herself standing outside the Ramses III pyramid in Egypt as a guard. He is a male royal sentry wearing ankle-wrapped leather sandals, and a gold-pleated fabric skirt with a diagonal piece of white fabric hanging on one shoulder, with an angled collar piece. His black squared-off shoulder-length hair is adorned with a gold band across the forehead and around it, hieroglyphs relating to the Pharaoh. Looking inside the pyramid, he watches a solemn coronation ceremony of Ramses.

Dressed in a long robe, walking up a flight of stairs, Ramses' installation ceremony is attended by his private officials. The pyramids are used for ceremonies and burial purposes, according to this guard. Guarding the pharaoh is a day job for the sentry. His personal quarters are quite humble.

LAST DAY OF THAT LIFE…

While leading Ramses' body, a group of guards go into the pyramid with him. The door is closed behind them, as they will stand guard until they physically die.

I move him forward in time to when he leaves the body. He goes into the light. We could explore this area more; however, an hour has passed by, and it's time to move onto the Higher Self.

HIGHER SELF

All of these past lives were imprints because Dorothy has had only ten Earth lives and they were all as a human, according to the HS. With the dragon imprint lifetime, the Higher Self wanted to show Dorothy how to feel her power and apply it in her current lifetime.

Dorothy was shown the lifetime as a dolphin to see herself as the jewel that she is. The Egyptian guard life was for her to know the honor of serving and holding that station and position. It was also about standing her ground.

Dorothy's star family is located in the Orion constellation. She is from Sirius. Her soul mission is to fully embrace her divinity, and to be gentle with herself by relaxing and allowing things to occur in their own time. She is teaching others about the state of sadness and feeling alone. Her purpose here is to express emotion and to heal herself.

The HS finds a density on the left side of her brain from the concussion she experienced earlier in life during the auto collision. That accident's purpose was a way to change the path she was on. Right then and there, the HS repairs the brain with a beam of light and re-wires it to stop the migraine headaches. They find a density in the right brain hemisphere also and remove this.

The HS finds that her jaw was severely injured from the TMJ dysfunction, which was a result of her not speaking her truth since age fourteen. During her hypnosis, the HS shows her the inside of her jaw, where the HS places cross pins of cartilage so the cartilage grows fully back to full health—all during the session.

"My whole cheek bone tingles and feels electrified," she exclaims! Then, all of sudden, she adds, "Whew! The whole left sacroiliac joint just tightened up. It's a weird faraway feeling, like I want to scratch inside the bone."

I knew this was a physical sign of new bone growth. I ask, and the HS confirms it to be true.

> HS: The TMJ work went behind the cheek bone to the eye. This is causing the headaches. Barbara is part of the healing.

> Barbara: *She mentioned her right eye felt icy cold while you were healing her. What was that about?*

> HS: The removal of scar tissue under the cheek bone and the eye socket.

The HS gives Dorothy dietary modification recommendations and another modality to use for detoxification: a sauna. She no longer needs to do the liver and gallbladder detox procedures because these organs and systems are completely healed. The HS heals all emotional trauma and defeating mind programs. They install six new gateways in her Human Design[20] for the heart-to-mind connection, through the throat chakra area.

Prior to this session, Dorothy received a group of thirty symbols to open her heart chakra. She had brought a piece of paper with the symbols given to her. Per her request, I ask for an explanation of this grouping of symbols and their meaning for her.

> HS: The pyramids of white light going up to the universe as geometric patterns connecting to her Higher Self and seeing all of those opening her heart chakra.

At this moment, Dorothy says, "My heart chakra exploded wide open!"

I can feel the burst of energy. She is overwhelmed with emotion, in a good way. Smiling and crying at the same time. Surely, this is a client experiencing the ecstasy of loving herself.

Regarding a new relationship with a man...

Dorothy will be moving her residence. She is given the name of the town and state, and what she will be doing for work. Her employment will be hands on, teaching women how to heal deeply. Dorothy will

---

20 http://humandesign.net/human_design.html

thrive abundantly and find the community she's longing for. We are given the first name of the man who is her soulmate, and the where, when, and how they will meet. Dorothy is given a special sign so that she knows without a doubt that he's the one. She knows when she will move, and she's already packed to go.

PARTING MESSAGE

HS: You are always loved. You have mastered Self Love.

Throughout the hypnosis session, at various times, her entire body would shake momentarily. This was releasing toxins, blocks, and old programs. I am familiar with this type of body activity during healing sessions. It's perfectly normal.

Right after the session, Dorothy demonstrated how her mouth now opened and closed in perfect alignment, smoothly, without pain. Prior to the session, her mouth had made a zigzag movement when opening and closing.

Dorothy also explained how during the hypnosis session, she saw and interacted with her parents. This shows that, during these sessions, the client is seeing and experiencing a whole lot more than we practitioners are aware of. Surrogate healings for friends were done, too, during the session.

In the next story, we meet a character that has great responsibility, knowledge, and power.

12
GUARDIAN OF THE KNOWLEDGE

I facilitated this session for a middle-aged man named Charles, with a specialty in communications. Since he lived across town, we met halfway at a relative's rental home undergoing remodeling. The whole two-story house was upside down in reconstruction. I love how the external reflects the internal!

The amount of inner work this man had done in his life was impressive. He meditated regularly and made mindful dietary choices. In addition to food allergies, migraines, and exertion-induced asthma, he asked to explore a missing time episode in his life. Charles also mentioned that he often felt as if there were something blocking him from going further on his ascension path, and he wanted to find out what it was.

PAST LIFE

During the QHHT® session, he finds himself standing in the middle of a garden with stone statues all around, along with varying-size pyramids.

Beyond, are large buildings and flowing water. He describes himself as a very tall muscular male with olive-colored skin. His feet are bare, and his white sleeveless garment hangs down to his knees, with a belt tied at the waist. His long dark hair is topped with a white cloth and metallic-decorated triangular headdress. There are colorful jewels hanging from the neckline on his garment.

When I ask Charles what his job is, his voice changes; it becomes authoritative and strong. He is the guardian of a complex in this garden where scrolls, scripts, and books are kept for people seeking knowledge, initiation, wisdom, and understanding. He says he is a form of human and also another form of being; however, there are no words to describe himself in the human language.

The complex is in Egypt. It is called Khem, and many other names long ago, according to him.

He was born to be a keeper of the knowledge. All the books, teachings, and knowledge contained in these buildings, he attained. If there are questions that need to be answered, he helps the seeker because he knows where the information is located in the building. He doesn't help them on their path. It's very important that he not interfere. He helps them to know where to go to get the information.

"There are seekers who are not seekers. This is the guardian's special task. There are those who wish to attain this knowledge and use it for less than wise purposes. Some folks call it evil, negative, and others call it darkness."

He can see through this darkness. He does it through a feeling, then sight follows. There is nothing he doesn't see or not know. He feels humble, honored, and privileged to do this job. He says that we are all equal.

"We are all in this together; in the ascension. I do this job to the best of my ability so that others can ascend too."

At this point I ask if he has a name. He replies:

"I am energy, or vibration, I don't take any credit or form. I observe. I'm the guardian, to help and to serve. If you have a name that's in your mind, you can call me that."

This energy being is now communicating to me telepathically as I sit here on the ottoman. I hear the name "Karlos" in my mind. He replies:

"That suits perfectly."

I ask Karlos, "How do you redirect the ones who are not here for the highest good?"

Karlos replies, *"The light comes in. It's indescribable. I sense, I see, then the light comes in. There are beings that follow. When they follow in, the energy is transmuted, so there is no confrontation. It just looks like a conversation. I step back. The energy transmutes. The beings without good intentions leave without any confrontation."*

ANOTHER IMPORTANT DAY

He goes into the Oneness. Pure white light. Pure energy. "No words to describe further," he says, enjoying this experience because it feels like absolute bliss.

HS: His life is about service toward others, to be strong when others cannot, and to let the light shine forth. This is in alignment with the fact he was a "whistle blower" at a former employment, where he was fired for exposing his superiors' immoral behaviors. His career is done, and this is why he is moving on.

The move is favorable to Charles, according to the HS.

HS: His monetary investments will do well. He is to pay attention to his intuition and not doubt himself.

My clients find it comforting to know their career change is in order. The knowledge gives them strength and clarity to step into their next adventure. Another benefit for Charles: Because of this session, Karlos becomes a trusted guide to whom Charles can turn.

The HS works in Charles' chakras, making energetic adjustments.

HS: Charles is very warm, and the energy is working.

I ask if I should remove the bed sheet from covering him, and the HS say no.

HS: Emotionally, socially, physically, pressures can come. Just as Jesus went through the initiator process in the ancient land, so do we go through this, in a more spiritual form. There is a non-physical form of initiation, and it creates pressure. Just like finances, it creates pressure, but it will not remain.

Because Charles expressed a vague memory of something perplexing happening in his childhood, I make an Akashic records request.

HS: The records indicate less than human beings communicating with a small child. Their intention was to do harm and block the coding. Some call it deprogramming. They only partially succeeded. If they had totally succeeded, he would not be living in this initiated path of ascension right now. It's taken many lifetimes to deprogram the coding that they blocked. We are almost complete with it. Their intent was to do harm. The plan was diverted.

The HS transmits healing energy into his star fields, and then tells us that the transmission went extremely well.

HS: There is much heat in the physical body. There is a sense that reprogramming may take place. There was a program within a program that could be relaunched. We sealed his fields so that no one can come near or interfere, [Charles begins to cry] manipulate, attempt to block, program, or deprogram. It is done. It is so.

Charles: [Charles' voice changes to one of intense emotion.] It is closed! Such relief! [tears and more tears] Such profound relief!

I wait in silence, then ask for permission to continue to ask more questions. Charles' voice changes back to the powerful SC in the affirmative.

I ask about Charles' food allergies.

HS: Yes, there are allergies from head to toe that have been plaguing him for many years, mostly in the upper body near his heart and soul [solar plexus] chakra. The allergies came about from foods, environment, and being, the being, the person, the programming. That is gone now. The purpose is to ascend, enlighten, and uplift. Those substances are no longer needed by this vessel.

I ask about his migraine headaches.

HS: Migraine headaches are associated with the climate changes. The root cause was the programming. This was partially to blame. Environment yes, it can be favorable and unfavorable. As you begin to take on new forms of sustenance, these episodes will be less and less. The intent now is to purify the physical body as much as possible. In this time, day, and age, it is essential to intend to purify the body, the mind, and the heart. Communicate with us, the Higher Self. Follow that intention, then all manners of sickness and illness will cease to be. One sees themselves as pure, they are pure. There is no other way of being. So, we would say to this vessel today, continue to see yourself as pure. And you will live no other way.

Exercise-induced asthma is a narrowing of the airways in the lungs. It's triggered by strenuous exercise, causing shortness of breath, wheezing, coughing, and other symptoms during or after exercise. I ask about Charles' exertion-induced asthma.

HS: We would say the same as we just said. The environment and programming are largely responsible for this condition. See yourself as pure light, walking your path of initiation, then these forms cease to exist.

B: *What about the missing time episode?*

HS: Two minutes was actually two hours. You did this to yourself. You didn't realize what or why you did. The few instances this occurred, you actually stepped out of space and time for a moment. It's not permissible for you to know what had occurred outside in those moments, but we would say it was very loving and purposeful. Nothing darkness. The moments were accurate, according to the physical vessel. There was time missing, but the purpose was beneficial, and you, this vessel will know when the time is right. It is not necessary to dwell upon the why. Be grateful that it occurred and move on. All will be revealed and fall into place when Divine Timing occurs.

The HS scan Charles' body, bringing forth more energy. Powerful energies run through my body too. This is one aspect of a QHHT® session: The practitioner can experience magical and mystical energies flowing in the room and in his/her body.

HS: The downloading and coding are taking place. Every cell in the physical vessel is receiving new information right now. This vessel is eternally grateful for the energy you brought forward.

The HS express their gratitude for my allowing their energies to flow through me too.

PARTING MESSAGE

HS: Listen to the recording, as many times as need be. Those codes are already in place. The programming that once controlled him are no more. All will be revealed in divine timing. His eyes to see, will not fail. This vessel chooses to walk in the light, to follow the path of initiation. There are more words to be said, but are not in this language. It is not necessary to speak in another language. To utter them, it would be counterproductive. It would be a distraction. This vessel can now go forth in a deeper understanding of purpose, initiation, with a stronger sense of balance. Communicate well with others. Focus more intently. Love greater than words in any language could ever express. Be the guardian, the keeper, the servant that you have been in so many lifetimes. Nothing was in vain. All shall move forward in divine time. There is no more fear. See yourself as pure, and you are. The White Light of the Great Brotherhood, the higher consciousness of the Divine Creator. All is well.

I express my gratitude to them, and they say in return:

HS: We are the ones who are most grateful, for the work being done. For it is we, that see the dawning of the new age of man. We see the Christ Consciousness coming forth in the work you do. We have nothing but love and gratitude for the love you do. We only encourage you to do more, as long as you are physically able to do. There is much work to be done.

When the HS speaks directly to me, about me, in sessions, my heart chakra opens more and I feel a oneness during the vocal sound transmission. Since the room was filled with immense love, I use this opportunity to speak directly with Source and ask about Dolores.

Source: Dolores is with you and all of you [the practitioners]. She is very pleased. She sees what she envisioned years ago.

The presence of Dolores was palpable, and the amount of unconditional love from her was almost overwhelming.

LATER...

Charles shared his testimonial several days after his session:

"Over the years I've had many energy clearings/healings. Nothing, and I mean absolutely nothing, has come anywhere near what I experienced with Barbara. The healing and energy integration was so intense that when I came back into the conscious waking state, I could literally feel every cell in my physical body vibrating and teeming with energy."

Charles' testimonial is an example that everyone is responsible for their own healing and perceptions. Ninety percent of the session is up to the client in how they want to experience the session. The QHHT® practitioner comprises only ten percent of the session. This is an important understanding for the QHHT® client. It is the client's responsibility to follow through with the recommendations of the Higher Self, and if there are obstacles met during the session, then they truly are a wonderful discovery that more inner work needs to be done.

This is one of the reasons why we incarnated on Earth as humans. To do the work to perfect ourselves. The work continues even after our passing from the Earthly plane. I encourage QHHT® clients to listen to their practitioner's recap of the hypnosis and follow through with any inner work that is either stated or revealed in the hypnosis.

Out of curiosity and inspired by the session, I looked up the word "Khem." It is the origin of the word Egypt, meaning the black land.

13
CREATOR BEINGS

HE GOT THE GIGGLES

Walking across the hotel parking lot with my rolling briefcase and purse, for the first time since becoming a QHHT® practitioner, I sense Dolores is walking beside me in her previous human form. The awareness and sensation feels comfortable. It's a nice feeling, nothing to get excited about nor off-centered. We practitioners must be mindful that our energy is calm and reassuring for our clients. My excitement for Dolores' presence will have to wait for later.

I arrive at the fourth floor hotel room. The client and I sit, and I give John the overview of the session. He places his hand over his heart while conveying his admiration, love, and gratitude for Dolores and her work. I share with him that Dolores is here with us. He replies, "Yes, she walked with you across the parking lot." I am impressed with this remark, as it confirms without my prompt that Dolores is with all of us practitioners. And it is with John's statement about Dolores that alerts me that this session has a special element to it.

John doesn't remember much of his early childhood. He was told he had a viral lung infection and was not expected to live through it. He was also told of a twin brother that didn't live. When he was a child, he remembers very tall, large beings coming into his bedroom with space suits on, picking him up and taking him into the hallway. The only thing John remembers is being returned to his bed by them. This occurred repeatedly. He didn't dream these memories; they happened. He's always wondered why they came. He said after a couple of times, he decided not to fear it. They would only come after everyone in the house was asleep. John said he would like to find out what this was about. I agree.

Growing up, his body remained healthy except for sport injuries to the ankle, knee, and low back. He had surgeries on his right knee and ankle.

He is a tall, husky-appearing man with a great deal of energy emanating from him. He shares with me that there are people that see him and run away. He also has people he has never met come up to him and tell him they work together in the other realms, and that it is a great honor to meet him. John is a spiritually awakened person.

WE BEGIN THE HYPNOSIS

John is able to answer the first initial questions, then he begins laughing. He tries really hard to suppress his laugh, but he can't. The more I read, the more he laughs. When I turn the page of the induction script, I think surely he will stop. He continues. We all know laughing is contagious. I have to do something or I will end up laughing too. And then, where will we be!?

I stop the relaxation script and ask him what is happening. He tells me he can't stop laughing. I share with him this could just be his ego interfering. We start again. This time, he goes deep and fast. He is nearly snoring! I'm impressed with the speed and depth of his relaxation. John is at the bottom of the ocean, admiring the fishes and the coral. We explore the sea life, and he thoroughly enjoys it. We leave this scene and go to…

ANOTHER IMPORTANT DAY…

He is a business man who sets up medical centers for a living. He is on his way to work, when his intuition tells him to return home. Upon entering the home, he can hear a hair dryer upstairs. He walks upstairs and finds the girl he lives with nervous that he returned home. This interaction is how he learns that she is having an affair.

HIGHER SELF

> Barbara: *Why was John shown the scenes of the underwater ocean fishes?*
>
> HS: For peace. This is where peace is.
>
> B: *What were the lessons he learned?*
>
> HS: He can be an observer. He doesn't need to do anything.

B: *How do these lessons apply to his current lifetime?*

HS: He needed to be part of everything. This is not necessary. He just needs to be an observer. Be an observer, not be a part of it. He's evolved enough at this time.

B: *What is he to observe?*

HS: Everything. Nature. He needs to change the world. He needs to see the change of nature.

B: *How is his father?*

HS: He's at peace.

B: *Is his father available?*

HS: Yes, he's willing to come over.

If there is a loved one who has crossed over and is available to visit during the hypnosis, I will ask on the behalf of the client for their loved one to come forward. I sit in silence while the client engages in conversation. Sometimes the client will talk out loud, while others are silent. Having this silence affords the opportunity for the soul on the other side to convey more messages each time the client listens to their recording.

B: *Why did you show him the scene of the unfaithful woman?*

HS: He doesn't trust his instincts. Still, he caused it himself. He's helping her to be a better person. He had to learn.

B: *Did he learn it?*

HS: Yes.

B: *The twin that did not form in the womb. Would you tell us what happened?*

HS: He had a twin. They shared the same body for a while. The twin's out there right now. At some point in life, he will come back. The twin is watching over John.

B: *John told us when he was quite young he almost died from an illness? Can you tell us about that?*

HS: It was a bacterial infection. Normally it should have damaged his brain. We didn't let it happen.

B: *Was he considering leaving the body?* [Sometimes when a lifethreatening illness or injury occurs, the original soul will leave and another soul will swap places. These are known as walk-ins and walk-outs.]

HS: No. More energy had to be put into the body in order for him to survive. Normally, it was not supposed to be this much energy. It was too much for a normal body to handle. In order for him to survive, we had to put in more energy there. He created other problems. He was a hyperactive child.

B: *Was he able to dissipate that energy when he needed to?*

HS: Oh, he has excess energy still!

B: *When he was that young child, did he stay in the body? No walk-in?*

HS: No. More of his own soul came in. He's the same soul.

B: *How many times has he incarnated on Earth?*

HS: Hundreds and hundreds.

B: *What about other places, other planets, total?*

HS: Countless lives.

B: *More than thousands?*

HS: Yes. He's been to many planets and star systems. He had lives there. He had lives in the ships. He's a friend of yours, Barbara. You're old friends. He's a captain. He's working on peace missions. He's commanding a war ship. Never had to use the weapons because he likes to make peace.

B: *Who is he negotiating peace with?*

HS: Races who have been fighting for eons of time. They never get tired of it. This is another universe.

B: *These other universes, do they have the contrast and concepts where people don't get along?*

HS: Not to this extent. Wherever there's trade, there's a problem. Here on the planet, there are a lot more things going wrong than trade. But the other galaxies and other universes, there are always problems. Even the higher dimensional systems and beings get into problems with other races. It's part of creation.

B: *There's no right or wrong?*

HS: Right, everyone is doing what they're supposed to be doing.

B: *Could you share with us what is John's life purpose in this lifetime?*

HS: He came to the planet to say farewell. To say goodbye.

B: *Is this his last lifetime on Earth?*

HS: Yes. He asked to come. Just one more time to say goodbye. He's done a lot of work.

B: *Is there anything for him to accomplish while he's here?*

HS: You know how curious he is? [Yes] He will write. He will write a lot of stuff. I'm not sure if he can write what he will think he will write about. He has a lot of followers. People trust him. He just doesn't know. People will follow him when he starts broadcasting that information.

B: *What is he to write about?*

HS: He did express he wants help in writing. He wants to know history. All his life he wants to know about history. Maybe some history, Earth changes, more people will listen to him because he will have a unique style of writing. He will teach in a hilarious way with humor. Especially the young children will love his writings. It's better to educate them than trying to educate non-listening adults. It's for all ages. The children will resonate, and they will understand better than the adults.

B: *Yes, these are the new children here.*

HS: Exactly!

B: *They are very very advanced.*

HS: They know who he is! They vibrate at the same frequency as him.

B: *Will you help him with that writing?*

HS: He already knows everything. We just need to remind him.

B: *He would like to know, does he have a relationship with the Annunaki?*

HS: Yeah, he had a few lives with them. He doesn't actually like them.

B: *What is it about them doesn't he like?*

HS: They claim that they generated modified humans and created the gods. He knows it's not true. He knows that they were part of the creation, but the real work was done by other races. He was other races, helping to create man.

B: *Well, isn't that part of you?*

HS: Yes.

B: *What we call our Higher Self?*

HS: Yes. So, he knows this, but he doesn't like to claim this, but he had lifetimes with them. Not as an Annunaki. But when they were on the planet, he was in a human body.

B: *So he knows better?*

HS: He knows them personally. He was a high priest for them.

B: *Did he have a name as the high priest?*

HS: He does but I don't want him to go there. Because I know him, he will start researching and he will get into this. He needs to cool down.

B: *Does John have any karma to balance?*

HS: No. He came this time with karma protected. He has nothing. We used him in some missions; he thought he created karma. It was our missions actually. He's free of karma.

B: *Do you have any more missions planned for him?*

HS: No. He has done more than usual. He has helped a lot of animals. He helps a lot of people. He raised a lot of children, sponsored them. He worked with environmental issues, governmental issues, anything we told him not to do, he did it anyway. He didn't have an easy life, you know.

B: *From what he's shared with us, he's had a very fulfilling life, and he's done very well to be of service to humanity.*

HS: He's that guy. He goes till the end. This time he was supposed to just watch and have fun. Well, now at least, he can do it from now on.

B: *That will be good news for him. Thank you. He shared with us since he was a small boy, he was approached by these beings in what appears to be environmental suits and was taken to the hallway, and later brought back. Would it be possible to let him know what that was all about?*

HS: They were just scientists doing their job. His body couldn't fit the energies. The body couldn't handle the energy so they needed constant progressions, cell deformations was happening. So, they needed to add cells, stronger cells to his biological body all the time. So, what he isn't supposed to remember, he does.

B: *Is it permissible for him to remember?*

HS: Oh, it doesn't matter. It's old stuff. We didn't think he would remember that.

B: *I know you have the ability to erase our memories. Was this something you forgot to do or something?*

HS: Maybe we left a little reminder that we are here for him.

B: *Very nice. He did share with us he doesn't remember much of his childhood. Was it because of that or something else?*

HS: No, there was, we needed his presence up here for some special missions, so his body was there but with a little energy.

His presence was up here, then when he was finished, we sent him back.

B: *When you say "up here," does that mean a higher dimension?*

HS: Yes, a couple of higher dimensions. He had to work on several missions. He has specialties.

B: *Is he to know about those? He is curious: Would it cause any harm for him to know?*

HS: There's some very complicated physics. He's one of the very few beings that knows about it. He is also a teacher here. He needs to train people and there was some issues, physical issues in some dimensions. He had those repaired. So, we needed him for a while. And he didn't want to go back to the same time he left the body because he wanted the body to grow a little older. So we put him back at age five and a half, something like that.

B: *Is he sharing a soul with anybody else on the planet?*

HS: He's sharing the soul of everyone. He's too old with the planet. The first moment this planet was created, he was part of the project. So, actually every soul walking on the planet today is somehow stepping [on] a part of him in the past. He loves Earth. So he respects the very soul of the planet. He respects Gaia, and they are good friends.

B: *Do John and I see each other at night in the other realms, doing our work?*

HS: Oh, you're old friends. You will keep communicating on the planet. And please keep up the good work.

PARTING MESSAGE

HS: Enjoy the life. Enjoy being alive. Yes, he always must keep writing.

The concept of a soul being in a human body with little energy, while the other part is in a higher dimension or realm, is a new concept for me. It shows us we really don't know what's going on behind the scenes until we explore it, such as in a QHHT® session or through shamanic meditations, for example. I also find it comforting that the creator beings are here with us in the most exciting times of Gaia's lifetime. People such as this man bring a sense of order and structure in their aura that permeates the environment. My soul recognized him, and it felt awesome to hold him in my arms while expressing my gratitude to have this experience as humans.

FLYING CREATOR BEING

Before the session, on the phone, Charles says he uses both sides of his brain and wants a session for health concerns. He's a retired hypnotherapist and has had many traditional hypnotherapy sessions himself.

He was never nurtured. In his entire life, Charles' parents never told him they loved him or showed any affection toward him. By the time he was eight years old, he wanted to commit suicide. He talked himself out of it.

Charles' health concerns include left knee pain, both hands and feet hurt, his abdomen hurts, his right shoulder hurts, and he's losing his teeth. He is homebound and has no energy. His mind is foggy. The one question he gave me to ask his Higher Self, "When will my Higher Self fully activate into me?"

PAST LIFE

From a beautiful tropical waterfall with lush greenery, Charles goes straight up in the air! Amid the swirling clouds, he looks back at himself and sees large white angel wings. Wearing Roman soldier body armor, carrying a shield, wearing sandals, Charles describes himself with short, curly dark hair and a matching short beard. He is flying over the Earth, observing.

In a totally different than the voice I listened to during the interview, he shows angst, but no tears. As I watch him, his abdominal muscles quiver almost constantly. His right hand, which is near me, gently massages the bed mattress, back and forth, in constant motion during the entire regression. I attempt to give emotional support, but he won't give me any information to clue me in on the emotion's root cause.

Then, suddenly, he moves below the clouds, looking up at them. I ask him how it feels hanging out here below the clouds. He says it felt better at home. When we move to his home, he replies, "Fog." He is stuck in the fog, so I ask him to move to…

ANOTHER IMPORTANT DAY…

Flying over Earth, Charles sees a tall pyramid made of dirt, towering above the forest. The pyramid base is located on the ground. The pyramid is helping Earth to grow itself with plants and trees. When I ask about his role in this, he begins to sob greatly, without tears.

I ask the HS to dial down the emotional charge. His voice changes slightly, as he tells me that he is a member of a group of creator beings who created the Earth. I ask him who gave the call to create the Earth. He replies, "The All." It took about an hour to get to this point, with not much information coming forth, so I ask for the HS.

HIGHER SELF

The client's voice changes again, becoming stoic. The reason why the HS showed Charles that life was to show him the progress being made. The application of that life story, as a prime creator being, in his current life, was to show him he needs more help in completing the task of evolving the Earth, by maintaining focus and anchoring the energies. They were showing him who he is, his true self.

He's learning patience in this current lifetime. The special message for him was to remember the call. He has not only created this Earth, he works with others creating other worlds.

The HS say his time on this Earth plane is limited but will not divulge anything more about his work. The HS say that it is always present; however, for this soul, there's a disconnection.

Charles' voice: His Higher Self are not engaged.

Could this mean that he's a backdrop person like Dolores spoke of in her *Convoluted Universe Book IV*? I ask if the original soul walked out and another came in.

Charles' voice/HS: No.

With every question I ask, the HS give me short, cryptic answers. This is a communication style we QHHT® practitioners notice in some sessions. I share a portion of his session to give you an idea of what I'm talking about.

B: *Why did you show him that life as the creator being?*

Between these questions and answers, there are long silent pauses.

HS: To monitor, check the progress, to help.

B: *How is that applying in his life today?*

HS: Needs more help.

B: *He needs more help? What does he need more help with?*

HS: Completing the task.

B: *What task is he completing?*

HS: Evolution, the Earth.

B: *Evolution of the Earth. And how is he doing that?*

HS: Maintain focus, anchor energies.

B: *Does he anchor energies for the Earth here?*

HS: Prime energy.

B: *He's anchoring prime energy. The life you showed him, is that a past life, parallel life, or what?*

HS: True self.

B: *True self. So, you're showing him he's a creator being. Is that correct?*

HS: Prime creator.

B: *Prime creator being. And what are the lessons he's learning in this lifetime?*

HS: Patience.

B: *Patience. He's learning patience. Has he learned patience, or is there more to do?*

HS: Time is limited.

B: *Time is limited. And how does that apply to his patience?*

HS: The work is almost done.

B: *The work is almost done. Is that his work here?*

HS: Both.

B: *Both. Is there anything you'd like to tell him about this and help him to understand?*

HS: Remember.

B: *Are you showing him what to remember at this time?*

HS: Remember it all. Remember the call.

B: *Remember the call. Dear Higher Self, could you please do a body scan at this time? Energy fields and chakras? Are you able to do this at this time?*

HS: [silence]

B: *Dear Higher Self, may I speak with you?*

HS: [silence]

B: *Is the Ego interfering at this time that prevents you from speaking?*

HS: [silence]

B: *Alright, dear Higher Self, I'm asking you to do a body scan of Charles' body and look for anything that needs to be removed, healed, altered, modified, dissolved, and if you would tell us what you find and what is the root cause of it.*

HS: [silence]

I wait several minutes for the HS to say something, then suddenly:

HS: Always here.

B: *Yes. Everything that he's shared with us. We are very grateful that you're able to heal his body, his emotions and any mental patterns, and neural pathways that may need to be modified. I have a couple questions he'd like me to ask. He shared with me he feels a disconnection, and yet, you're always present. He would like to know when are you going to fully activate into his beingness?*

HS: Soon.

B: *Soon? Is his healing complete in this session?*

HS: No.

B: *How long will it be before it is?*

HS: Soon.

B: *What will he notice after this session as a result of this healing being done?*

HS: His memories.

B: *His memories?*

HS: They will become whole. [his voice shows momentary angst]

B: *Is there anything he needs to do in his conscious awake state to support this healing?*

HS: Visualize his true self.

B: *Visualize his true self. Can he see his true self to visualize?*

HS: Wings.

B: *Wings. What is it that will surprise him the most about what was said here today?*

HS: That he already knows.

B: *And when he contacted me for a session, what did you hope he would receive from this session the most?*

HS: Help.

B: *And did he receive that help?*

HS: Begin.

B: *Is there anything you wish he could have asked about today?*

HS: Will he hear the call?

B: *And what is your answer to that question?*

HS: Oh, he's heard it. Time is irrelevant.

B: *And dear Higher Self, could you explain what the call is about?*

HS: To create, to help.

B: *And is that creation and helping for this planet or another place?*

HS: Everywhere, anywhere.

B: *And so if it's anywhere, are you talking about his multi-dimensionality?*

HS: We're all everywhere. All focuses. All me. All us.

B: *Will he understand what you're talking about?*

HS: He's already did.

B: *Thank you. What is the most important thing he didn't know about himself that you would like to explain to him?*

HS: Already knew it all. Already does the job.

B: *Dear Higher Self, are you always connected to Charles?*

HS: No.

B: *Could you explain how that occurs—the disconnection?*

HS: Many tasks, many problems.

B: *It's my understanding that people have to have a Higher Self to be in this human experience. And that it's always connected. Would you help me understand how that disconnection can occur? Are there any ramifications for it? I'm very curious.*

HS: Prioritize. Achieve the goal. Not the most important.

B: *What is not the most important?*

HS: The body.

B: *So, is he considered one of the backdrop people that uses the body to do a certain task?*

HS: Just the focus.

B: *Is the original soul that came into this body still here, or did it leave?*

HS: No.

B: *So another soul came in?*

HS: No.

B: *Could you please explain further?*

HS: Other duties, other goals, can always come back when the time is right.

B: *So the duties and the goals always come back when the time is right? Is that what you're saying?*

HS: Have to create. Have to maintain. Have to heed the call. Always come back to this later.

B: *And what is he coming back to?*

HS: When the time is right, soon.

B: *When the time is right. But what is he coming back to? To what?*

HS: I will come back when I'm ready.

B: *So you, dear Higher Self, are leaving? Is that correct? Is that what I'm understanding?*

HS: Many duties. When the garden, help the planet, help the sun, help the creator.

B: *Thank you very much. Would it benefit him to know when you are connected to him?*

HS: Soon.

B: *Okay. Would it be helpful for him to really know and believe when that connection occurs?*

HS: When the time is right. When the Earth is ready. When the garden is green.

This dear Higher Self is so cryptic, not giving me easily understandable answers. I know Charles will listen to this recording, and receive more information and put it all together. This is another important concept about the QHHT® session. The client listens to the session recording over and over. The client figures it all out. More information and insights come into the client's consciousness, because the Higher Self is working behind the scenes even when the client is listening to the recording.

PARTING MESSAGE

HS: Stay the course. It will be revealed. Joy will come.

The HS finally says they will connect soon with the client, when the Earth is ready.

Charles did share with me in the interview he felt his time on Earth was almost up. What was interesting for me to observe in this client, during the entire hypnosis, his right hand was massaging the bed mattress. Since this session, I've come to understand that this is not unusual. Even in my own fifth session, I noticed I was moving my left fingers in a repeat pattern under the blanket.

14
EXTRATERRESTRIAL LIVES AND ALIEN ABDUCTIONS

We consider ourselves coming into the human experience from God Source onto Earth through our biological human mothers. Those who are enlightened understand we also come from other places in the universe. If this concept resonates with you, then you can understand that we humans are extraterrestrials too. When the call went out into the universe after the atomic bomb was detonated in 1945, souls came from many places to help the Earth and its inhabitants and save Earth from total annihilation. Dolores wrote about this call in her book, *The Three Waves of Volunteers and the New Earth*[21].

If we are to become advanced souls as humans, we must learn to get along with each other and with our extraterrestrial neighbors. One way to accomplish this goal is to explore reality inside a QHHT® session. Observing lifeforms foreign to our experiences helps us to break down the programming of fear and separation. Even observing procedures and processes unfamiliar to us helps expand our awareness of a greater concept outside of our limited human influence.

The following session stories help us to comprehend the struggles and successes that exist for others in the universe, making them relatable to us and our journeys. For some people, their role on Earth may not be in their consciousness. Until they explore through hypnosis or Higher Self dialogue in meditation, they may not be aware that they came here to complete a mission for the greater good of others and the planet. It is possible what would appear to be an "alien abduction" is really an opportunity for learning, or communications, or a light code upgrade for the human body. The Higher Self has the ability to "step in," so to speak, and alter our reality for the purpose of making sure we complete our missions and projects in the human experience. For

---

21 *The Three Waves of Volunteers and The New Earth*, Dolores Cannon, 2011

those who don't feel quite at home here on Earth, it could be a result of not knowing what they are really accomplishing here in this Earth dimension. In other words, the true mission is not within conscious awareness, giving an unsettling feeling of not belonging.

CLINK CLINK

Amanda was born into a large family. She never married and was not interested in doing so. Her family was extremely dysfunctional, and she endured a childhood of trauma and abuse by family members. Amanda never fit in. She felt she needed to leave home as soon as possible, and she did, while a teenager.

Amanda has had extraterrestrial contact and wanted to know more about these ETs. One was a grasshopper ET. The other was an ET with orange skin with a long face, with the front of its face appearing missing when looked at from the side. During the interview, she showed me a picture she drew of a red-colored extraterrestrial being that she had seen too.

Amanda had been working hard on forgiveness, evolving spiritually, and had a plethora of physical ailments: bilateral sciatica; anxiety about driving a car and taking the driver's test; fused Lumbar 4-5 vertebrae; fibroids discovered in 2012; ovaries ache when she did her own energy healing; jaw, neck and shoulder pain; and such severe back pain that she couldn't sit up on the sofa, so she laid on the sofa, and I sat in a chair facing her.

About halfway through the interview, she said, "Wow! My back pain is gone!" She sat up for the remainder of the interview. While listening to her, I heard a lot of anger and victimhood. Amanda cried while telling her life story. These emotional releases during the interview were therapeutic and very much part of the healing process.

Amanda didn't have a car or know how to drive. She failed the test three times, driving up and over the sidewalks, without any steering capability at all. Amanda was white-knuckled while driving and almost catatonic, completely out of her wits. She wanted to find out why.

PAST LIFE

Amanda is standing in a forest, looking at a red-colored human-shaped being sitting at a table.

Amanda: The trees are tall, elongated and tapered at the tip. It's like it's sunrise.

Barbara: *What kind of table is it?*

A: Like a picnic table. Let's see. It looks like it's between wood and metal.

B: *What do you see for feet?*

A: My feet look square. Like box shaped. I look red too.

B: *Is the box what is on your feet or is it part of you? You can look at your whole body and describe.*

A: It's human shaped. I have legs. Thin, very thin. Much thinner than a normal human. Looks like shoes I'm wearing. Not human shoes.

B: *Are you wearing garments?*

A: I don't wear any clothes. I don't look like a gender of anything.

B: *Do have a skin covering of some form?*

A: It's like the texture of scuba gear, skin suit.

B: *Describe your face.*

A: Similar to the being. I'm related to this other being at the table.

B: *In what way?*

A: The same. It's hard to describe in human terms. When we say family on Earth, it's family as collective. The relation doesn't matter.

B: *Are you wearing any ornamentation on you?*

A: I'm having a hard time seeing that, for some reason.

B: *Are you carrying anything at all?*

A: It looks like a garment or staff. Like a mop. It's something significant. I can't place it right now.

B: *What happens next?*

A: I communicated telepathically to the being on the table. I greet hello. He answers back and invites me to sit down.

B: *Is that what you do?*

A: Yes, that's what I do. I sit down. We're at the end of the table. We're sharing a meal.

B: *What type of food do you eat?*

A: Um, I need a moment to tune into what is in front of me. It's not human food. It looks like striations of energy. And it's like the way it's formed. It looks like the way DNA is shaped. But the striations of energy, you can break them off like crackers.

B: *Nice.*

A: [Amanda laughs and relaxes more with a deep breath.]

B: *What type of things do you talk about?*

A: He's telling me about my mission here.

B: *What is he saying to you?*

A: I don't want you to go. [Big sigh]

B: *Is he saying that to you?*

A: That's what he's saying to me. I'll need a moment. It sounds like I may have to relay to you what's being said.

"I want you to be at your highest best way to go to Terra[22]. I don't want you to go. But I will love you and miss you. I know you volunteered, and I will honor what you desire. I will honor your desire to see Terra evolve. I love you. Although I don't want you to go. I'm sad." That's the message. He's really sad. Lost for words.

B: *It sounds like he's going to miss you.*

A: Yeah.

B: *Will he be able to visit you from time to time?*

---

22 Mother Earth

A: I'm sorry, I didn't hear your question.

B: *Is he able to visit with you from time to time in other realms?*

A: Um, I need a moment to tune in. It's many light-years away. I'm [big sigh]… I'm sorry.

B: *It's alright.*

A: He put his hand upon mine as an assurance as well as some sadness. My head is down. Because I know I'm going away and I don't know when I'll be back.

B: *Are you able to visit each other in the other planes?*

A: The density is so [crying deeply]… [Crying deeply] I want to see them ascend.

B: *You're helping a lot of people.*

A: [Crying] I hurt extra now.

B: *For the people on Terra?*

A: Yes, for the people who want to know about themselves.

I give Amanda comfort and support to help lessen the emotional charge so she could keep talking about the experience. Her crying stops and big releasing sighs follow.

We leave that scene and go forward to when she departed for her mission.

A: I'm having a hard time seeing.

B: *What does it look like?*

A: I'm seeing a haze.

B: *That's all right. You can be in this haze and rest in it.*

[silent pause]

She needs this time to rest after the emotional release.

B: *How does it feel to be there?*

A: Okay. I don't feel like I have a body. I'm just in a haze. I see a being's head. Different from earlier.

B: *Please describe it for me.*

A: This form is a egg-shaped head. The eyes are big, white almond shaped. There's an indentation down the middle of the face. The eyes are black.

B: *Are you able to communicate with it?*

A: It's like its tapping at me, and it sounds like glass. [clink clink] Somehow, I'm in a glass jar.

B: *Is it trying to get your attention?*

A: I don't have a way of seeing that clearly.

B: *Okay. Look at your body. Describe to me what you see.*

A: I am a fetus that looks like a form of the being who is viewing me in the glass jar. I'm in an incubator, being born, I guess, and I am being taken out! I guess because I said hello telepathically. I was ready to come out!

B: *Can you communicate with the being who took you out?*

A: I'm being taken out of the jar and taken over to the other side of what looks like a laboratory.

B: *Describe it.*

A: A laboratory that's all gray metal and dimly lit.

B: *Are there others in incubators?*

A: Yes, there are. There are a lot of beings like me being born.

B: *Is there a name for the place you're being born?*

A: Where I'm being taken? I'm going to be implanted in a human. I'm a template, a hybrid template. So, there is a human in the room. It's a woman and I'm going to be growing inside of her.

B: *Do you recognize her?*

A: It resembles a human being like me, laying here. This is a different type of incubation where the soul wraps around to interface with the being, and after a time, I'll be taken out. She doesn't know it.

B: *Is this a human mother from planet Earth?*

A: It's from here.

B: *From Earth?*

A: From Earth.

B: *Is this for your current incarnation as Amanda?*

A: Yes.

B: *So, how are you prepared before you are born?*

A: Well, as a being, I will be inserted into the human. And incubate for a period of time, then removed. And the process is done.

B: *Then what happens to you?*

A: I will live amongst the other beings. I look like the person who took me out of the jar, but I will have a soul of the human I was taken out of.

B: *Do you share that soul or what?*

A: She doesn't know, but we do. I try to visit her. She saw me but she didn't understand.

B: *Amanda saw you?*

A: She did. I'm not sure how to feel about this. I think she'd be happy for me. I don't know if she would want to understand.

B: *How does Amanda become prepared for her journey on planet Earth? Is that taken care of by someone?*

A: I need to clarify. When I say the human I was taken out of. The one I saw—the women you see right now speaking these words, she's where I came out of. I'm existing here. I'm that being.

B: *So, is this another aspect of Amanda?*

A: No, separate.

B: *So, Amanda has a soul. Is that correct?*

A: She will always have a soul. It's that she shares it with me.

B: *Did you leave Amanda before she was born or later?*

A: [Deep sighs] I'm sorry, what is your question?

B: *Did you leave Amanda before she was born or after?*

A: When I was out of her, her body was an adult. We are separate. So to answer your question, after she was born and after she became an adult.

B: *So what was she going through in her life at the time you left? What was she experiencing in her life?*

A: [Silence] She was in her twenties. Twenty-one. Her energies are very sad.

B: *Is that why you left?*

A: [Big sigh] The state of her emotions was very sad. I say this because her body memory doesn't know what's going on, but her Higher Self does. She was taken—just, the word, abduction, in your language. That's how to describe even though I don't like that word. I would say sequestered to come and have her soul wrapped around me, for a time, and then removed from her. I can sense how she feels when I was in her, growing. She didn't like her mother very much; she wanted to go away. She didn't know where to reach out. It had nothing to do with me. I know why I'm here. I'm here to be just like her.

By now, this was getting a little convoluted for me. Although it sounds as if I'm speaking with an emotional attachment or entity formed due to the difficult childhood. I decide to talk to the HS to get clarity.

B: *Thank you so much.*

HIGHER SELF

When I call in the Higher Self, the voice change is remarkable.

Barbara: *Why did you choose to show her the life that started at the picnic table in the forest?*

HS: It's time for her to find out where she comes from. This is her question all her life. Because she felt she did not belong.

B: *Where is she from?*

HS: Andromeda.

B: *That's a galaxy. Is there a particular planet that she is from?*

HS: I could try to say it with her language.

B: *Do the best you can.*

HS: En-nay-han (phonetically spelled).

B: *Thank you very much. One of the lessons she's learning in this lifetime—*[HS interrupting]

HS: Consciousness. Consciousness in this third dimension, to merge in the third dimension.

B: *You also showed her the being in the incubator, being born and placed into Amanda's body. Why did you show her that?*

HS: She has a connection with the grays.

B: *Who are the grays?*

HS: The B variety. This is the one who is most evolved from this species. We have more than one variety of gray.

B: *What do you want Amanda to know right now?*

HS: That she is connected. That she has a family. That she has an origin, even though her soul is different than the others. It's part of the creation and part of the ascension process. A density energy humans cannot take along higher consciousness, and these beings assist. Much better because of experience and level of ascension. It explains why she is able to navigate in this density so readily. It's time for her to ascend, advance, and move forward.

B: *How best will she be doing that?*

HS: She will meet us soon. Soon. It's time for her to meet us.

B: *Who are you?*

HS: [Deep sigh] I have a name. I can't say it in this being. She wants to come home.

B: *Dear Higher Self. [client moaning, but not in pain] Dear Higher Self, may I please speak with you?*

HS: Yes.

B: *I asked who are you. Why did you give me this answer instead of telling me who you are? I'm curious.*

HS: I'm sorry. This is new. A new na–a.

B: *Dear HS, I notice that Amanda's body is twitching at this time. Can you tell me why this occurring at this time? I know you're monitoring her body.*

HS: Entity.

B: *There's an entity someplace? Dear Higher Self, is there an entity here?*

HS: Yes.

B: *And what do you want to do about that?*

HS: It's interfering with the conversation.

B: *Well, I know you are very powerful and can remove entities. Would you like to do that right now?*

HS: Please. [The Higher Self is being very courteous in their communications with me.]

B: *Let me know when you're done.*

[Amanda sighs repeatedly.]

HS: Done! [It took less than thirty seconds]

B: *Would you please share with us, where did this emotional attachment come from?*

HS: From the embryonic implant we mentioned earlier.

B: *What was the purpose of it?*

HS: Experience.

B: *Experience what?*

HS: Of children. Birth. You can go. She doesn't want any children, human children because of her experiences. It's a fulfillment of karmic contract.

B: *So she fulfilled a karmic contract with that. Does she fully understand it now?*

HS: She understands now.

B: *Has this been released completely?*

HS: No.

B: *What else do you need to do?*

HS: There are other ties that need to be untangled.

B: *Can you do that at this time?*

HS: Yes.

B: *Thank you so much. How many?*

HS: Four.

B: *Can you tell us about them?*

HS: Number of times embryonic implants have been inserted here in this body.

B: *Are they for other reasons?*

HS: Yes, she's not aware of.

B: *Can you share this at this time?*

HS: No.

B: *Can you share this with her later?*

HS: Oh, yeah.

B: *Thank you so much. Are you removing them now?*

HS: Yes.

B: *Would you let me know when you're done?*

HS: [Three seconds later] Done.

B: *Thank you. Are there any other missions she's to embark upon that she hasn't completed?*

Amanda: My head hurts.

B: *I'm asking the Higher Self to please dial down the head discomfort for Amanda.*

HS: Yes.

B: *Dear Higher Self, what is the root cause of the head discomfort?*

HS: She doesn't want to see it. She's afraid.

B: *Is she running a fear program?*

HS: Well, yes.

B: *Could you please go into her mind and look for any programs running fear and doubt? Do you find any?*

HS: Her mother keeps telling her things are not nice about what her abilities are.

B: *Could you go in there and remove this program? You're really good at this.*

HS: All right. Done.

B: *Thank you so much. Would it be possible to download and install new programs?*

HS: Oh, yes, she's been wanting new programs anyway.

B: *Receiving affirmations of who she is, her abilities, her skills, her innate gifts, of what she brings to the collective table of life here? To give her self love, self honor and respect, happiness, joy, balance, harmony and worthiness, and anything else you feel would be beneficial for Amanda?*

HS: Done.

BODY SCAN

B: *Her left ear has been ringing for three weeks with heat, what is the root cause?*

HS: Antenna.

B: *What about the antenna?*

HS: [Big sighs] Alien antenna.

B: *What's it for?*

HS: The first being, as the red being, they have antennas and it runs laterally through the head. The reference point is the top of the ears. The axis of the brain transverses the pineal gland. This is for her third eye sentience.

B: *Everything is normal?*

HS: Yes, for her origin.

B: *Nothing to be concerned about?*

HS: For comfort she can add ice on her ears when she runs hot.

B: *As you look inside, she feels she's carrying extra weight. What is the root cause?*

HS: Sadness. Her experiences. Self soothing. It's misdirected but, it is what it is.

B: *She would like to lose weight. Can you help her with this?*

HS: Yes, she'd like to let go.

B: *Looking at her nutrition, digestive system and nutrients, is there anything you'd like her to do or modify?*

HS: She says she's sweet enough. She loves sweet things. Not as much as she used to. She's aware of her blood sugar. Vegetarian is better for her. She can go vegan if she wants too. She's done it before. This body talks to her a lot, so it's just a matter of her willingly complying. There are blockages, emotional blockages.

B: *She has emotional blockages. Are you able to clear those out?*

HS: Yes.

B: *Thank you. As you do that, would it be possible for her to have weight range between 125 and 130 pounds (client's preference)?*

HS: 130-135 pounds.

B: *Okay. Are you able to program her body with that weight range?*

HS: Yes.

B: *Is there any activity you would like her to engage in to support her body?*

HS: Cardio.

B: *Which one?*

HS: The elliptical is the best for her.

B: *Does she have one here?*

HS: There is one here.

B: *Looking into her mind. She shared she has anxiety regarding driving a car. What is the root cause of it?*

HS: A car accident at twelve. She was the passenger. Father was drunk. Her consciousness was between, because she was asleep.

B: *She had to come quickly back into her body?*

HS: Yes, it scared her.

B: *Are you able to make an adjustment with her cellular memory?*

HS: Hmmm!

B: *What is that?*

HS: Right shoulder.

B: *Is that from the auto accident also?*

HS: Trauma memory.

B: *Are you making an adjustment for that? Are you bringing it to her consciousness to she can become aware of it so it can go away?*

HS: It's going away now.

B: *Can you remove that cellular memory so she can take that driving test and pass it with flying colors?*

HS: Done!

B: *Thank you so much. She shared with us that she has sciatica nerve discomfort, numbness and spasms, in her hips, buttocks, etc. What is the root cause of it?*

HS: It's trauma.

B: *Is it all from the auto accident?*

HS: No.

B: *What kind?*

HS: Emotional.

B: *What about the lumbar 4-5 vertebra?*

HS: They are fused together, and there's slight inflammation.

B: *What caused that?*

HS: The auto accident.

B: *What emotional trauma occurred?*

HS: She doesn't remember all of it. She had to probe really deep.

B: *Is this when she was a child?*

HS: Yes.

B: *All right. How do you want to address this? What is the best way for her?*

HS: As those memories are released. The pain will be… it's deep. [Swallowing]

There is silence for several minutes.

B: *As you continue to work on this, may I continue to ask questions?*

HS: Yes.

B: *She's shared that there's discomfort in her neck/jaw area. What is your assessment of this area?*

HS: It's all emotional trauma. Anger. Being on pins and needles. Living in a house with angry people. Not knowing what they are going to do or say next. Defensiveness. Just not being able to relax at all.

B: *Sounds like she was on high alert.*

HS: Constantly.

B: *Hyper-vigilant, and the ego had to develop quite well to help her.*

HS: Yes, unfortunately.

B: *Thank goodness the ego was there to help her to continue to live and for us to have this blessed opportunity here today. Is it possible for you to remove all of that cellular trauma?*

HS: It's all in the muscles. Yes.

B: *Thank you. How are you doing that?*

HS: Just seeing it all disappear. Just dissolve. She's going to go to the bathroom again. It's working right now as we speak.

Amanda had gone to the bathroom during the past life and excuses herself to go now too. The urination is the release of toxins from cellular memories and stored emotional traumas. This is why I don't mind when the client needs to use the restroom during the session. It takes only about a minute and a half, and the benefits are exponential for the client, in my humble opinion.

B: *The bladder is filling from your work. Are you recommending she drinks extra water after this session? Will this help her release even more?*

HS: Oh, yes!

B: *Have you taken out any self-doubt programs?*

HS: We see it in a way… it's an attachment. No longer a program, but an attachment. An illusion for her.

B: *Will you be able to remove that from her at this time?*

HS: Yes.

B: *Thank you so much. How are you doing that?*

HS: It's disappearing, dissolving, floating away.

B: *How is she going to feel after this?*

HS: More confidence.

B: *At nine or ten years of age, she felt she entered an inter-dimensional portal through a vent in the kitchen of the house she grew up in. Is this something of a one-time occurrence, or is this something she can do?*

HS: It's a one of—she hasn't seen any more. Once her consciousness expands, it will happen more. Her meditations will help her. Getting the attention, she'll relax more.

B: *She would like to know if her mother was happy at the moment of her conception?*

HS: It was her mother's version of happiness.

B: *She was wondering: Does or is the baby affected by what the mother is going through during the pregnancy?* [I already knew the answer.]

HS: Always. There's no language. Baby doesn't know language. There's vibration, emotions.

B: *Is it to Amanda's benefit to re-engage with her family back in her home state?*

HS: No.

B: *Is it best to continue on her journey?*

HS: Yes.

B: *She also shared with us that she doesn't want to work with anyone who is ego driven. Would you explain to us why she's feeling like this?*

HS: She's clairsentient. She understands people's emotions, not the senses per say. What drives a person, things people are programmed to behave. Since she's not had a nurturing environment, other than the one she's created for herself, she's very sensitive to negativity. So it's important for her to be in the most peaceful and supportive environment there is. Understandably with this world, and the energies that are shifting here and there, there's just more navigating to do. She'll have that information.

B: *Would you look at her Divine feminine and masculine energies in her body? What is your assessment?*

HS: She is really grasping the understanding of what creation is, not just polarities. But the expression… there's more consciousness to expand, but she's grasping very well.

B: *She would like to know why humans are engaging in destructive and negative behavior towards one another? Could you enlighten us as to why this is occurring on planet Earth?*

HS: As above in consciousness, so below in matter. What your consciousness engages in, that is what you actually do. There is a separation. There is a total separation from the person's Higher Self, which is connected to God. When a person is not connected, they act independently. And so in the minds of these people who are engaging in the negative behavior have deluded themselves into thinking God has sent me to do this person a favor by doing x,y or whatever. God is not a bully.

The Higher Self is giving us an example of a person who is narcissistic, a sociopath or psychopath that has delusions that God is telling them to harm someone.

B: *Does God experience through these behaviors?*

SC: There are behaviors that run a thin line between consciousness and what the separate human is doing. There is no justification for any harm to another soul. When a soul suffers, it decreases the vibration of Gaia. And one feels that. It is up to the people who have a will and consciousness and use it actively enough to speak up.

B: *She said several times in her life that she almost left the human experience, through her depression, her despondency. She knew she had help from the other side that intervened. Were these exit points in her life?*

HS: These are not authorized exit points. Not for this soul. She has to stay.

B: *Did someone step in to help her?*

HS: Her description of who showed up and people who happened to show up are safety mechanisms for her. Because of the densities, what was mentioned earlier.

B: *Did you help provide that?*

HS: Of course. She knew that the being of what her mission is. Planning everything, no exit points for this soul. [By seeing herself in the extraterrestrial form, she is reminded of her mission here on Earth.]

B: *Were you able to remove all blocks for abundance of prosperity?*

HS: There's more to remove.

B: *How would you like to address that?*

HS: It will disappear.

B: *Will it be helpful for her to listen to this recording repeatedly?*

HS: Yes.

PARTING MESSAGE

HS: Until I will speak with you again, and it will be soon, just keep your heart open. We're almost there. [whispering] We're almost there.

From this session, Amanda now understands why she has had extraterrestrial contact. She knows more about herself. She also learned more about the human condition and its role in consciousness and behaviors. Amanda now knows the root cause of her driving anxieties. Having brought them to her consciousness, she can now release those anxieties. As Amanda listens to her session recording repeatedly, she'll receive more information and insights of what was revealed in her session.

In the next session story, we see the struggles of extraterrestrial beings who lost their home planet. We learn about the importance of getting along with others different from us.

UNITY CONSCIOUSNESS

I facilitated this session for a delightful star being in her mid-thirties from another country. Patricia had read my blog article, "QHHT® session story: Before my birth."[23] She received a healing while reading the article. She flew to Phoenix, and we met at one of the airport hotels where I facilitated a QHHT® session for her.

She was born the first child of parents who were emotionally unavailable to her, and the parents divorced when she was very young. The father was a physically abusive alcoholic. The mother developed multiple sclerosis. The children became the parents. There wasn't much food in the house.

In grade school, Patricia was bullied. She befriended a girl who wasn't popular, and for this, Patricia was chastised by other classmates. The mother became involved in cult religions, giving all her money and household items to these cult people. This included the children's

---

23 https://barbarabeckerhealing.com/qhht-before-the-birth-of-barbara-becker/

beds and bedroom furniture. This behavior was very stressful for the two daughters.

All through childhood and even now, Patricia sees ETs and spirits. She uses all of her extra senses for communications and guidance. She is able to channel people who have crossed over. She does psychic readings and energy healing. All of this work is one-on-one.

Meanwhile, she is dealing with her own self esteem issues, including feeling too scared to speak her truth. She never had established boundaries as a child, so she recently has begun to form them and feels she is doing quite well. At times it doesn't feel good. We talked a bit about this being because what is familiar feels normal; the new familiar feels different, and takes time to get used to it.

PAST LIFE

Patricia: I'm on a planet. It feels like it's gray. I noticed it when I was flying over. I see gray alien beings with dark eyes. I'm standing on the planet.

Barbara: *Describe the environment.*

P: It's barren, and dark. Feels not like Earth at all. No ecosystem. Feels like it's the moon with craters, white and gray. Atmosphere is not oxygen. I'm breathing fine. Clear atmosphere. Sky is dark. I'm just standing on a crater, not moving. Fixed in place. Feels like blackness with little stars in the distance. Whole environment is like this. There are others with me. My feet have three toes. No clothes. My skin is smooth, rubbery with thin legs. I'm tall. My eyes can see multi-dimensionally. My head feels larger. Upside down triangle shape. Smooth skin, eyes, and the mouth is not for breathing. I have three long fingers. No gender. Middle-aged. Healthy. I have a tattoo on my chest, wrapped in a circle; inside there's a V.

I'm on a mission. We are explorers. Five of us. We are exploring a new planet around our own. We're checking out the land. We are looking for more life-sustaining homes. Our home is in jeopardy. [emotion released with tears]

B: *What happened to your home planet?*

P: Some sort of disaster is happening.

B: *Is it an ecological disaster?*

P: It feels like it's the environment, yes. Things are not lining up with the planets and the stars, so it's affecting the environment.

B: *Do you have family back there?*

P: Yes.

B: *Are you able to communicate with the other team members of this group?*

P: Yes.

B: *How do you communicate?*

P: It's not with words. We simply send a vibration of information. Like telepathy. It's almost like we use our mouths for sounds, not for words, but sounds that carry a vibration of information.

B: *You are able to communicate with thought and the sound vibration. What is the purpose of that?*

P: It carries information.

B: *What is your group finding out so far?*

P: That this place is not sufficient. We won't be able to live there.

B: *What type of environment are you looking for?*

P: Blue plasma environment that needs sun. It feels like where we are, is not conducive to that. It doesn't get enough exposure.

B: *Do you spend a long time exploring here?*

P: We just landed, and it feels like we're going to leave soon. [emotionally] It feels like a failed mission.

B: *Is the mission just to go to that one planet?*

P: No, we have a few to go to.

B: *So the mission is not done. Is that correct?*

P: Yes.

B: *At least you have information that this planet is not available for your civilization.*

P: Yes.

We move forward in time to when she's on her spaceship.

B: *Please describe your craft.*

P: We move really fast in this ship. We are exploring the outside of our galaxy. It's a long ways from home. It feels like we just want to find a place.

B: *How do you determine where to go in your exploration?*

P: We have maps. It's not a normal map. It's like an energy grid where we know—we have a rough idea of where we can go that should be conducive to an environment for us to live. The sun is really good for us. It's something that replenishes us. We need to be near the sun.

B: *Where does that information come from that you use to determine where to go?*

P: It feels like that is information from a council of beings. It was given to us to use. I feel it's why I'm an adventurer. We are a team that was put together to explore other avenues for where we can live. Yup.

We move to the next destination.

P: I feel like I'm on this star system that is completely white. The purest of white. It doesn't look like much with the physical dimension, but on the higher vibrational system, is beeeauuuuuutiful! Full of color and vibrancy. Everything is moving and shifting. People are happy.

B: *What do the people look like?*

P: It's really, all different beings, actually. Not just the ones that look like me. Like every being together. It's like a hub of most of civilization, in a sense that there's beings from all over in communion and unity with each other.

B: *It sounds like a happy place.*

P: It is a happy place.

B: *Does this look like a place where your people could live?*

P: Yeah. It feels like we're coming here. We found it. We're happy we stumbled upon it on our journey.

B: *Sounds like the mission is not a failure at all.*

P: Yeah!

B: *How do you determine to establish your colony? Do you have to talk to somebody about this?*

P: This planet is like a non-regulated planet. It's the people that regulate it, the beings that regulate it. It is all of the beings that vote to allow you in, and the beings back at my home just have to make the decision to come. Then we come and we integrate with everyone. We don't just stick to ourselves.

B: *So what happens next?*

P: It feels like we can establish a home here. It feels like home is a little more regimented, and it's going to take us a little bit of time before we can actually move in. Now we know there's space for us to go to a happy place. [smiling and laughing]

B: *What happens next?*

P: There's a unity sensation that occurs and we collaborate together on how to make our galaxies align. We collaborate on how to help other people. We are helping ourselves, people, and the universe—multi-dimensions coming together. The unity sensation is the place that begins the journey for us. We're able to be shipped out to do missions elsewhere.

B: *Is there an opportunity for you to do more missions from this planet?*

P: Yes.

B: *Did your family join you yet?*

P: No. Now I feel a sensation. This is what they told me to do. This is what they proposed to me, for this is what I did. This is where I landed, and this is me finding a new home for us. This being a part of the journey that links me to Earth and why I'm here. This is that planet where we've grown in unity together and come up with the next mission. That mission is why I'm doing this Earth mission I've been cycling through for a little while now. Yeah.

B: *How does it feel having that clarity?*

P: It feels really good. I can see how it came together now and why it is the way it is. I wasn't just forced to do Earth without my will. It's that I came together with the council of people on this other planet to decide on what the mission is… I did agree to it. For my family, it was the initial finding a new home that they told me to do and explore. They knew I love the adventures and exploration.

B: *Let's leave that scene to go to another important day.*

P: If feels like I'm returning from my Earth mission. It feels like I'm coming back with knowledge for everyone and information I've gained to share. It feels good. It's done. It feels like the future. I feel like I've grown a lot. It feels like light years of growth. Now I'm able to advise the council more knowledgeably because of this mission I've been on for a while now. Yup.

B: *Can you describe the council?*

P: In the galaxy that I'm in, there is a representative from each of the planets and star systems. They all look very different from each other, but they all have the same alignment of belief systems, although they may be different. They all bring that difference in their nature. We all have that common agreement in what we are doing and why we're doing the missions.

At this point, Patricia explains that although the beings all have their own languages and dialects (not in words, but in a sort of telepathic manner), they can communicate in a multidimensional vibrational language.

We're all sitting around a table [laughs] even though the table isn't real; it's just like the visual they're giving me so I can interpret it.

B: *Leaving that scene and we're moving to the last day of that life. You can see it as an observer.*

P: It just feels like it's a cycle of energy really. It feels like I haven't lost anything. I've gained more than anything I could imagine. It feels like the dimension I'm on. It's like I'm going to dissolve and just go to my light being body.

B: *You're out of that ET body?*

P: Totally.

B: *What happens to that ET body?*

P: It just dissolves.

B: *What were the lessons you learned in that life?*

P: When you live for the greater good, your life is fulfilling. When you learn from a place of service to yourself and others, you live a fulfilling life.

To see the world beyond what we were. When we integrated with the light planet that had all species on it, we found unity. All of us found unity, and it was helping us to evolve and get out of our selfish way of living. We saw life was more than just our planet.

B: *What do you feel was the purpose of that life?*

P: Seeing the Oneness as everyone. We feel like our species came to know that in that lifetime.

Just as Dolores asked her clients in hypnosis what they thought the purpose and lessons were of the life shown, she also asked the Higher Self the same questions. Often times, the Higher Self answers are different from the client's answers.

HIGHER SELF

Barbara: *Why did you show her that lifetime?*

Higher Self: 1. So that she could see she's had an extraterrestrial lifetime. 2. So that she could see the explorer/adventurer is a part of her soul.

B: *What were the lessons in that lifetime she was learning?*

HS: One of the key lessons was to have faith. Because their journey was multiple Earth years. Before they came across the white light planet. She needed to see that things don't happen in a flash. They take time. You just have to keep on going. She eventually had that realization. We just wanted to bring that to her attention.

B: *Thank you. She shared with us she's working in a corporate job. She has been preparing herself for a spiritual career, in alignment in her soul path. What do you recommend?*

HS: Keep a balance between both. She's not ready to jump into a full spiritual career.

B: *Is she on track with her education training that she's engaged in right now?*

HS: Yes.

B: *Will it be psychic medium work or healing work, or what?*

HS: It's going to be. Right now it's the gateway. She'll be working with energy on a much deeper level than what she knows at this point.

B: *What form is that energy work?*

HS: Working with vibration, with hands, not only shifting energy. Painting is very important for this.

B: *Is she to continue with the light work painting she's doing?*

HS: Yes.

B: *Are you recommending that she continue moving forward in a format where she's able to sell these paintings, integrating with the healing that people are receiving from these?*

HS: Yes.

B: *She gave me a demonstration of the light language she speaks. Where is it coming from?*

HS: This is the light language that she was born with when she came into conscious being. She came into it from her light family that brought her forward. It's a vibrational language. It emits a feeling and is currently not placed in her vocabulary. Halcyon [pronounced hail-see-on] is the first word that comes to mind.

B: *What is Halcyon?*

HS: It is a dialect of her initial species. It's part of who she is.

B: *When she speaks this language, what does it do for other people?*

HS: It brings them back into alignment. Their energy comes back, blockages are cleared.

B: *Is this something she can do in private sessions? In small groups?*

HS: Just one-on-one for now.

B: *She also writes a light language. Can you tell us about it?*

HS: Seraphim. This is a vibrational writing that emits an essence. It is continuous different patterned words. It is an expansion, just as color does. It's vibration that emits sensations. It's new, and she's hesitant about sharing it.

B: *She puts it in her paintings. Is this appropriate?*

HS: Yes, this is how to incorporate it for now.

B: *Do children recognize the writing?*

HS: Yes.

B: *Is she to go back to school to obtain a counseling degree?*

HS: No. The wisdom that is from her family will come through. Different workshops are okay. No formal education is necessary. This incarnation was not the easiest to get into. Her counsel felt this was the best. She's working out the karma with her father right now, and in the next year, it will be balanced.

B: *What is the root cause of her receding gum tissue?*

HS: Resentment towards herself, of not believing in herself. This is located in her teeth. This is in the area of self acceptance and becoming the whole body, mind, and spirit. In three years time it will integrate. Work still needs to be done internally around her tuning into, where she doesn't feel acceptance... allowing herself to express those parts and loving herself. This is when this will shift.

B: *Is she running a mind program of no self love?*

HS: Yes.

B: *Are you able to change that mind program?*

HS: Yes.

B: *And how are you doing that?*

HS: Energetically I'm working her energy from her third eye down to the heart chakra. Right now it is pulling out those programs running in her grid and affecting primarily through her mind that are stuck in this part of her grid. We're unweaving it from where it's stuck.

B: *You're really good at this.*

HS: Yeah. It's done.

B: *Can she feel that?*

HS: Yup! She's been feeling some tightness in the back of her neck, and this is what it's from. Repairing the grid right now.

This takes a couple of minutes.

HS: It's good now.

B: *What can you tell us about the allergies to certain food substances?*

HS: She has been protecting herself from fully integrating with the Earth. This has been a manifestation of that protection mechanism. As she does her exploration of self, she's breaking that down. In the next few years she won't have any more allergies.

B: *How is her nutrition?*

HS: She's not eating enough light vegetables and fruit. Start with lunch and supper, then breakfast also. It can be a smoothie, but we need this balance of fruits and vegetables. Vitamin E, more salt. She didn't grow up with salt. Himalayan Sea Salt is recommended. Vitamin E: one capsule a day.[24]

B: *How is her digestive system?*

HS: She has a tendency to eat candy and junk food. Trying to numb her experiences. It's the only thing that affects her digestion, throws it off balance.

B: *Can you adjust her food cravings?*

HS: I'm calming down that part of her brain that wants that comfort, and she will crave meditation in place of it. That sensation will be filled in her meditation sessions.

B: *What will she notice after the session as a result of this healing?*

HS: This depth of relaxation and this comfort in her body she hasn't felt before. And the integration of her soul and her body, not feeling the separation of it, but the Oneness of it.

B: *Will she need to have surgery on her gums?*

HS: No.

B: *What is her soul purpose?*

HS: Teaching.

B: *What will she be teaching?*

HS: Working through the complexity of how the mind thinks, helping people get through to see their energy bodies, to heal themselves. It's bringing her home species to humanity. This is what she's bringing forward.

---

24 Appropriately so, most of my clients are concerned about their physical health and want to inquire about their nutrition. For many clients, the HS recommends more water, fruit, and vegetables. In addition, exercise through hiking and walking in nature is often suggested. Avoiding junk food and sugary foods is mentioned repeatedly.

B: *Is this past the conscious mind?*

HS: Yes.

One of her angelic guides comes through.

B: *Do you have a message for her?*

Angelic guide: I want her to know that I'm with her and when she works with me, this will begin to expand her mind so that she can open the door further into this healing career she wants to do. She has some hesitation. This is normal. Once she chooses to do this regularly, she'll see more shifts. She will bring forward more messages of light to people who have had similar experiences as her in this lifetime. I want to work with her once a week and gradually build up. Practice meditations and record the sessions so she can observe the energy I emit through her.

I ask to speak with the Higher Self again…

B: *She's had five lives prior to this one on Earth. What can you tell us about this?*

HS: The first three are very short. She exited fast on the first three, on Earth.

B: *The other two?*

HS: She woke up in her fifties in the last life. [She became aware of her spirituality and focused on evolving her spiritual self.]

B: *What type of lives has she had outside of Earth?*

HS: She has been in the elf species, working with trees. She's been energy in a lifetime on Earth. This was in Atlantis. The energy outside of Earth are three different alien species so she could explore and see different lives and what they bring and share among multiple beings and dimensions.

B: *Is she Pleaidian?*

HS: In the most recent one, before this current Earth life, [she] was Pleadian. However, she is part Pleadian, but she is [also] multiple species. Casiopia star system is the closest to what she knows at this point. All of these make up the whole, that no one amount of knowing one species or another will be a gold ticket to that understanding.

B: *She shared that she can see and sense her star brothers and sisters?*

HS: They are part of her team. She has several species helping her, from her previous incarnations.

B: *Will she be working with children in the future?*

HS: Yes, she will be instrumental in helping children remain open to the spiritual gifts they have. She will help children feel accepted and comfortable with their advanced knowledge and skills.

B: *What will surprise her the most from today?*

HS: The depth of information that has come forward.

B: *What didn't she know about herself?*

HS: The healing around her teeth and gums, and knowing this is going to be completely gone now. It's just a matter of believing it.

B: *She wanted to know if this is her last lifetime on Earth?*

HS: [It] has the potential to be. That's all I'm going to share.

PARTING MESSAGE

HS: I love her. Her connection is going to keep getting deeper and deeper. This is the beginning of sharing this experience and the growth that she is going through with others. [The Higher Self is expressing their love for Patricia, and letting her know her connection to them will grow deep. In this brief message, the HS is preparing Patricia for the changes that are about to occur in her life. They give her a glimpse of other people that are in her life and others that will come to assist in her spiritual growth.]

Post session: Because Patricia found her star being identity in this session, she could go forward with her healing gifts knowing what was behind the star language. After the session, she became even more creative in her art. She also met her sweetheart.

In the next session story, we learn of a soul's amazing abilities in a past life and his purpose in his current life. And we get insights into an extraterrestrial encounter he had in Mexico that left him in denial about what he saw that day.

ET PAST LIFE AND ET ENCOUNTER IN THIS LIFETIME

This session is with a man who works in construction and as a life coach. Bruce seeks direction in both his life and healing work.

Hurtling through space, seeing the color purple and flashes of electricity, we journey for about fourteen minutes. It seems the SC is still transporting Bruce back and back, to another time, another place...

After this long journey, I move Bruce to his destination. He sees himself as a strong, tall grayish-white being, with long blonde hair walking on a white cobblestone path, which is constructed from the ground, going upward to the stars in the night sky. A white robe is fashioned with a belt made of the same material.

He looks like he's in his twenties, but he's very old, and possessing immense power. For instance, he can jump a mile at a time in his healthy body. This thrills him.

His eye vision is extraordinary; he can see a star or a planet, a billion miles away, and they are very clear to him. He's in awe and speaks with reverence as he describes himself.

The cuffs on his wrists are made of gold. Underneath his breastplate there's gold-leaf embedded into the fabric. The huge sword he carries feels lightweight in his hand.

Walking through a large gate, he sees that the city walls are thick and made of a clear material. The streets are clean, and he passes a water fountain. Everyone knows him. The town folk are smaller than he is. His job is to help manage the city and surrounding areas.

> Bruce: We control. We have big meetings. We watch the doors when the rulers all come together. We're the caretakers. There's [sigh] a ruling class that manages the way things work. The energies govern. We, um, we work for keeping things in control and working correctly. It's hard to explain. It's a job that takes strict commitment.

To get more information about his job, I ask probing questions.

Barbara: *Does your job require discipline?*

Bruce: Beyond. We... WOW! [He's almost overwhelmed by what he's seeing and sighs repeatedly.] There's worlds, times, and dimensions all open to us.

He gets easily distracted by helping people and making sure everything is in working order. He's a very curious fellow.

We move to another important day where he observes the people on the planet split apart, with some being sent to a different dimension.

Bruce: It's like, I've just got to tell you. It's like there's Heaven. It's not what you think. It's millions of people, millions of souls. There's a decision that's been made. And those who don't want to follow the decision have to leave. [big sigh] They are cast out of that place into another dimension. [Bruce is moving his body because of everyone's pain]. They are separated from loved ones, those that they have connections to.

My speech is firm. I tell him to take a nice deep breath and remind him it's safe to look at this; we're just observing. He can talk about it. Bruce complies.

Bruce: It's caused wars, and we had to separate everyone. And there's hate and anger because of it. And it doesn't follow what the true Divine Light [is]. We separated them. There's anger and there's war. It forced the elite above me to leave. They're in this Earth, but it's not, it's different from where we're at right now. We're sad. I'm angry that they had to leave. But those that were unwilling to listen...

I ask who's in charge now.

Bruce: The God I serve. I love Him. He loves everyone.

The Higher Self showed Bruce this lifetime in order for him to find peace by accepting what's in front of him.

LIFE PURPOSE AND MISSION

Bruce's life purpose in this lifetime is to fulfill the healing for Earth. Many are involved in this cause, but those that come to help must first find healing. Only those already whole can bring healing to Earth.

His mission is to teach his children how to love. By doing this, he will stop the deterioration of both families he's part of. This problem has caused the breakdown of the souls life after life, as the pattern has repeated over and over.

The HS have agreed to repair the DNA lineage. However, Bruce must learn certain knowledge for himself and those around him in order to heal all involved and stop the cycle. He needs to follow his heart to learn this knowledge.

> HS: Walk away from those who slow you down. Accept this healing. Learn the modalities that bring healing. Bruce has power to bring great healing to people. That power will be greatly needed in the future. He has to accept it. He keeps putting it off.
>
> Barbara: *Will he be vibrating at a much higher level after this session?*
>
> HS: He will. There's more to come. You're helping with the ego as a separate entity, and so to say it's a roadblock that—the work you're doing helps remove that, so that people can progress. And that's going to help him.

When I ask about Bruce's healing gift, the HS says that Bruce has the ability to go into people, assume their vibration, and remove those dark emotions and entities that restrain them. He can guide people with their decisions by seeing what their guides are showing him. He helps them to develop their talents and to feel loved when they have given up. He also helps them raise their vibration so that they can contribute to the worldwide healing that needs to take place. He has many more gifts, too, which the HS will disclose at the proper time.

ET ENCOUNTER

> Barbara: *In Mexico, he saw white lights above the ocean. What was this?*

HS: He doesn't believe in that, but it's true. It's there. He resists it.

B: *What is he resisting?*

HS: The recognition of what happened.

B: *What happened?*

HS: He and his companion were there witnessing other races of superior intelligence and dimensions. The memory of the experience was not supposed to stay with him.

B: *Did he and his friend participate in this gathering?*

HS: It wasn't a gathering. They witnessed an exploratory work that the others were doing.

B: *What were they exploring?*

HS: The Earth has energy of its own, and within that energy, there are many fields of energy that can be tapped into to gain power—like refueling, as when you're closer to the center of the planet, the strength intensifies. The technology is there to communicate with that energy and regain alignment with the fuel that's needed for the craft they use.

B: *So they are refueling their space craft? Are you saying their craft can't regenerate energy automatically?*

HS: Yes, that type receives it from planets and stars when many things are happening at one time, in one space. People are very limited in their sight. Occasionally as the energy fluctuates, things become visible.

B: *May I ask where that star craft came from?*

HS: It comes from other galaxies, other creations.

B: *How far away from Earth's galaxy?*

HS: Further than light can travel at this time. Creator creates many worlds, many lives. It's ever expanding. Those lives are different from yours and have different realities and different effects.

B: *I'm curious to know. Did they receive permission to come here to get fuel for their craft?*

HS: Yes.

B: *Who gives them permission?*

HS: Council for the Source.

B: *Which council is this?*

HS: It goes back to the councils that manage higher intelligence and the workings of the energy. The universe is beautiful. It is a machine that is created and managed and governed by laws. Those with knowledge are allowed to govern those workings.

B: *Thank you. What will he notice the most from the session?*

HS: He'll find reconnection with his true self. He will start enjoying life the way it was meant to be enjoyed. Not only are lessons to be learned, but to feel joy is part of life. He has to allow himself to do that.

B: *What do you recommend he do in his conscious awake state to support the healing?*

HS: Be mindful, staying mindful of his thoughts and not allowing any kind of corruption to come in.... the corruption interrupts [healing]. The world is full of corruption.

B: *What will surprise him the most from this session?*

HS: His ability to remove the abundance blocks. He needs to spend his time talking to his body (and emotions), to bring up the power that is within him. He doesn't use that power except for right now. He needs to ask himself what can he be doing to spread the love and healing that the world needs. He has the answers within him[self].

B: *What didn't he know about himself that you'd like to explain to him now?*

HS: To not put limitations on his intellect—that part of his life is over, and new opportunities and doors have been opened for him; he needs to accept that. He needs to listen to his guides and let his fears go.

PARTING MESSAGE

HS: He already knows the answers to anything I say.

[To Barbara]: You need to know you're loved. What you are doing is important. And it brings energy and healing to you, as well.

Bruce's ego attempted to interfere with the session. I spoke with the ego and helped it to understand that we're all on the same page of wanting the best for Bruce. I helped the ego to understand that one of the benefits of a QHHT® session is that the ego doesn't have to work as much or as hard as it did before the session because Bruce will have a better understanding of who he is and why he's here. He'll have direction for his life. The ego settled down nicely after that talk.

15
WHERE A SOUL GOES AFTER LIFE ON EARTH

This session was facilitated for a woman in her mid-fifties. Born in the Midwest, Kim settled in Arizona. The fifth child in her family, she was bullied at school. It was a small school, and Kim didn't fit in. She graduated and went to college on a scholarship, obtaining her bachelor's degree, then marrying. Her health issues included swollen legs and ankles, and being overweight.

PAST LIFE

> Kim: I feel I'm dressed in the Civil War era. She has dark hair, parted in the middle, tied in a bun at the back of her head. The dress looks like a ball gown. She's Caucasian. The dress is very ornate, big puffy sleeves, low-cut front, multi-colored, green, red, black, white. A dress has many vertical panels in the skirt; it looks professionally made. She looks like a very elegant lady. There are officers around her. Some on horseback, some not. It seems they may be coming from some place, passing through. The soldiers are in uniform, looking clean.
>
> She's one of the townspeople, a town with a courtyard, court house, and a vast amount of grass in front. Brick facade, porches around it, white woodwork. Steeple on top. Some bushes around the courthouse building. Green bushes with trimmed foliage. A few trees here and there.
>
> I'm that woman. This dress with hooped skirt. White shoes, smooth, leather. Heel, go up the mid calf, buttons on the side on the inside. New shoes, comfortable. Rounded shoes, plain on the front.
>
> She has a young body, healthy, no ornamentation, no jewelry, nothing on head, blue eyes, not carrying anything. Majority of

time, lady of leisure, plays piano, takes care of house, not working, and has servants. Just watching soldiers going by. This is expected as they travel, similar scenes before in her life. Feeling sad for the soldiers, how many will come back, how many will lose their lives. Lot of fear in them, I can feel it.

Barbara: *Go to where you live.*

Kim: It's a small house, white porch, made of brick, comfortable, windows in front white window frames, front door is glass and wood, white, has a clear glass door knob on left-hand side. One story house. Long house going back. Many more rooms. Very little grass out front.

[Goes inside] To the right: a parlor, fireplace, on the wall, immediate right is the front window, sofa under the window near the fireplace, two chairs, a table between the two chairs that are at an angle to one another, coffee table made of wood. Side table between the two chairs. No pictures on the wall. Mirror on wall above fireplace—rectangular. Sitting room. As you come in the front door, there is a staircase ahead on the right, and a hallway. It seems there is a second story!

Note: This is not unusual. The scene can change and not make sense. That's okay. The Higher Self is showing the client subtle messages within the story images. The client will make sense of it later when listening to the recording.

K: Left of the front door is a dining room with a large table with many chairs. A large family, no, kitchen area is on the same side of the house as the dining room. Alone in the dining room, kitchen, a staging area, not a kitchen, no cooking in here. The cooking is done elsewhere and put on plates there.

B: *Go to where the food is prepared.*

K: Outside; it's a stone building. There's a woman cooking in there with a stew in a big pot. She recognizes me. She's wearing a plain dress and an apron over it. She knows what she's doing. She's happy and content to be doing this. She likes cooking.

B: *What is a typical meal with the family?*

K: I can see myself. Nobody else is around. I eat by myself. Food: stew, potatoes, meat and carrots—the normal thing I eat. Dishes: utensils are shiny, silver, fairly plain but sturdy with four tines. She drinks water from stemware in the form of a large goblet with clear glass. Her husband is gone. They are newly married. He went off to war. Lonely and frightened for him. "I want him to come home. There's been no correspondence and it frightens me."

We go to another important day in that life…

K: My husband comes home, and he's happy to see me. We embrace. It feels wonderful! He's the same, slightly different. Slightly older, hair is graying, and his eyes are sadder. He's seen a lot. But he still loves me.

B: *What happens next?*

K: We go into the house. We resume the life we had before. We have a child now. A little girl. She's learning to walk. My husband is somehow involved in education. He runs a school and teaches. He's been home for a while now. We're happy.

We go to another important day in that life…

K: I'm ill. I'm in bed laying down. Flu symptoms. Feeling weak, no more will to live. Sad. Body not old, but feels old. No discomfort. My husband is with me. My daughter is with me. She's fourteen years old. The woman who does the cooking is with me too. My husband is just looking at me, with a big concern that I'm not going to get better.

B: *Were you taken care of by a doctor?*

K: No.

B: *What do people do for treatment when they don't feel well?*

K: There's a doctor who comes around periodically. The doctor wasn't available. This ailment has no name. It came on suddenly.

B: *What happens next?*

K: I get up and my body stays where it is.

B: *Are you out of your body?*

K: Yes.

B: *Can you see your body?*

K: Yes.

B: *Is your family still there?*

K: Yes.

B: *What happened to the body?*

K: Everyone is crying, and I left so soon, so abruptly. I caught the flu and couldn't fight it off. Someone comes and takes the body away. It's put into a wooden casket. After a while, there's a funeral. It was buried in a cemetery a little ways out of town.

B: *What do you think was the purpose of that life?*

K: It seems to be to provide a good home and cherish those that I love. Be patient.

B: *What were the lessons learned in that lifetime?*

K: I learned patience waiting for my husband to come back from the war.

B: *What happens next? Where do you go?*

K: I go to a place that is kind of cotton-wool looking. It's indistinct. Kind of white, whitish. Everything is clearing up. It appears to be a grassy area with scattered buildings here and there. Buildings are white and appear to have cones on the front.

B: *Is anybody else there?*

K: There are people around, no one distinct.

B: *Do you see your guides or angels?*

K: There is one person coming up to me. This person appears to be male, but could be female. A fairly large person, light colored hair, white gown. It's smiling. "Welcome back." Laughing, smiling, hugging me. Welcoming me back. A very androgynous-looking person. It wants to take me someplace. We're drifting along a path of some sort. All around us is the greenest grass I've ever seen. The whitest buildings I've ever seen. It's beautiful. Blue skies, clear. There's a lake here and there. We keep drifting on. I'm not sure what our destination is.

Finally, we come to a huge building. Lots of steps out front. It's white, and there are also columns on this building. We go in the front. Not a door, just an opening. It looks like a library. I see lots of books on lots of shelves. We drift toward the back. There seems to be a roundish kind of room. It's empty, but there is a table to the right side. We go over to that table. We just stand there for a little bit. Other people come up to us, and a lot of those welcome me back. They're saying, "It's good to have you back." Everybody seems very happy. Easy going. Everything is easy.

B: *Do they have any plans for you at this moment?*

K: I have to watch what's on the table. It's almost like a screen. I have to watch what's on that screen. So I do that. And then, this person wants to take me to a different area. I sit and lay down on what appears to be a contoured sofa. It conforms to my body. It's very comfortable, and I rest there for a while. This area is darkened a little bit more from the area where I was looking at the table screen.

I thought this would be a good place to leave her to rest.

HIGHER SELF

Barbara: *Why did you show her this life?*

Higher Self: To show her she is a patient person. That she is a strong person. She is a person who can make a happy life for her family and not have to sacrifice any of herself for that peace, for that family. Even though all around her may have been conflict, she had a peaceful home in that area of conflict.

B: *Is she doing this in her life right now?*

HS: Somewhat.

B: *How is she applying it or not applying it?*

HS: She is a patient person. She loves to build a happy, peaceful home. She is somewhat successful in doing that in this life too. She could do more, though. Be more patient, more understanding, more caring, more thoughtful of other people's feelings.

B: *Is this also about speaking her truth?*

HS: Yes, she must learn how to do that on a regular basis, for her well being.

B: *How has this manifested in her life so far?*

HS: It has made her sad and sick at times.

B: *What type of sickness did she manifest from this?*

HS: She manifested fibroid tumors, pancreatitis, colds, and flus at other times, finally manifested as breast cancer until it got her attention to stand up for herself. She must do this.

B: *Do you have recommendations how to stand up for herself? Do you have examples to help her know how to do this?*

HS: She has to find a set of principles and beliefs she can live with, that are the truth for her. She needs to stands by those, and not allow others to sway her. She can see the other person's side, but she can't allow the other person's view to sway her to that other side. She must simply stand her own ground.

B: *Where can she acquire that information?*

HS: Through meditation, self examination. Through contemplation.

B: *Does she know how to do these?*

HS: Yes.

B: *She now has a healthy body?*

HS: She has a healthy body. There are no areas of concern.

B: *She no longer has breast cancer?*

HS: That is correct.

B: *Does she still need to keep taking the estrogen blocker medicine?*

HS: To be in her body is like poison.

B: *Are you recommending to stop taking it?*

HS: She can hold it for a while, but she won't even need to do that anymore because the cause of the cancer is not physical.

B: *So now we know the root cause of the ailments you shared with us, what about the cholesterol? Is that in normal range too?*

HS: The cholesterol is all right at the moment, because of the Lipitor. That doesn't need to be taken in as high a dose.

B: *What do you recommend?*

HS: Half the dosage, just for a little while.

B: *And then what?*

HS: Then she can stop.

B: *Will she know when to stop?*

HS: Yes, in her meditations.

B: *You'll be able to give her that information?*

HS: Yes.

B: *So the ringing in the ears is all gone too?*

HS: That probably will have to gradually disappear.

B: *When will she notice the ringing will be gone?*

HS: It may take a few months. Then it will gradually be gone.

B: *What is the root cause of the ankle swelling?*

HS: There was a weakness there from birth.

B: *What happened?*

HS: It was a minor birth injury, but it can still cause problems here and there.

B: *Can you tell us what happened to the ankle in the birth injury?*

HS: It got squeezed in an abnormal position. After birth it straightened out. But she's always had the weakness.

B: *What was the purpose of the weakness injury in the ankle?*

HS: It was just to let her know there would be other problems on the left side, and this was the first, if she didn't change things in her life.

B: *Was she aware of that when she was younger?*

HS: No.

B: *Now that she knows about it, will that weakness go away?*

HS: Yes, it will go away, gradually as well.

B: *Will she know a difference when she returns to exercising?*

HS: Yes.

B: *What about her low back tightness. What is the root cause?*

HS: Sometimes she is too stiff in her judgments, too rigid in her thinking. She needs to loosen up a bit.

B: *What's the best way for her to do that?*

HS: Listen to others without cutting them off. Listen to them actively. Hear what they actually have to say before jumping to conclusions or reacting.

B: *Can she practice that with her husband?*

HS: Yes.

B: *If she shared that with her husband, will he cooperate to help her develop it?*

HS: Yes. He wants to help her.

B: *Regarding the nutritional status in her body, what is the most beneficial diet for her?*

HS: Stay away from all types of sugar. Eat fruits that are in their native form, natural form. Don't eat so much in the way of processed foods. Eat raw foods, like fruits and vegetables. Eat simply, as close to nature as possible. Add Vitamin D. Either stand in the sun or take the caplets, quite a few to start because she's a little depleted, then gradually 1,000 units should be okay.[25]

B: *You say a bunch of tablets. How many at the beginning?*

HS: Five.

B: *What is her purpose in this life?*

HS: She is to serve others. She is to love others. She needs to show people her light.

B: *How best can she do this?*

HS: Live a positive, loving life, spread her happiness and love just by being herself wherever she goes.

B: *Is she on that path right now?*

HS: She is on the path, but she doesn't recognize it as such.

B: *Is there anything you recommend to bring this to her consciousness?*

HS: She must meditate. She must listen to herself and her inner guidance.

B: *That would be you, wouldn't it?*

HS: Yes.

B: *She would like to know if she can be shown her star lineage or the place where she has originated from, besides Source.*

---

[25] Although this is not meant to be medical advice, there is a common theme for people to eat more healthfully, simply, and supplement when necessary. Each individual needs to consult with their healthcare provider to determine what is best for them in their dietary choices.

HS: She comes from the Pleiades.

B: *Is there significance that she is Pleiadian? What does it mean for her?*

HS: It is just her lineage.

B: *Is that enough for her to know?*

HS: Yes.

B: *Would you give her more information as she listens to her recording?*

HS: Yes.

B: *She feels somewhat at a loss as far as what service to do at this time, in her life. Is there any form of service would be in alignment with her soul path?*

HS: Anything where she can be of service. No one is better than the other. In her meditations she will find the answers.

B: *Would you help us understand why she chose her parents in this lifetime?*

HS: They were chosen for her to stand on her own two feet. To be a strong, independent woman. They love her, but they wanted her to be independent more than anything.

B: *Is that the contract that was made?*

HS: Yes.

B: *What is the significance of hearing bells ringing?*

HS: That is her light council trying to get her attention, to let her know she is loved. She is cared for. She is taken care of. We love her dearly and want her to know this. So, the bells are a reminder that we are here. That her light council is here. She's not to doubt that we are here. She needs to trust us and herself.

B: *What is the root cause of the extra adipose tissue?*

HS: Partially to diet and not loving herself enough. Care for herself and her body. Loving herself is the greatest thing she can do.

B: *How can she love herself?*

HS: Contemplation. Review the good things about herself, keep those foremost in her mind. That's not to say to forget about the weaker parts of her; she just needs not to dwell on any of the weaker parts of her. Certainly, she can try to make those weaker parts stronger, but she needs to contemplate and always be a positive person.

B: *Why does she feel overwhelmed at times and a feeling of needing to be free from other people?*

HS: There were too many other lifetimes where she was controlled by others and lost her freedom for various reasons. The circumstances of each life were different, but in each life, she lost her freedom to a greater or lesser degree. And she was always rebellious of losing her freedoms. She wants to be a free agent, a free being as when she was with All That Is. When she was part of the One. She doesn't want to be controlled ever again.

B: *How is that applicable in her life right now?*

HS: She feels somewhat constrained by the circumstances in her life, as well as by her partner. But, it's mostly self imposed. She does have that freedom to be who she is and who she needs to be. She just needs to stand up again for her own self.

B: *Does that mean she needs to speak up for herself with her spouse?*

HS: Yes, and sticking to her beliefs. Just be unwavering. If it's important to her, whatever it is. She must always speak her truth and make sure that her partner knows that it is her truth.

B: *How will she benefit from speaking her truth?*

HS: She will gain that freedom that she desires. It will be an all-encompassing freedom that she desires. And she will have it if she speaks her truth.

B: *She has a feeling that time is running out. Can you help her to understand why she gets that feeling?*

HS: There is a new Earth coming, and time is short. She's feeling that urgency to think clearly, speak clearly, be a beacon, be herself. She feels that she must do this; subconsciously she feels that. But it comes out in various ways. She feels anxious, she feels like she must do something right now, and yet she procrastinates. She cannot procrastinate any longer because time is running out. The new Earth is coming despite what she does. If she wants to get to the new Earth, she needs to get on the bandwagon. Get on with her missions. Get on the path, stay on the path.

B: *Summarizing, you want her to meditate [yes], you want her to check in with you [yes], you want her to speak her truth [yes], you want her to explore what she believes in and what she doesn't believe in [yes], to express her needs so that she will feel the freedom she desires [that is correct], and not be afraid of what other people think? [correct] or what other people will do? [correct]*

B: *What were you trying to tell her in her dream of manifesting glass coins in her palms?*

HS: We were showing her an actual glimpse of what happens on the other side, when her physical body is sleeping. She goes to various places, attends various classes in schools. That was a glimpse of what she can do and is learning to do. And that was to give her hope that her life on Earth is not all there is, but that there is a full life for her on the other side of the veil.

B: *Can you tell us more about that life on the other side?*

HS: It's more than she thinks it is. Much more satisfying in some ways. Being on the other side and being in the physical, it's all a matter of perspective. She loves her time on the other side. But she is anxious to be here in the physical to fulfill those missions that she wanted to come to fulfill. She still wants to be here to spread her light, fulfill her missions, stay on her path.

B: *Will you continue to help her do that?*

HS: Yes.

Contacting her deceased dog is very important to her.

B: *Can Jake, her dog, come through for a little visit?*

HS: Yes.

B: *I'm asking the Higher Self to recede, while Jake comes forward. Take this time to talk with Jake, listen to his messages. Just let me know when you're done.*

When a client's pet dog comes through, I can literally see the tail wagging very fast, and the love feeling is very intense. I consider this a perk for the QHHT® practitioner.

After the visit was complete, I ask to speak with Kim's Higher Self.

B: *Would it be permissible for her to go to the Temple of Wisdom?*

HS: Yes.

B: *How would you like to do that?*

HS: I can be there now.

B: *Could you allow her to describe what she is seeing and experiencing?*

HS: It was the Temple of Wisdom she went to with her guide after she passed over from the life we showed her.

B: *I thought so. Is there more for her to see at this time?*

HS: There are many parts here. Healing parts, healing rooms; she can go there anytime she wishes.

B: *Dear Higher Self, may I continue to ask questions?*

HS: Yes.

B: *What will she notice after this session after this healing?*

HS: She will notice her lightness of being. She will be able to tap into her joy of life. She will be a lighter spirit. She will understand more about her partner and herself, because of this session. She will grow healthier each time she remembers our session.

B: *Will she have an easier time being around other people?*

HS: In time.

B: *What can she do to support the healing that was done here today?*

HS: She must remain positive and meditate. She must maintain a positive outlook.

B: *What will surprise her the most about what was said today?*

HS: Her physical ailments were not caused physically, as much as by other means.

B: *What did you hope she would receive the most from the session?*

HS: Complete healing of her physical body.

B: *How can she best connect with you?*

HS: Meditation, and the second way is to be out in Nature.

B: *What did she not know about herself, you'd like to explain to her?*

HS: That she is loved, dearly loved, and can tap into our love anytime.

Kim's Higher Self recommended meditation, enjoyment of Nature, and loving herself. This message comes up in many sessions. It is a simple recommendation; yet, we humans can make it complex through our excuses. I've done this, too. It does take a little effort to be disciplined to exercise and meditate regularly. Self love is very important in our soul's expression.

16
SACRED SOULS

In Dolores Cannon's *Convoluted Universe Book IV*, the fourth in her multi-volume series[26], she wrote about a phenomenon called backdrop people. Among other uses described in Dolores' books, the concept of the backdrop people is a way for the rest of us here on the old Earth to not notice the massive number of people who are ascending. I am very fascinated with this concept because it flies in the face of everything we've been told before. Things like: we die, there's no such thing as reincarnation, and that this reality is all there is. I asked my Higher Self about backdrop people in my QHHT® sessions with Virginia.

Virginia: *What is the purpose of the backdrop people? Why have them at all?*

HS: Because we don't want to cause concern. We do not want to cause heartache and sorrow when they see that most people are already on the New Earth, on new missions, in different areas of the galaxies. This is our way of doing a gentle and seamless transition.

V: *Will there be a time where the backdrop people will disappear on the 3D Earth?*

HS: They will be leaving. We have other assignments for them. We will disperse them throughout the universe. There will be those that will be transformed, or what we would say, shut down.

V: *When we see large calamities, like floods, tsunamis, one-hundred thousand people killed, is this one way backdrop people are "shut down"?*

---

26 *Convoluted Universe Book IV,* Dolores Cannon, 2011, Chapter 2, Section 38, pp.553-566

HS: Well, my dear, it's our way of clearing, and in that, there may be one or two, so to speak, a small number of those humans who are on their path and are ready to ascend. It's just a nice way of giving an excuse or reason so that others can talk and process, and come to an understanding and come to terms with the loss of a loved one.

V: *Is there anyway for Barb, as she walks around day to day, to know she's interacting with a backdrop person or an aware person? Are there any cues an aware person can use?*

HS: For Barbara, she senses. She has very acute sensory perception. So she can feel them. She also notices how they look, a lack of expression on many. She was near a couple of them this morning, at breakfast. What was she doing? She was preparing her coffee. They were complaining. That is what backdrop people do about the most simple, small inconveniences.

V: *Is this just part of the program of these holograms?*

HS: Yes! We do install those programs, so it would appear that most of humanity is used to "complaining," and this gives a background "white noise" that others are accustomed to. So it appears quite normal. Think of them as little actors in a play.

V: *We have become aware through Barb's QHHT® sessions with her clients, that there is a growing number of backdrop people on the Earth today. We'd like to know more about this phenomena. Of the seven to eight billion people on the planet, what percentage of these people are backdrop people?*

HS: [Fifteen second period of silence] 89.9 percent are backdrop people.

V: *Does that number refer to geographical region? Or are there some regions where there are more enlightened people and other regions having higher percentages of backdrop people?*

HS: Higher percentages of backdrop people are located in the cities, the large cities and large towns, that are occupied and pre-occupied with behaviors associated with the passionate and what would we describe as diversionary… diversions, my dear. Those things that would take you away from awareness and concentration on your path and the work one must do.

In Chapter 9, my Indigo client's guide, Sonar, told us that Phoebe can spot backdrop people instantly.

Sonar: In order to recognize a backdrop person, you must be conscious of where your level is versus the other person's level. When you are at a higher level, you understand the other people; they don't exist anymore, but they exist. Because we are in a multi-universe. It's like in the *Matrix* movie, where it's a hologram. They exist, but they don't. They will be existing in your consciousness for as long as you remember them. You see them, but they are not there. It's just to make it smooth. We're making it smooth—the change. The memories will be erased.

When we move to the other Earth, everything will be erased, and you won't remember all these people with low consciousness and low vibration. Right now, it's such a difficult time because everything is a melting pot. We are trying to discern and try to save them all, but it's really hard because they don't understand. They just don't get it.

At this point, Sonar said, "I have more people."

More beings of the SC showed up to help explain about the backdrop people. There was silence as I waited for the continued answers to come through. There was deep sighing and utterances of the SC talking with themselves.

SC: It's like a cell dividing right now.

Barbara: *Is it like a separation?*

SC: Yes. It's because if we disappeared everybody, we will create a shock. It's an emotional trauma, and multiply it by all the people... if we did that, it will lower the vibration of the Earth, then all the work we did will be a waste.

I ask Sonar about my personal experience in the fifth dimension at home, in December of 2014. I am curious if I were definitely in the presence of a backdrop person.

It was the work of Maureen J. St. Germain[27] that acquainted me with the concept of the fifth dimensional expression. I recollect she said we aren't aware of being in the fifth dimension until after the experience. In the fifth dimension, there is no duality, and there is no fear or reason for protection, because there's nothing to be protected from.

Since Phoebe had given me permission to ask my own questions while she was under hypnosis, I thought this would be an appropriate time to discuss with the HS about my personal experience. I don't ask my own personal questions while facilitating sessions for clients, unless the HS directly converses about me and/or with me during the session. The only other time I might ask these types of questions is if the client has given me express permission, as with Phoebe. Overall, it is quite rare because the session is about the client and the time devoted under hypnosis is most appropriately theirs. Here's the background story of my experience I shared with Phoebe:

I was in the fifth dimension when a woman came into my bedroom at the ranch during an open house. My boyfriend in the living room told the woman that she could walk through the house and that she would find me in my bedroom. I was sitting in the middle of my bedroom, typing on my computer. She did not see me when she entered the room. She was in the third dimension.

I did not see her either, but I did hear her disgusted sigh in the room, from not finding me. I remember Dolores said in her *Convoluted Universe Book IV*[28] book that the backdrop people are angry. This was the demeanor of the woman when she returned to the living room and told my boyfriend she was frustrated that she could not find me. Naturally, she didn't like the house either.

> Sonar (client's guide in contact with the Higher Self): This is an accurate description of a backdrop person.

TALKING WITH GOD ABOUT BACKDROP PEOPLE

I facilitated the following session for fellow QHHT® practitioner, Virginia, in a hotel room. After exploring her life as a large (four-foot tall), strong,

---

27 www.maureenstgermain.com
28 *Convoluted Universe Book IV*, Dolores Cannon, Section 2, Chapter 38, p. 565

young male fruit bat, she continued on to the angelic realm, all the way to Source. I found myself with the opportunity to speak directly with God Source.

I wanted to know more about the backdrop people concept Dolores shared in her book. Virginia was curious about someone in her life who had an abrupt personality change. We both were wondering what really had happened to cause a personality change without a prior traumatic event, such as a brain injury.

> God Source: He was not a backdrop person, but now he is. He is one of the individuals who has transcended, and the body that remains will continue a normal human life without the soul engaged.
>
> Barbara: *Is this like the "walk-in" concept?*
>
> GS: Yes, it's a "walk-out." And this is what is happening for many people. There are many ways to transition to the new Earth. One way is to die, and then you can go anywhere you want. Another way is the physical body is transported through inter-dimensional travel flight. It's happening today on a regular basis. The third way is to transcend spiritually, while the body remains physically on the Earth. In this case, we just can't have thousands and thousands and thousands of people appear to die in this transcendence. So we have programmed the body to continue. The body will continue on its journey while the soul continues. Virginia noticed this by the dramatic change in the personality.

There are beings from other planets who are in human cloak while they do their work on Earth. They are considered extra-dimensional beings. There are many here on Earth.

I ask about two specific people in my life and if they are backdrop people.

> GS: They are sentient beings. They are not backdrop people. I need to explain. There are different varieties of backdrop people. Like the one we mentioned. They live sentient lives, then leave; the body remains. There are holograms of humans that give the appearance of human activity, productivity, that are hollow shells. There are

suits, human suits, human shells. They are not holograms. They are living humans. They are vacant and allow for other entities to come in at will. [This is done] for work that needs to be done, or for that being to experience the "suit."

There are sentient humans that are not enlightened or transcended, that are wavering in their commitment to the human life. Their Higher Self is playing with being human; not yet committed to a plan, contract, or karma. It's like the suit, but a suit for only one Higher Self. This is what the specific people you asked about are. The Higher Self has not committed to the human experience yet. They appear to be resistant or reticent. They are undecided. Until the Higher Self commits itself to this human form, they will not participate in any activity that will elevate them to an enlightened state.

B: *Does this mean they will not do the inner work that needs to be done to become enlightened?*

GS: Yes, there are many souls that are playing with the human experience at this moment. During this transition time, now it's a good time to do this, due to the flux and the dynamics in the movement. It's an easy time. There aren't a lot of implications, if we play with these human forms.

B: *How do Virginia and I identify a backdrop person? What are the interactive cues?*

GS: An easier question is, "How do I recognize an enlightened person because there are so many backdrop people?" It would be easier to find the points of light among the points of dark. This comes from the connectivity, the energetic connectivity. Virginia was shown a methodology this week, the infinity [symbol]. This energy is resident in other enlightened entities, individuals. However, it's important to understand, consider the backdrop people as holograms that you have created to serve a purpose like a bed, chair, or a lamp. The enlightened entities on the planet are merely wearing a suit, are merely participating in the hologram. So, they aren't that much different from backdrop people. It's the experiences outside the human experiences that make the difference. The experiences inside the human experiences are the same.

B: *About how many people on the planet of more than seven billion, are backdrop people?* [I'm asking the same questions Virginia asked my HS to see if there is the same, different, or additional information. The HS is aware we are asking duplicate questions.]

GS: The vast majority of appearance of humans are holograms. Virginia has had a hard time processing this information. Because one of the biggest problems on the planet today is overpopulation. So, if most people are merely holograms, then let's get rid of them, restore the Earth to its balance. However, if the overpopulation did not occur, the evolution of the Earth would not have occurred. So it was planned. Mother Earth came into being with a life plan, and part of that plan was to have the experience she has right now, experience the overpopulation, the need for excessive numbers of holograms, polluting, and seeming to harm the Earth. This was her plan. Her purpose in that plan was to see where to exercise her self healing ability, for her to sense her own power in the ability to manifest healing for herself and her evolution for herself. It is also the program that creates the excessive amount of backdrop people. Although this causes the enlightened people to exercise their strength, as well. And that is another purpose of these holograms. Of the 8.2 billion, 7.6 [billion] are holograms.

B: *Will Virginia and I have backdrop people come to us for sessions?*

GS: The only way this could happen is if the client came to you pressured by someone else. It could be a spouse demands that the client have a session, or even out of some peer pressure or narcissism, the client of their own accord comes to you for a session. You could find backdrop people coming to you for a session. You will most assuredly have clients that are playing with their human existence.

B: *Is the HS installing a program for these backdrop people to come to us for QHHT® sessions and having good sessions? Is this possible?*

GS: No. The technique is perfected, and it simply will not work on backdrop people.

B: *I'm asking, because I had a [left brain] client who was pressured by a girlfriend and he had a fabulous session. You did a wonderful job with him.*

GS: He was not a backdrop person.

B: *So, it's not in every instance with the parameter you gave me?*

GS: No, you will have enlightened beings that are pressured to come. But the only way you will get a backdrop person to come is if they are pressured to come.

B: *Will a backdrop person who is not enlightened, not on the path, or may be even sitting on the fence trying to figure out if they will continue as an enlightened person, always have a difficult session?*

GS: They will not have a session. The Higher Self is not present for the interaction.

If the Higher Self is not available, then no matter how many tricks we employ from our bag, a successful session is just not going to happen, or at least it will appear so. We won't know this until we are in the session, or after the session. We must look at what our definition of success is. We know every client receives exactly what they need, and healing occurs even if it's not apparent at the time. This is just one more element that makes this work exciting.

For the concept of backdrop people, in addition to the above descriptions, there are holograms of people existing in our third dimension. They don't have a spirit inside of them. They are energy. It is my understanding that even they are considered to be a form of the God/Source/Great Central Sun/Creator Source, or whatever name you use. They have importance and value, as they are helping us to remain calm and at ease because most souls have ascended. They also help us to learn our lessons.

Although they can be negative, angry, and annoying, it is one more opportunity for us to learn to be positive, happy, and patient. They are not to be looked down upon or considered to be less than.

I'm still learning about these concepts. I don't have all of the answers to my many questions yet.

In one of the sessions I facilitated for Virginia, Dolores came through and spoke about the name "backdrop." She recommended I come up with a new name because people are attaching a bias to it. The name didn't bother me, nor cause me to look down upon those with that identifier. It was after that session, I dialogued with Dolores while I was consciously awake. I asked her what would be a term that identifies the concept and doesn't color it with prior perceptions of being less than. The name I was given via clairaudience is "sacred souls." The way I understand this new name is that the spirit/soul/program is considered an aspect of God Creator Source; therefore, they are sacred.

In the next session story, my client surprised me by introducing me to the "human suit" concept.

THE HUMAN SUIT

George works in the healthcare field with the human skeletal system as his specialty. He came to a QHHT® session with health concerns: vision disturbance, low back pain, and social withdrawal tendencies. In addition, he expressed the eternal question: What's my life purpose and mission?

Coming into the first scene, George floats over New York City's skyscrapers. Landing on the sidewalk, he finds himself observing people, mostly men, walking around in different directions, wearing dark overcoats. In a human body, he is wearing black suede shoes with dark grey plaid pants and an overcoat. His hair is black at a medium length, combed to the side, and is covered with a dark blue hat. The hat style is similar to the other men on the street. He is wearing a gold ring on his left ring finger. There is no significance of the ring to him, although it feels as if someone gave it to him. From his pocket he retrieves a brown leather wallet, with a moderate amount of cash and credit cards.

I ask him how he's feeling. Calm. His body is healthy, in his fifties. He isn't sure what he does with the majority of his time. He doesn't know where he is going. He doesn't have an appointment. He observes people. No family. He feels like he's a visitor, but doesn't know from where.

I ask him to move to the place where he lives and wait for his response. There is no place [on Earth] he calls home. He doesn't know where he lives.

Barbara: *Do you come from this planet?*

George: It doesn't feel like it.

B: *Are you some form of observer?*

G: It feels that way.

B: *Do you know where you come from? It's okay to share it with me. It's very safe. Many of us come from different places in the Universe. Can you see where you come from?*

G: I see something out in the solar system.

B: *Is it a distant planet?*

G: Uh-uh.

B: *Can you take a look at it? It's okay to see it.*

G: It has a yellow glow to it.

B: *Do you have name for it?*

G: It seems something like Uranus.

B: *Would you like to go there?*

G: Sure.

We leave NYC and go to his home planet.

B: *Let me know where you'd like to go. What would be your favorite place? Let me know when you're there. What are you seeing?*

G: Just a dense yellow foggy surface.

B: *Do you have a form or body when you're there?*

G: I do have a body. Twelve toes on each foot. Looks like a statue—white porcelain type skin. No garment is necessary. Each hand has six fingers. My face looks like a monster!

B: *In what way?*

G: The shape. Two eyes, mouth with saber-tooth teeth, no hair.

He goes to a little cave where he lives. It's dark, but he can see stalactites and stalagmites inside. He's all alone. Others like him are outside. He's not part of the community. The others look similar. He doesn't have a name. He doesn't eat food. Nourishment is obtained through light. His body is healthy, but old and of male gender. He has no family here either.

B: *Tell me about your trip to New York City.*

G: It feels like I go on trips like this to just observe.

B: *Do you know how you were created?*

G: It feels like I was created from the stars.

B: *From the observations of NYC, what did you observe?*

G: People are going out in different directions. There is a lack of togetherness and communication.

B: *Is there a sense of community on your planet?*

G: I feel very alone there.

B: *Can you tell me why? Why are you by yourself in a cave?*

G: I'm supposed to be there.

B: *Did someone tell you that you had to be there in the cave by yourself?*

G: It's my appointed place.

B: *Do you have any special gifts or attributes that others don't have?*

G: No.

B: *What do you do in your cave?*

G: Sleep, heal, and regenerate.

B: *Do you only stay in your cave? Do you go out?*

G: Yes.

B: *What do you like to do?*

G: Explore land and watch the sunsets.

B: *What are they like?*

G: Pretty bright, and the color is orange.

B: *What's a typical day on your planet?*

G: It's short.

It is close to the hour point in the hypnosis, so I ask about the purpose of that life shown.

G: The purpose was to spend time by myself to reflect and think about things and learn about patience.

HIGHER SELF

The HS says the lifetime was shown so George can know what it feels like to be alone. The lessons to learn were about comforts.

Barbara: *Would you look into his eyes and the optic system and tell us what is the root cause of his vision disturbance?*

HS: The fibers are spread apart.

B: *How did that happen?*

HS: Stress on the eyes.

B: *From what?*

HS: Trying to look too hard. To find the answers what he's going through. It parallels. The recommendation for perfect vision without fluctuation is to see the bigger picture.

B: *Can you recommend how he is to do this?*

HS: Stop trying to get it all perfect. Be willing to be wrong. Be willing to be vulnerable, in every area of life.

B: *Are you able to heal that blurriness at this time in the session? You've done it for others.*

HS: We're working on it now.

B: *How are you doing the healing?*

HS: We're removing the swelling and repairing the fibers.

B: *What is his purpose in this lifetime?*

HS: To serve others. To show them their higher path in wellness and balance.

B: *Is he doing this through his work and modalities?*

HS: Yes.

B: *Are there any other modalities for him to acquire?*

HS: He's on the right path.

B: *What is his main mission in this current lifetime?*

HS: To show others they can see their lives differently; they can experience a sense of happiness and wellness that they did not know they can tap into. He's to remain patient, to trust his inner voice and instinct, and take action on those.

B: *Why does George prefer to be alone and not in a relationship?*

HS: He avoids getting hurt and disappointed by the way people can be. His consciousness is much higher than the average person.

B: *Is this why you showed him the being from the yellow planet?*

HS: Yes.

B: *Is this a past life or parallel life?*

HS: Parallel life.

B: *Is there a name for the planet he's from?*

HS: There is no name. Not Uranus.

B: *In a different solar system?*

HS: Yes.

B: *The community he's from, are these highly evolved beings?*

HS: No.

B: *Do they have the ability to go to other places to observe and learn?*

HS: Yes.

B: *Is this what he was doing in New York City?*

HS: Yes.

B: *Connecting with that part of him, would that be beneficial for him?*

HS: It can be useful.

B: *Can you give us a name he can use?*

HS: We don't understand that question. Not necessary to contact with a name.

B: *That aspect of him is something that he can just know about? Where he comes from and how that part of him is experiencing life?*

HS: Yes.

B: *What was the purpose of the parallel life you showed him?*

HS: To show him patience.

B: *You mentioned in another answer that he is to gain new friendships and engage in activities in order for him to trust himself and take chances. Will you put those ideas in his mind?*

HS: It's all there for him. He just needs to take the steps.

PARTING MESSAGE

HS: You're here in this body for a short time. Finish your mission; you're not coming back.

For George, he learned his life purpose, and the root cause of his low back pain and vision disturbance. He was given the guidelines to trust himself and take chances. He learned he comes from another place in the solar system.

It's not unusual for the client to receive the name of their home planet or star later, after listening to their recording in private. People who are resonating with the QHHT® method often are wondering about their own life purpose and missions. This is the perfect point in their life to go into deep level trance hypnosis with a trained QHHT® practitioner.

17

THE ETERNAL QUESTION: WHAT IS MY LIFE PURPOSE?

Do you wonder why you're here on Earth? Do you know what you need to do in order to accomplish your missions? What if you have contracted agreements with other souls and you don't even know it?

These are the typical questions that can be answered in a QHHT® session. Dolores commented on the eternal question in her book *Convoluted Universe Book IV* that the same answer she heard over and over was, "She/he is here to help." I agree with Dolores. I've never heard the Higher Self say the client is to party their life away, make a lot of money, drink alcoholic beverages, and engage in wanton sex.

At the least, the client is told to "just be" because their light is bright, and their mere presence is affecting change in others. On the flip side, a client receives information about their mission, which could be writing books, giving public presentations, and creating specific projects, such as healing businesses and/or healing centers.

I like to think we're all doing our part to raise consciousness and assist in the ascension. Through our own healing and self love, we are the solution to the problem created long ago. A QHHT® session can help people create the roadmap for their missions. At the same time, in a session, people also clear remaining karma and heal themselves. Often times, they also find out they are healers.

BECOMING A HEALER

I facilitated this session for a middle-aged married female, mother of five beautiful children; she's very intuitive and clairaudient. We'll call her Sarah. Starting at a very young age, her verbally abusive father told her he did not love her and blamed her for everything that had gone wrong in his life. Sarah's third eye chakra closed shut at that time, according to her.

Sarah never felt any support or love from her father her entire life, and he made sure she knew it. Two psychics told her to leave her husband because he doesn't support her spirituality. I was eager to hear what the Higher Self would say regarding this guidance, because I was trained to never say this to a client during an angel reading. If the woman is being physically abused, then that's another story. There, I will help the client see her options and develop a strategy for change and safety.

At precisely one hour and forty minutes into the interview, I experienced a very loud tone in my right ear. I heard Dolores talking in a loud, matter of fact voice saying, "We have a lot to do here, Barbara, let's wrap this up." Five minutes later, Sarah felt energy movement going through her body. I shared with her "they" are already working with her. This is typical in QHHT® sessions and in my private channeled healing sessions for clients. The Higher Self doesn't wait until the hypnosis starts to begin the client's healing.

PAST LIFE

Sarah is in medieval England, in front of a cathedral, as a young man who hunts small game with a bow and arrow. He brings rabbits to the priest, who appreciates and values this young hunter. He also lives with and provides for his mother in a nice cottage.

In the next scene, the young man is getting ready to marry a beautiful woman of higher social status named Elizabeth. He feels lucky and loves her very much.

The third scene reveals his wife delivering a stillborn son because of nutritional deficiencies. Food was hard to find, so the growing fetus was unable to thrive in the mother's womb. He cries. I give him emotional support. Although they have a healthy four-year-old daughter, Elizabeth blames her husband for the stillborn child's deficiencies because of his lower social status. She no longer loves this hunter. On the last day of his life, he dies of gangrene of the arm that became infected from a dirty arrow striking him during a hunting accident. The mother, wife, and daughter sit at the bedside while he chokes and suffocates. He leaves his body.

I ask the man what he thought that life's purpose was. He says, self worth. "You are only as good as you think you are. Love can exist with your children. Love comes in many forms. Self love must come first."

HIGHER SELF

The Higher Self, in its infinite wisdom, chose that lifetime to share the message that the client must always love herself, by helping herself first. Sarah does too much for others. The life purpose in that lifetime was to learn to love another person, even when that person doesn't reciprocate the love. In her current life, the HS said she is to learn to heal, be healed, and then to heal others.

The HS reveals that Sarah is an expert at reading runes, and this is why she is seeing runes in her dreams at night.

The purpose of Sarah's father's current abusive behavior towards her is to remember she must love herself enough to walk away. Sometimes we must forgive someone even if they don't want our forgiveness. We can forgive without being forgiven.

Sarah's father was the priest in the past life, and he saw the value in her then. In this life, Sarah must see her own value. She must forgive herself first. She must keep her distance from her current father. She's not to associate with him at this time.

Regarding the two psychics who told her to leave her current husband:

> HS: There is nothing wrong with her marriage. Her husband is insecure at this time. He's struggling with what to believe and what not to believe. She's trying to force him to believe. He's not there yet. Be patient. He will see. He will know.

This information from her Higher Self gives Sarah great comfort. About her career path? She is to be a mother first. After her children are grown, she should become a healer. In the meantime, she can study and enjoy being the good mother she is.

HEALING DURING THE SESSION

Right knee nerves were unbundled. The HS did this by pulling on the nerves. Sarah could feel the sensation inside her body. Her emotional issues were removed from her abdominal area. Her third eye was worked on, and her chakras were aligned. After the session, Sarah's eyes sparkled, and she glowed with high energy. During the debriefing after the session, Sarah shared with me that she heard the very loud tone coming out of my ear that I heard near the end of the interview when Dolores spoke to me telepathically. Sarah was seated five feet from me!

BEING AN ADVOCATE FOR WOMEN

Even if a client can't "see" with their third eye in their everyday life, in a QHHT® past-life regression, their other senses are enhanced to where they can feel, hear, and know the information they are seeking. Images are conveyed in vivid detail, just like watching a movie. The following session story is a good example of this. Look for how the client "felt" her way through this past-life regression experience.

I facilitated a QHHT® session for a delightful single woman named Marge who works in the corporate environment as an advocate for women's rights. Marge is in her mid-twenties and loves to travel. It's her opinion that emotions are unnecessary. She has been suffering with depression since she was a small child and wants to know why. She has a hard time committing to relationships and legal contracts, such as housing leases. These things provoke anxiety in her, and she would like to remove this stressful feeling. She has been hypnotized before for a past-life regression.

During the interview portion of the session, I tell Marge that I do not hold judgments. The example I give is that I don't care if she is a prostitute in this current life, nor was one in a prior life. This was the first time I used this example to explain my unconditional love for my clients.

PAST LIFE

Marge comes gently into the death scene. She is looking at a road stretching into the distant red rocks of the Southwest. She isn't associating herself with a body. Looking around to the left, she feels the presence of people arguing. Marge sees that she is part of the argument and got punched. She doesn't feel any discomfort experiencing this scene. This was my cue to go back before the death scene, further back so we can find out what caused her death.

Moved back, Marge finds herself as a young, barefoot man, dressed in rolled-up pants and a shirt covered by a vest tied with a leather string. He's sitting on log next to a campfire, eating mush with pieces of meat in it. His hat is off. There are others eating; however, the group doesn't have a sense of community. He is a hired hand involved in moving horses across the country. It's almost nightfall, and he will later sleep in his tent. For the majority of the time, he travels with this group of men and does various other pursuits like pan for gold. When I ask if he is married, he says, "There's a connection to a woman, but it's not marriage. Romantic of some sort."

B: *Is this someone you have relations with when you come to town?*

He in Patricia's voice gives a coquettish smile and laughs. "Yeah."

B: *That's okay.* [conveying my non-judgment]

We move forward to another important day…

He finds himself in a lively, but not crowded saloon, sitting at the bar, inebriated, enjoying his drink and talking with Mac, the bartender.

Marge: I think that's where the girl connection is.

Barbara: *Is your lady friend there in the saloon?*

M: I think so. I'm sitting by myself; I'm fairly drunk. I wander on my own. I don't feel connected to things. I like to walk and smoke cigarettes.

B: *Besides cigarettes, drinking and walking, what else do you like?*

M: Women come to mind. That's another thing I like.

B: *Do you help women to feel good?*

M: I get the impression it's a mistress thing, not of substance, like flings. I might have a fondness for one. I'm outdoorsy. I'm smart and quiet. No one knows I have initiative.

He doesn't have any family because they were killed in a fire when he was teenager at the time and his younger brother was five years old. His mother was a prostitute who worked in a brothel. Some town folks burned down the building where she and her children lived. People used the term, "whatever" when referring to prostitutes. They felt women who sold their bodies were not important.

We leave that scene and move forward to the last day of that life. Reminding him that he can see it as an observer, without physical or mental discomfort, I ask, "What is happening?"

He is by a river, lush with a green landscape.

M: I get the idea someone came out from behind, hitting me, and I fell into the water.

The assailant knocked him out, and he drowned. Once out of the body, a soul can look back at the life and share what they learned.

M: I didn't respect women, not that I was mean. It wasn't an equal way of thinking.

B: *What was the purpose of that lifetime?*

M: Not being able to save people, because I couldn't save my brother. I can't save everyone.

HIGHER SELF

I ask the Higher Self why that lifetime was chosen for Marge.

HS: Let go of the brother. Plus, part of the work now involves being an advocate for women.

B: *What was the purpose of that life and lessons of that lifetime?*

HS: It was an important opportunity to connect with nature in that way. That independence was important to learn.

B: *Can she apply that in this lifetime?*

HS: Yes. Nature needs to become a bigger role.

B: *What is her current life purpose?*

HS: She needs to learn to float on the water, stop trying to work so hard as if she needs to swim to somewhere. The water is symbolic of the connection and understanding that she has access to. Discussions are occurring with her guides at this moment. She's always on track. She needs to be easier on herself, in that thinking that every step could be a misstep.

B: *Can you help her with this?*

HS: Yes.

B: *Are you performing a healing for her?*

HS: Yes.

B: *What can you tell us about her childhood depression?*

HS: It hurts us to see that. We want to comfort her. We're pulling it out. [Marge sighs.] It was a hanging, and this is why there is a problem with her throat, because it closes off.

B: *Are you able to heal it now?*

HS: Yes.

B: *Is it gone?*

HS: Yes, and her depression will be an ongoing healing. We will continue working on her at night. We will give her a symbol so she knows the depression has lifted. It will be lilacs.

During the debriefing, Marge and I were amazed that I had used the prostitute example in the interview without knowing what, where, how, and who the other life would be. This could very well be an example that the Higher Self places these thoughts into our consciousness or we access the Universal Mind to draw upon to communicate our perspectives.

We found it enlightening that the life of a man who used women for sex and referred to them as "things" in the current life is an advocate for women, in a woman's body. It illustrates a beautiful karmic balancing and shows that Marge has learned her lessons and is now right on track with her current life purpose, as she is already a women's advocate in the corporate arena.

DISPERSE THE KNOWLEDGE

I facilitated this QHHT® session for a fifty-six-year-old woman. Valerie's mother never loved her. Her mother told her she didn't want her and that Valerie ruined her life. Whenever her sister or brother did something wrong, Valerie was beaten. Valerie's mother would purposely push her out the door while a storm came through, and lock her out and not let her in, even when Valerie banged on the door begging to come inside.

Valerie has been through years of mental therapy without appreciable improvement, according to her. She's done considerable inner work through several modalities. I include the healing part of Valerie's session below because of its valuable information. You will read how the communications were conducted between the HS, Valerie, a specialist healer in spirit that was called in, and myself.

PAST LIFE

Valerie finds herself up in the clouds as we explore the scene. She sees other swirling stormy clouds over the ocean and the ash-ridden sky from a volcanic eruption. The land sinks into the water. The air is filled with dirt, soot, and ash. Looking down over the ocean, she sees through the crystal clear water what looks like snow-covered mountaintops. The ocean is churning with big waves, because it just happened.

V: It's Lemuria! So many caves.

B: *Tell me about the caves.*

V: [Talking in retrospect] They were living in the caves, and part of it is carved out. There were walkways, round, smooth areas where, waist high, there was a display of things. They would put some kind of reeds like curtains that hide the things in the dugouts. That's where stuff was kept.

B: *What color are these reeds?*

V: Brown. They are held together with a string, like a drape on the walls.

B: *What type of objects were on display behind the reeds?*

V: Amethyst, crystals of various colors.

B: *Were they large or small?*

V: Large ones, and there were metallic round objects for ceremony with engraved symbols on them. They were the symbols of a…

The scene abruptly changes…

V: I'm seeing a long table with elders. There are, let's see, [counting] 1,2…7, 8, 9 elders. They all look different. Some look alien.

Each one has its own symbol. I've seen these people before in a dream.

B: *Now, looking down at your feet tell me what you see.*

V: I'm wearing sandals.

B: *Are they the feet of a child or adult?*

V: I think they're a man.

B: *A man. And looking at your body, does it have a garment on?*

V: Everybody is wearing white robes with leather belts. Leather straps for belts.

B: *What is the fabric made out of? You can touch it and feel it.*

V: It's like silk.

B: *Silk. And as you look at your hair, tell me about it.*

V: It's long. It's gray. I have a beard. A full beard. The hair is kind of curly. Bushy eyebrows.

B: *What color of eyes do you have?*

V: Blue.

B: *Blue, and looking at your body, any ornamentation or jewelry?*

V: I have a large medallion like the others do.

B: *What does the medallion look like?*

R: It's gold and… [long silence]

B: *Does it have any inscriptions or designs on it?*

V: Can't tell. The letters are unfamiliar to me. It's like it's possibly leaves, but in the middle it's kind of like it's not a crescent moon, semicircle shape with almost like, a dagger shape. As I look down on it, it could be more of like a nail. It's a different shape.

B: *Did someone give this medallion to you?*

V: It's a symbol of who I am. My pattern.

B: *Does it help to identify you to the others?*

V: Yes.

B: *Is your body healthy?*

V: It's old and worn out.

B: *Do you carry anything with you?*

V: No, my hands are empty.

B: *And you're sitting around this table?*

V: I'm standing.

B: *You're standing. You're there with nine other elders. What is happening now?*

V: I think I'm being chastised. I'm not one of them.

B: *In what way?*

Valerie becomes emotional and tears fall.

B: [Giving Valerie emotional support] *It's safe to look at this.*

V: I was a teacher, but I had gotten... something had happened to the body, where it was in pain, and I had become critical, and stubborn, and didn't ask for help. They expected me to ask for help, but instead, I became critical and not nice.

B: *Who were you critical of?*

V: Those I was overseeing.

B: *You said you were teaching. What were you teaching?*

V: I was teaching life. I was teaching those on the surface, but I wasn't on the surface.

B: *What was your environment like where you were doing the teaching?*

V: Pleasurable.

B: *In what way?*

V: There was no hunger. Everything is comfortable. All you had to do was think about it and it came. Telepathy instead of talking. I was resentful and angry that the body was hurting and everything else was perfect.

B: *What did you need help with?*

V: I was servicing too many souls. It was too much.

B: *It was too much for you?*

V: [I'm] being told the critical thoughts were causing the pain.

B: *Were you able to change those thoughts?*

V: I'm angry because they didn't automatically know I was in distress and help me, and I am angry because I was expected to ask.

B: *And was this how it was done, that you're expected to tell someone how you're feeling?*

V: I'm expected to let them know because everybody had a lot, everyone was doing a lot.

B: *And so what are they saying now about this, at this council meeting?*

V: That I've forgotten what it's like to be on the surface.

B: *And what is your response?*

V: I don't want to go. I don't want to go back. I don't want to be there.

B: *And why don't you want to be there?*

V: Because I don't like the pain. I don't like the heaviness. I don't like being trapped. I don't like having to... it's too hard.

B: *And what do they offer you now, as they are discussing this with you?*

V: They're discussing among themselves. I can hear what they're saying, but I don't remember. It's like they're talking kind of soft.

B: *They're talking soft? Can you look at their body mannerisms and get a feel for what they're discussing?*

V: They're discussing what would be the most appropriate, the most appropriate action.

[silence]

V: We're going to have to come back. They're going to send me down to experience, experience the things people I was overseeing and little bits, but so many, so much of it… it's just going to be too hard. I think it's going to be too hard. Some say that, "He can do it. He's got enough learning, he can do it."

B: *Sounds like they have a lot of confidence in you. Do you consider these wise members of this council?*

V: [Mumble in the affirmative]

B: *Are there any plans in how you are going back to experience?*

V: That takes place somewhere else. I keep telling them, "Please don't."

Valerie is now sobbing. Emotions surface.

V: Sorry.

B: *It's all right.* [said with an empathetic tone] *Do you feel like you disappointed someone?* [I'm exploring the root cause of the emotions]

V: [sobbing] I just want them to let it be enough, and I'm sorry. I don't want to come back. I don't want to come back.

Valerie is now deeply sighing while sobbing.

V: I'm just so tired of everything hurting and being in pain.

B: *You will not feel any discomfort at this moment, as you are experiencing this.*

Valerie's sobbing eases. I note her breathing is slower.

V: It's the whole life!

B: *Are they listening to you as you tell them you don't want to go back?*

V: They said, "Just try to do this, just one more time. Just do it all. Just try to do it all in one. Just do it all!"

B: *Can they share with you what is the purpose of this experience?*

V: [deep emotional sigh with no answer]

B: *How does it benefit you?*

V: Yes, I'll ask.

B: *Go right ahead.*

[Silence with repeated deep breaths]

V: I forgot it wasn't real. My teachings had become too harsh because I had gotten drawn into the drama of those who I was overseeing. I was forgetting it wasn't real. I'm supposed to take that with me and keep it with me. Keep that in plain [sight] with me. And just not to get sucked into the drama. [Big sigh of relief]

B: *Yeah.*

V: They're admiring me. They said I will be [laughing]. "We're helping you every day!" [Big sniff, and big sigh of relief]

B: *Ask them who they are to you? What is their relationship to you?*

V: [silence] They're my guides to my soul group. My teachers.

B: *Your teachers and your guides to your soul group.*

V: They've been with me from the beginning.

I recognize we have the beings who can answer Valerie's questions. I continue to direct my questions to Valerie, without having to contact the Higher Self directly.

B: *So they never leave you?*

V: [Affirmative mumble] They all do different things. They have an expertise. There's not much longer. The main one said, "There's not much longer."

B: *Would you ask them about your missions here? What are your missions? They will tell you.*

V: Stop listening to everyone else. For one thing, reconnect to my inner guidance. I ask too many people what to do. I seek outside instead of seek within.

B: *Are they referring to people like the psychic you spoke of?*

V: Yeah, and others.

B: *Do they remind you that you have all the answers within you?*

V: Yeah, that all I have within, to ask.

B: *How would they answer them for you?*

V: They're discussing. They'll answer some things.

B: *Ask them about your path right now, regarding you making a living in this life at this time. What do they say?*

V: They see me speaking on a stage. I'm seeing a memory of when I went to another town and saw a famous psychic healer. I listened to him talk. I stood in line to get his latest book, and when I looked into his eyes, I could see forever. I could see the other place, the other plane.

B: *Ask them what does this mean?*

V: "You know what you need to know. I'll tell you what to write."

B: *They'll tell you what to write. Does this mean you'll be writing?*

V: Yeah.

B: *In what forms will you be writing? Ask them.*

V: Three books.

B: *Three books.*

V: They need somebody to take the teachings mainstream because people are in tunnel vision. People are into Zen or they're into Hindu or they're into Christianity. They're not getting the full teachings and the full words and the full messages. Time is running out for the planet. There's some kind of a timeline. That if humanity doesn't start getting it, they're going to have to start over again. I have to be, do what… I'm seeing Eckhart Tolle, it's gotta be taken out of religion. It's gotta be taken mainstream, so it goes in to all consciousness without the ties to any particular dogma.

B: *Can they give you an extra boost of enthusiasm for writing and for being at your present employer, now that you have this direction? You can ask.*

V: The employer is clearing up the last karma of service, because they need me so desperately.

B: *Ask them if you're providing more than the clerical work at your employment.*

V: I'm raising the energy levels of the people there.

B: *You're raising the energy levels. That's very important work.*

V: There's something of the energy I put out that stimulates seeking so when they do they will already have found direction and sought solutions. Helps connect them to themselves and to the Divine energy. They're very depressed. They have low self esteem. Worried, afraid.

At this point in the session, I feel comfortable to speak directly to the Higher Self. Watch how pronouns come into the conversation.

Barbara: *Is there anything in the physical realm she can do to help them?*

HS: Be positive and offer suggestions when asked.

B: *Is this part of her skills that she has?*

HS: A connector. A channel for God's energy.

B: *Thank you for that. Is she supposed to develop a product for her skin aberrations that come up from time to time?*

HS: If she does the one product for the over-sensitized skin of cancer patients, it will be a small niche cream that will sell.

B: *Could she get a patent on that if she pursues that?*

HS: Yes.

B: *Will you help bring that information into her?*

HS: It's already coming in.

B: *Would you be able to do a body scan at this time? Is that permissible?*

HS: [Big sigh] No.

B: *And why not?*

[silence]

HS: The right person is not here to do that.

B: *You mean the guides? Can we ask that person to come forward? You're always so good at this. It's so beneficial.*

HS: She's attending to somebody else.

B: *Is she multi-dimensional and can also come here?*

HS: Yes.

B: *I'm seeing the whole room here fill with white light.* [The office filled with light]

HS: She's very bright.

B: *Yes. Thank you for being here. Would you please do a scan of her body now?*

HS: Yes.

B: *Thank you. And please let me know what you find and the root cause. And of course, let me know when the body scan is complete.*

HS: There's some veins in the brain that are not in good shape. Possible place of stroke in future. It's the way she's going to go. Nodules on the thyroid, benign. Benign growths in the breast. May be beneficial not to do the mammograms because they'll pick them up, but they're benign. Mostly on the left side. Uterus is still enlarged, but the cysts on the ovaries will shrink.

B: *Are you doing that now?*

HS: Would you like it done now?

B: *Yes, I would like everything to be addressed at this time, so she'll no longer have to take the supplements and the medicines. You're really good at this.*

[silence]

HS: Lowering eye pressure [glaucoma]. Going to have to change the diet even more for the neck and spine.

B: *What do you recommend?*

HS: She's still too acid. No sugar. Start adding in vegetables, no grains at all. Give up the cheese. Eggs are okay if cheese is given up. She doesn't have to eat everything at once.

[long silence]

B: *Is the body scan complete?*

HS: Just saying that she's got to go somewhere else. The healing will continue throughout the night.

B: *The healing will continue throughout the night. Would you expand upon what you found in her body and what modifications can occur now?*

[silence]

Now, Valerie is listening to the specialist healer being and telling me what is being said: "The thyroid thing. Some kind of other issues with the thyroid. I was taking iodine and I stopped."

I continue to ask questions directly to the healing specialist, and Virginia tells me what the healing specialist is saying and doing.

B: *Does she need to resume the iodine?*

V: Take it in the evening instead of the morning.

B: *How much?*

V: Just a dropper. My throat hurts now.

B: *Are you able to make an adjustment in her throat there, so there's no discomfort?*

V: Yeah.

B: *Is that part of the healing process?*

V: Yes.

B: *Yes, I've seen that before. Will you help her to release that now?*

V: Yes. She's doing something with her hands.

At this point, Valerie's hands are resting on her lower abdomen. She shares that they were very hot and vibrating. Taking them out from under the covers helps her feel comfortable again.

Now the healing specialist communicates directly with me.

Barbara: *What is the root cause of the thyroid being out of balance?*

Healing Specialist: Not speaking up.

B: *She shared with me that she's speaking up. What is your assessment of her voicing herself, her opinions, her thoughts?*

HS: Still too quiet. Still too afraid of offending. She needs to release. We need to do releasing on that.

B: *Are you going into her brain at this time and helping her release those patterns that cause that fear?*

HS: She said, she can do that.

B: *Very good. Thank you very much. Will she need to continue taking her thyroid preparation? Is she able to wean off of it after this healing?*

HS: Go slow.

B: *What do you recommend?*

HS: Try half a tablet, if the iodine is at night.

B: *Okay.*

HS: The problem is that the other hormone preparation, now that everything is in balance, discontinuing the thyroid will affect the others.

B: *Did you heal her hormones?*

HS: That wasn't requested.

B: *Would you please do that? Would you put them into balance where she doesn't need supplements? You've done it for others; I know you can do it for her. You're really good at this.*

HS: Give it a couple of weeks.

B: *Will you continue to work at night?*

HS: Yes.

B: *How would you like her to wean off her hormones?*

HS: Every other day progesterone. Stay twice a week on the DHEA.

B: *And then, before the middle of next month, she'll be able to be off of these medicines and feel perfectly normal?*

HS: She needs to cut back and give it some time, and then have the blood tests. She has a hypersensitive system.

B: *Why does she have a hypersensitive system? Is there a purpose for this?*

HS: It's a byproduct of the terrorizing by her mother. Living in fight or flight the entire life.

B: *Are you able to make an adjustment in her brain pattern to remove that?*

HS: Yes.

B: *Are you able to install a program where she's living and perceiving in affluence, ease and joy, balance, and harmony?*

HS: Yes.

B: *Thank you. Are you doing that now?*

HS: [Affirmative mumble]

B: *Thank you so much. And what about her migraines. Can you tell us about that?*

HS: It's connected to the veins in the brain.

B: *What purpose do these migraines have for her?*

HS: To remind her that there's no control. There's no control over life. It's Creator's movie.

B: *So, she has no control over it. Do you have a recommendation for her how to live her life now?*

HS: In the now and in the now and in the now.[29]

B: *Do you want her to continue the Propanolol[30]?*

HS: Yes.

B: *Is that causing any problems for her at all?*

HS: It affects the thyroid.

B: *I understand you have the ability to make the chemicals that come into our body—whether we take them or through water, food, or the environment—not affect us. Are you able to make an adjustment so that this medicine, this chemical doesn't affect the thyroid?*

HS: Maybe taking it at noon, a different time of the day.

B: *You want her to take it at noon instead? Will this help you make adjustments for her?*

HS: It should.

B: *Could you help us understand how does the time of the day affect the chemical structure of the medicine and its effect on the body?*

HS: She's been taking it at night with wine that she drinks with dinner.

B: *So it's the wine that's affecting it. Is it the alcohol?*

HS: Yes.

---

29 Recommending we humans live in the present moment is a frequent message in QHHT® sessions, by the Higher Self.

30 Beta blocker medication used to treat chest pain, high blood pressure, irregular heart rhythm, tremors, migraine headache prevention.

B: *Thank you for that information. And what about the itching between the eyebrows from time to time. Can you tell us what that is about?*

HS: It's connected to allergies and perpetual sinus inflammation.

B: *And what is this sinus inflammation about?*

HS: It's about the trees.

B: *The trees. Are you able to make adjustments at this time so that they no longer affect her?*

HS: I could try.

B: *You're really good at this. How are you healing this?*

HS: I have to heal the inflammation, and there are some growths, benign growths in the sinuses. They're pressing on nerves and causing the itching between the eyebrows.

B: *Okay, I know you're really good at dissolving growths, even Stage IV malignancies. Are you able to dissolve these at this time for her? Have they served their purpose?*

HS: So, the pattern connected to these, the irritation to being close, the thought pattern must be dissolved as well.

B: *Thank you. Are you doing that now?*

HS: Yes.

B: *Thank you so much. So after this session, will that feeling no longer be there?*

HS: It should go away.

B: *Very good. When will she know that it's gone?*

HS: Tomorrow.

B: *Tomorrow. Thank you so much. She shared with us she has the inability to stay asleep at night. Would you tell us the root cause of that?*

HS: If she would write, she would sleep.

B: *What does the writing provide for her and helping her to sleep?*

HS: Everything is getting bottled up; it's not being expressed.

B: *So she'll feel less stressed?*

HS: It's the only time we can talk with her.

B: *Does she find comfort in that?*

HS: Yes.

B: *She'd like to know if she's behind on her life purpose, what she came here to do?*

HS: She's doing better than we hoped. This is all clean-up time. Everything moves forward after [age] fifty-eight.

B: *Are there any missions she hasn't completed yet, besides the writing and getting the information out to the public?*

HS: [silence, big sigh] She will be required to place her mother, her mother is placed in a facility after her father dies. Because there will be no one else. The mother is developing Alzheimer's.

B: *Will this be easy for her to place her mother in a facility?*

HS: Her mother will make it difficult. Her sister will help.

B: *How can she feel more safe and secure in the world?*

HS: Take more time every day to reside in this space in which everything arises and everything appears, everything comes from the empty space that is full.

B: *What will she notice after this healing being done today?*

HS: She'll feel lighter.

B: *When she contacted us for a session, what did you hope she would receive from the session the most?*

HS: Just that we're still guiding her, and we are with her. She's still on the right path. It doesn't look like it, but she is.

B: *Is there anything else you wish she would have asked about today?*

Valerie: They're discussing.

HS: How to approach her death.

B: *And what is your answer?*

HS: Without fear.

B: *Does she know how to do that?*

HS: She will.

B: *What is the most important thing she didn't know about herself that you would like to explain to her?*

HS: Just want her to know she's doing good, and that she has more strength than she knows. And that some of the depression and fears are just childhood patterns installed and given by parents. And that she knows all that she needs to know. She doesn't have to keep seeking. It's time to turn around and disperse the knowledge.

B: *Thank you.*

PARTING MESSAGE

HS: If you seek guidance from the psychic, you should give him up. If you see the psychic as a peer, then keep him as a sounding board, because there are no others available at this time.

Although we spend our formative spiritual journey seeking guidance and direction from others more advanced and with knowledge that benefits us, at some point we need to look within ourselves for the answers to our questions. Through meditation and self reflection, we receive our answers and build trust within ourselves.

18
THE HEALING PART OF QHHT®

In *Convoluted Universe Book IV*[31], Dolores writes of the story of her client Ann who was healed of her insulin dependent diabetes, during a session at Dolores' home. As long as the healing is not interfering with a person's lessons and contracts, it occurs because the intention and willingness to let go of the disease or condition is decided by the client. Finding out the root cause of the problem is the key to releasing it in a QHHT® session.

In my own healing practice, clients have spontaneous past life recollection and/or I see the past life in my mind's eye while the client is in an altered state on the healing table or chair. I innately work with the client's Higher Self, Ascended Masters, and benevolent beings in the other realms, assisting the removal of distortions causing illness and pain, and re-aligning the star codes in the client's star fields and energy fields. The stories of healing are shared in my autobiography.

What I find fascinating the most is the Higher Self doesn't wait until the QHHT® session to begin the healing. A case in point is a California client whose abdominal pain abated just as we hung up our phones scheduling her appointment three weeks later. She had traveled all over the world for a year, seeking world-renowned healers to cure her pain. It was her Higher Self who resolved the pain during that one phone call.

The following session stories illustrate the client's Higher Self healing when and where appropriate.

GASTRIC REFLUX AND INGUINAL PAIN

Charlene enters the past-life scene seeing little boys running around. She thinks and feels it's a church. They wear coveralls, off-white shirts, and brown socks and shoes. It feels like France or Italy during the Renaissance.

---

31 *Convoluted Universe Book IV*, Dolores Cannon, Section 2, Chapter 37, pp.525-551

Barefoot, dressed as a female peasant, she's short and fat, wearing a white hat with ruffles and pompoms around the edge. Her hair is curly and red. Charlene is watching about twenty children. She has four children of her own. For the majority of her time, she is watching the children and listening to their antics. She giggles. Her husband is away at his job at sea. She feels comfortable in this life. She prefers not to wear shoes because it's more comfortable.

WE MOVE TO THE HOME...

Charlene is busy getting children to do their homework. She's preparing a stew, and making homemade bread. Her husband is not around enough. It's a simple home, a thatched cottage out in the country. The furniture is made out of wood, nothing ornate about it. It's a five-room, two-level home; however, from the outside, it looks like a single story home. The house sits on one to two acres with a grass lawn. She grows flowers and places them on the dining room table. The littlest one keeps bringing flowers into the house. Charlene laughs. Zekiel, Marna, Josha, and Lily are the names of the children. Her name is Marie. Lyle is the husband.

MOVING FORWARD TO WHEN LYLE COMES HOME...

He's more excited to see the children, picks them up and hugs them. She is excited to see him.

MOVING FORWARD TO LATER IN THE DAY...

The children are tucked into their beds. Marie feels nervous. He's been gone for so long. She doesn't know what to do. He's getting ready for bed. He motions for her to come over.

[We all know where this is going, so I give them privacy.]

MOVED FORWARD TO NEXT MORNING...

Marie feels that she doesn't know Lyle. He feels like a stranger. He's around the table with the children. She brings him oatmeal. Everyone appears happy; however, Lyle is distant.

AN IMPORTANT DAY IN THAT LIFE...

Utter disappointment. No one remembered her thirtieth birthday. Sitting in a field, feeling sorry for herself, Marie is crying. No one understands why she is distant and quiet. She doesn't share why she's feeling this way with her family.

MOVING FORWARD TO ANOTHER IMPORTANT DAY IN THAT LIFE...

No important days. Sees robotic movement, everyone doing their thing in the cottage. She's in her forties. Boys are taller, fourteen to fifteen years old.

MOVING FORWARD TO LAST DAY...

She's by herself, having a heart attack. Not scared. Laying in a bed on the first floor. A mist is coming in, and she knows she's leaving. It's easy. She's over looking where she was, out of the body.

> Barbara: *What lesson did she learn in that life?*
>
> Charlene: Children are the greatest blessing.
>
> B: *What was the purpose of the life?*
>
> C: I don't know.

HIGHER SELF

> B: *Why did you show her that lifetime?*
>
> HS: She needed to see that. She's dealt with this in many lifetimes.
>
> B: *What were the lessons to be learned?*
>
> HS: The only one who is going to make her happy is herself. And to see the joy she gets out of children.
>
> B: *Is her mother playing a part in keeping Charlene and her daughter, Lauren, apart? Can you help her to understand what is going on?*
>
> HS: [silence] Her mother is selfish and jealous. Her daughter is the only thing that can keep the mother down. The mother wants to be the queen.
>
> B: *Is this mother's role that Charlene is learning from?*
>
> HS: Charlene needs to depend on Charlene, not on what her mother or daughter think.

B: *Can you help Charlene understand her financial abundance?*

HS: Fear. Many lifetimes she's had people take from her. And she's afraid if she has money, someone will take it from her. There's also a component if she has a lot of money, her sisters will let her be, but they help her and then she feels they recognize her. If she had money, they would disappear. It's all about the money.

B: *Is this something Charlene needs to come to terms with regarding money?*

HS: [silence] She needs to relax and to enjoy the money and not worry, once again, about others and whether they will stay or go. Let it flow, and enjoy, not cripple.

B: *She would like to know why she's had so many life challenges. Can you help her understand about this life?*

H: She chose it. She's always got to help people. Somebody needed help, and [she] volunteered.

B: *What is her mission in this lifetime?*

HS: Main mission: making people happy and getting them to love themselves… less chastising and more joy.

B: *Is she accomplishing that?*

HS: Except for two young women who are opinionated and she can't do anything [about them]. Everyone has free will. Nothing that she has done.

B: *Where is Charlene from?*

HS: A planet that I don't know the name of.

B: *Can someone look up the name of the planet for us? You're really good at this.*

HS: Something like Aquarius.

B: *Aquarius. Do you know what star system or galaxy it is located in?*

HS: Jupiter.

B: *Jupiter star system?*

HS: Yes.

B: *Is there a name of the species or culture she is?*

HS: Just a higher being. I know not the language.

B: *A different dimension?*

HS: Four or five.

B: *Thank you. She would like to know her life purpose and is she fulfilling it?*

HS: Yes, and she should slow down.

B: *Her mission?*

HS: Her whole life. Most of her mission is done. It's time to calm down. Which she is. She's left and done a good job with her career. Now it's time to regroup and move. We'll give her signs when it's time to move on.

B: *So this is a resting time for her?*

HS: Yes.

B: *Why can't Charlene remember her dreams?*

HS: She goes far out. She's way out in the universe. There are times it's hard to get her back. And she pisses and moans. "You brought me back too hard!" [laughter]

B: *Is she doing work out in the universe?*

HS: She's in exploration.

B: *Is this something not to be concerned about?*

HS: No. We will guide her.

B: *You will guide her. You may have partially answered this. She feels she needs more time alone, especially around the time of the Super Bowl; she decided to stay home.*

HS: There were a lot of people going after her energy. They like her energy. Some are sucking on it. That's why she's retreating. She no longer is allowing and shouldn't allow anyone that is taking her energy, anymore. She needs to regroup. She needs to change the people she surrounds herself with, so there is a balance.

B: *She needs to set up some healthy boundaries?*

HS: Yes.

B: *She saw space ships just north of here, in the sky. Can you confirm this?*

HS: Yes. She's a nosy one.

B: *Is she seeing these space ships through her third eye or physical eyes?*

HS: Both.

B: *Are these spaceships of ET origin?*

HS: They are protecting her. When it's time for her to come home, they'll be there.

B: *Are these beings from her home planet?*

HS: They are a group working together. They are home. The space ships are working in conjunction with each other. They seem to be on a protective mode.

B: *Are they hearing what Charlene is saying to them?*

HS: Yep! [laughing]

B: *Very good. And what do they feel about that?* [Charlene says hello]

HS: They are all happy about it, and that's what all the squiggles are for.

B: *Thanks for the tingles of confirmation in my body about that. Looking into Charlene's brain is there any…*

HS: Fog.

B: *You see fog. Where is that coming from?*

HS: Too much thinking.

B: *What do you recommend?*

HS: Meditate and sit still.

B: *Is her brain healthy?*

HS: Yes.

B: *Pineal gland?*

HS: We're going to fine-tune it a little.

B: *What needs to be done?*

HS: There's something interfering. A little bit of fear, but curiosity too.

B: *Is the fear surrounding the third eye.*

HS: Of the dark side; let's put it that way.

B: *Can you help her understand what that is all about?*

HS: Yes. She certainly is nosy. Things are bigger than they really are. She thought that people actually saw, and some do. It will take time.

B: *Is her pineal gland healthy?*

HS: Yes.

B: *Are you going to help her see through her third eye easier?*

HS: In time.

B: *Does she need to do something to help?*

HS: Trust.

B: *Trust in what she's seeing?*

HS: Trust in everything, in the process.

B: *Charlene shared that she enjoys smoking. Is this a problem for her?*

HS: Other than the one she created. She was doing fine. And then she started taking in what everyone said, and she's holding onto it. If she would let it go, we could do something about it.

B: *Can you look at her lungs and tell us what you find?*

HS: She's got tension in there, which she needs to let go of.

B: *And what is the tension about?*

HS: Multiple things. What people are saying about her. The push about smoking. The relating to others and her father, and the cause of their death due to smoking. It wasn't the cause of their deaths.

B: *If she could let go of these other programs and just enjoy smoking she'll be okay?*

HS: Take walks in the woods or whatever.

B: *Thank you. Can you look into her ears?*

HS: Right ear is better than left. She's got good hearing.

B: *Can you do something now to improve the left ear?*

HS: Yes.

B: *May I continue to ask more questions?*

HS: Yes.

B: *What can you tell us about her gastric reflux?*

HS: Too much orange and grapefruit. She knows her body.

B: *She needs to cut back on those. By how much, do you recommend?*

HS: Stop for one month; eat more olive oils, grape seed oil, and cooking and salad oils. She'll be fine. Her body is high in iron and Vitamin C. She should watch those levels.

B: *Charlene has intermittent discomfort in the lower right abdominal inguinal area.*

HS: The root cause is money worries.

B: *Is that your way to communicate to her she's feeling the worry?*

HS: Yes.

B: *Is this connected to the root chakra?*

HS: Yes.

B: *What about her left ankle?*

HS: She's an Aquarian, so she needs to watch her ankles and toes. She's broken two toes.

B: *Is her ankle okay now?*

HS: Yes, we've been working on it.

Upon scanning Charlene's body, the Higher Self finds that only her sacral chakra and heart are still mending. The sacral is about the worry.

B: *Can we do anything at this time to help those areas?*

HS: She can stop worrying. We'll continue to work on the heart.

B: *During the night?*

HS: Yes.

PARTING MESSAGE

HS: Take care of yourself, my dear. Be kind to yourself. You listen well. Just pay attention and be yourself. We love you.

Charlene sent this email message to me later:
"*Thank you for the QHHT® session. It was intense, but the results were amazing. I cleared a lot of old hurts, as evidenced by an angel communicator I see, who said she doesn't see any more dark areas as she had previously. I feel spiritually lighter. I also no longer have stomach or lower quadrant issues and I feel so much lighter.*"

HEALING HEARTACHE OF LOVED ONE WHO CROSSED OVER

I facilitated a session for a delightful middle-aged woman who lived near the famous Superstition Mountains in Arizona. Since this was a three-hour drive for me, one way, Diana graciously offered her guest room for me to spend the night. The veil between the dimensions is very thin in this area of the Sonoran desert. I experienced confirmation of this phenomena later that night.

Two years prior to the session, Diana's husband of thirty years died of cancer. They had a loving relationship, and she continued to communicate with him telepathically. She was interested in making contact with this dear soul during the session.

Diana also wanted to address her insomnia, headaches, neck discomfort, right knee injury, dream time interference by spirits, and specifics about her relocation to another state. She was self-employed, and a Reiki Master.

PAST LIFE & FUTURE LIFE TOGETHER

We begin the session, and Diana finds herself standing in the middle of a town with lots of people walking around. Her healthy body is in its mid-thirties. Her name is Sistina. Wearing a reddish pink long dress with a white apron and a matching round headdress, she looks down and sees brown leather boots. Sistina is wearing pearl bracelets and a ring on her right middle finger, with a blue stone. Her wedding band is a plain gold ring. She's carrying an ornately tooled leathered satchel that contains a round gold disc as big as a typical dinner plate. The border of the plate has inscribed symbols that look possibly Arabic or a Russian language, at first glance.

Sistina exclaims, "It's really special! I'm not sure why I have it." I ask her to put the gold disc back into the satchel. She does and journeys to town.

> Barbara: *Do you have an appointment, mission, or reason why you're in that town?*
>
> Sistina: I'm to meet someone.

I move Sistina forward to the meeting where she walks up to a stone building that has a series of entrances. She knocks on the carved wood door. As the door opens, Sistina sees an old man with white hair and a white beard. His name is Ithar (pronounced ee-thar), and he's wearing a brown tunic and trousers. Smiling at her, he beckons her to enter. He knows who she is.

The room is simple, with a plain wood table and wood chairs. Sistina notices that on top of the table is a large golden disc surrounded by small crystals, looking like sparkling brilliant cut diamonds. It feels wonderful in this room, and her disc in the satchel is now vibrating! Sistina says, "The disc wants to come out of the satchel." Removing the disc from the bag and placing it on the table, the larger disc begins to glow.

S: I glance over at Ithar. His eyes are so alive, even though he's pretty old. He's here to guide me. [Diana is laughing now.]

B: *Guide you, for what?*

S: He says, "To take you back to where we came from, out there, not on Earth." She looks up and sees the stars in the night sky as the ceiling and roof disappear. I want to go, but I have someone who—I'm not sure I can leave yet. There is someone pulling me back. It's my husband! He needs me to stay here for a while until his Earth journey is finished. [Sistina sighs deeply.]

We move forward, and now Sistina is back outside in the marketplace, looking around. We move forward to meet her husband, Aarn, in the marketplace. He's tall and young like her and happy to see her. They have a happy marriage, but he's never understood her. He doesn't know who she really is.

B: *Who are you really? It is safe to share this information with me.*

S: I have a lot of knowledge. He couldn't understand this. It's magic; that's what they call it here. This is nothing people can know about. It helps everything, all the Earth. It's so grand, so tremendous. It can't be put into words. It feels wonderful. But, I've come here to help him and others. Until his Earth journey is done, I can't go back. I have to finish my mission before I can leave. They sent me to do this mission. This husband, I know him from this life. He's my first husband in this [current] life. He didn't understand me then, and not now. I made that commitment [to him].

Moving to a new scene, Sistina shares:

D: I'm alone in a forest, at night among the beautiful trees, dressed in the most beautiful dark blue cloak with a hood. There is silver embroidery along the edges sewn in the language that's on my disc. My disc is in front of me, on a tree stump. It's dark, but the area is lit up from the glowing disc. I can see all the stars in the night sky. My hands are held up toward the sky. I can feel the energy and a very strong pull.

It's pulling me! I'm ready to go. I'm going back now! [There's] a big glowing light in the sky, of the same energy. I'm taking my disc and holding it. I'm going up. It's gentle and such a strong pull as if someone is lifting me. I feel very safe.

Now, I'm there. It's really beautiful and peaceful inside. Like a beautiful marble temple. I see others I know there. They're waiting for me. They're dressed in white. They have gold; some have white cloaks with gold embroidery like mine. They are my family. They are my people. They look like humans. They are smiling. I feel wonderful. Now, under my blue cloak I'm dressed in white like them.

Diana gives a big sigh and begins to cry. It's obvious to me that Diana's soul has already gone to a place where we all come from.

D: I was gone for a long time.

I give her emotional support.

Diana: There he is! My love. [referring to her current life husband, crying very loud now, tears of joy are streaming down her face] He's waited for me for so long. He's bright. He's happy to see me. We don't even speak. And all the ones I love are here. Ithar is here, although he still looks the same, but dressed differently.

Diana and Sistina enjoy this time with Sistina's husband and soul family. Diana's husband from her current life comes through too. This feels like a possible blending of a past life, parallel life, and future life scenes. We must remember that time doesn't exist in the other realms, only in the third dimension.

I give Diana time to enjoy a private silent conversation with her deceased husband. This is very healing for the client. When the recording is reviewed over and over, it is possible for the client and loved one/s to have new conversations each time.

I ask Diana what she learned from that lifetime.

D: I learned understanding. They are not able to understand yet, that they can be very afraid. The purpose of that life was to serve even when your service is not understood nor appreciated. Be patient and know that it's all for a higher purpose.

HIGHER SELF

When her Higher Self comes through, Diana's voice changes to a lower tone. I ask the HS why they showed her these scenes.

> HS: We want her to understand that she has gifts that are needed. She has been reticent to bring them forward. She has been afraid of being too different. Now is the time.
>
> Barbara: *What were the lessons in that lifetime?*
>
> Higher Self: The lessons are to subjugate her gifts, her knowledge, to bring healing to those around her. The purpose of that lifetime was for her to understand she had to bring healing in a way that it could be accepted.
>
> B: *In the past life regression part of this session, she mentions her husband didn't understand her, and she had special knowledge. Is this what you are talking about?*
>
> HS: Yes. It was knowledge that could not be spoken to the people in that time. It had to be conveyed energetically.
>
> B: *Can you help us to understand what she was doing in that lifetime with that disc?*
>
> HS: It was her connection to us. It contained all the knowledge, all the magic that she brought with her. The inscription on the disc is in our language.
>
> B: *What was the disc made of?*
>
> HS: It is like gold, but it is higher than gold in its energy.
>
> B: *Can you tell us the name of the metal?*
>
> HS: [Silent pause] It is Alutron.

REGARDING RESIDENTIAL RELOCATION

> B: *Diana shared with us that she has a compulsion to move to [a certain town in the U.S. that we will keep confidential in this book to protect her privacy]. Is this appropriate in this lifetime for her to move there?*

HS: It is not only an inner deep desire, it is a place where we make the contact. It is a place where she is closer to us.

B: *Are you able to share with us when the move will occur?*

HS: When the trees blossom.

B: *That tells me spring. Is this confirmed? This 2015 spring?*

HS: Yes. This is the last part of her soul path. This is where the path has led. She will know when she arrives.

REGARDING HER DREAM TIME AND THE INTERFERENCE SHE EXPERIENCES

B: *Recommendation for her dream work?*

HS: She must set a boundary. She must tell them, "Not tonight. Tonight I need to rest." She must let them know when it's appropriate for them to come in. They feel she's an open door. They crowd in. She has the ability to say no. And when we [HS] want to give a message, we will be able to come through.

BODY SCAN

B: *Could you please go into Diana's body for a scan?*

HS: Yes, we are there.

They first work on her vision.

HS: The vision began to blur when she went to school when she was young. It was a way to help her see inside, always inside. To see with the inner eye, not what the physical eyes see on the surface.

B: *Is she seeing inside?*

HS: Oh, yes.

B: *Are you able to improve her eye vision at this time during this session?*

HS: We will consider it.

[Breathing, breathing. No response from the HS as I wait. I intuitively sense they are in a conference.]

B: *Are you talking among yourselves at this time?*

HS: Yes.

[More silence]

HS: We feel she has been given a very strong body. It is not untoward that she should have a little problem with her vision. She has many physical blessings. These things will remind her that there is much, much physical suffering in the world, and these are small in comparison.

They next work on her neck discomfort and headaches.

HS: This is to give her patience and understanding.

B: *Are you able to give her adjustments in her spine?*

HS: We made. [Meaning yes, they already did it.]

B: *Was she able to feel it inside?*

HS: Yes.

B: *Should she continue chiropractic adjustments?*

HS: Yes, to realign the energies. In addition, the massages are beneficial. The current program is good.

Now they work on her right knee injury.

HS: This occurred when she was not paying attention. It was very painful at the time.

B: *What was she not paying attention to?*

HS: Where she was going. So she collided with a very strong object. This is a lesson to be aware of situations and people, to pay attention. Do not assume that everything is the same as you. So, only with the aging of the vehicle, that difficulty has come, some pain, in that area. This serves as a reminder in the physical body.

B: *Is it for her benefit?*

HS: To slow down. To pay attention.

They comment on the residual grief from the loss of her husband.

B: *Can you make adjustments in her heart chakra?*

HS: We are working with that. She should know that they have not left her. Only in the physical. [Deep breathing.] We are sending a crystal light to heal this loss.

[Deep breathing continues for about 30 seconds]

HS: Now the tightness is going away.

During the crystal light healing, I feel pain in my left hand. I intuitively pick up my left hand and throw energy out the window. The discomfort in my hand stops instantly. I ask the HS why I had pain and how I knew what to do.

HS: [Silent pause] It went out through the left side of her body. You are sensitive. You felt it going.

B: *Thank you. As you scan her body, please let us know if you find anything that needs adjustment. And let us know when the scan is complete.*

HS: All the problems in this physical [body] stem from the heart. She must let go of the pain of the loss, of the anger sent toward her, of the misunderstandings. [From a family member] She must not hold this in her heart. She can do it. We are filtering it out.

B: *Thank you.*

HS: We are filling it with healing crystal light. She must know that she is loved. That all that she puts forth is being replenished, is being returned. We have completed [the scan].

B: *Thank you.*

PARTING MESSAGE

HS: She is on her path. She knows she must hold to this path until this life is over. We are showing her the way. We are giving her all the signs. We are bringing the other beings, the other people into her life. She will know them. She must finish her work. We know she wanted to go, but she must stay. She must help others. She must be strong. She must not waiver.

Diana thought she was under hypnosis for a brief time, although it was two hours. This perception of time being shortened is confirmation that the client was deep in hypnosis and that we travelled through time. She really enjoyed being with her husband, and the recording allows her to relive it over and over. Alutron is not on the periodic table. Not yet. The last time we spoke, Diana is doing very well. In the spring of 2015, she relocated her residence and business to the town discussed in her session.

INSOMNIA

This forty-three-year-old female psychic medium suffered with an intense fear of speaking her truth, along with insomnia. The conditions affected Margaret's mediumship career. Additionally, she was afflicted with the pain of endometriosis, a condition where the body makes extra endometrial cells inside the uterus. These cells can also develop implants and spread throughout the body causing problems such as collapsed lungs.

I used to have endometriosis and was all too familiar with the painful menses every month.

Margaret also had constipation, asthma, and allergies. Of note, too, was that she grew up with abusive parents. Emancipated at the age of seventeen, she went to college and carved out a public career.

Margaret already knew she would be doing platform work (this is where the psychic medium performs on stage giving messages to people in the audience.) She was very concerned that her fear of speaking would interfere with her psychic career. Certainly, this is a valid concern for anyone who does public speaking.

PAST LIFE

We begin the regression, and Margaret sees an old white church with stained glass windows and a cross on top. No one is here. Wearing a robe, tied with a blue rope around her waist, she sees herself as a slightly overweight middle-aged nun. A fabric hat goes around her hair. She spends the majority of her time praying for people who live in the small community. She lives in a dirt hut by herself. There's one other person who helps the community: a bald monk, wearing a robe. Her hut is sparse. Seeing just a chair and a little cot with a blanket, there are no eating utensils. She uses her fingers to eat food.

Nothing much is happening, so we leave that scene…

Margaret sees nothing; however, she hears chaos and destruction from bombs. Hiding in a cave with other people, surrounded by the children she teaches, she feels scared.

Abruptly, Margaret jumps into another life scene as a tribal runner in Africa. She's a young man, wearing animal skin leather clothing tied at the waist. This young man is running through the trees to fetch the medicine person for a woman who is about to give birth.

On the last day of that life as the messenger boy, he is grown up and shot with an arrow through the heart by a tribal soldier, killing him. He floats up out of the body.

HIGHER SELF

The Higher Self shares that the lessons he learned in that last life was to love people. The purpose of that life was to provide for his tribe as a hunter. He also learned that food wasn't available everyday. Additional learnings include: The purpose of the life as the boy messenger for the tribe was an expression of freedom. The lessons were about responsibility to the tribe.

The HS tells us that they showed her the life as a nun so she could see the work she did in helping others. She was light and pure. The lesson she learned was to give to others.

Barbara: *Has she completed all her karma in this lifetime?*

Higher Self: Most.

B: *What else does she need to do?*

HS: Work on family connections. Forgive. Release and let go.

B: *What is the purpose of her current life?*

HS: To help others. This is not for her.

B: *How many lifetimes has she lived on this Earth?*

HS: Thirty-six.

B: *She feels like she's here to do some extra credit. Would you agree?*

HS: Yes.

B: *She feels she's lived on Pleiades, Sirius, and Andromeda. Can you confirm these for her or not?*

HS: Multiple times.

B: *Is there any particular planet or star system she is from?*

HS: Sirius.

B: *What is her connection with her mother in this lifetime?*

HS: [big sigh] She's amending karmic debts. It's not about a mother-daughter relationship. It's about relationship. Getting along. Forgive.

B: *Margaret knows she's here to do work as a medium. Is she to do platform work[32]?*

HS: Yes.

B: *Are you able to tell her when to begin this?*

HS: In a year.

B: *In a year. Will she be traveling around the country?*

HS: Yes.

B: *Will she be able to make a living at this in service?*

HS: Yes.

B: *Will she leave her current job?*

HS: In a year.

B: *What incident turned off her clairvoyance in this lifetime?*

HS: Childhood.

B: *Can you tell us what happened?*

HS: Her mother conducted séances, and this scared her. She was told many things. She couldn't get around that. She picked up hearing instead.

---

32 Platform work is giving readings and channeling information in front of a live group of people.

B: *Is there something she can do?*

HS: Practice. It will open.

B: *Is there something she's supposed to learn in this lifetime?*

HS: She's an overachiever. Doing a great job. Beyond all expectations.

B: *Was she a psychic in a past life?*

HS: An oracle in Greece.

B: *She was wondering if she were a witch before.*

HS: Yes, in Salem. She was persecuted for her gifts. She's worried about judgment.

B: *Can she now know she's safe?*

HS: She's surrounded by the people who make her safe.

B: *Why is she scared of bridges?*

HS: She fell off of one.

B: *When?*

HS: 1800s France.

B: *Did she die?*

HS: Yes.

B: *Is this causing a fear of heights?*

HS: Yes.

B: *She wants to know why she doesn't sleep well at night.*

HS: We work on her.

B: *Are you the ones waking her up, doing your work?*

HS: Yes.

B: *Is it because you want her back in her body?*

HS: It's the only time we can work on her. She's too busy.

B: *So she becomes aware that you're there.*

HS: Yes.

B: *Can you look at her recent neck pain that is radiating down the left arm to the deltoid and biceps.*

HS: Working too much. Stop carrying people. Let others do their work. It's a lesson to remind her. Let them walk their own journey.

B: *Can you heal her neck?*

HS: Yes.

B: *Are you doing that right now?*

HS: Yes.

B: *Thank you. She has allergies to dogs, cats, grass, and other things. Can you tell us about that so she can understand?*

HS: She's going to be working with many people. Try to be in many environments. Trying to let go of that.

B: *Is this about being in those environments and not being affected?*

HS: Yes.

B: *Can you help her with that?*

HS: Yes.

B: *Are you able to heal that at this time?*

HS: May I look? It's in her chest. We're taking a look now.

B: *Okay.*

HS: Her chest is very bad. But I can adjust.

B: *Very good. Are you healing it with the white light?*

HS: Yes.

B: *Thank you.*

HS: Give us a moment.

B: *Yes.*

HS: We're done.

B: *Thank you. Has that taken care of her asthma?*

HS: Yes.

B: *Thank you so much. Will she need to use her Alvesco anymore?*

HS: No.

B: *Will she need to use the allergy medicine anymore?*

HS: We don't think so.

B: *Do you want her to wean that off?*

HS: Yes.

B: *And what do you recommend for weaning?*

HS: One-half pill; try that for a couple of days, and then try not to be on it.

B: *She's been taking part of a sleeping pill at night when she needs to sleep. Will she need that anymore?*

HS: Sometimes. We'll try not to wake her up in the middle of the night. That's the problem.

B: *If she understands it's you working on her, will that help her to go back to sleep?*

HS: Yes. She'll need the medicine when she travels. She's very sensitive to environments.

B: *Do you still want her to take the sleeping medication, or is there something else you would like her to take?*

HS: It's okay. She takes only a small bit. It's okay.

B: *For her painful stabbing in the right pelvis, severe menses, and iron deficiency—Western medicine would label this as endometriosis. Are you able to go in there and heal that?*

HS: We're looking at it now. It's from a past life. The wound has been opened from a past life. We're working on stitching it up right now. Healing is occurring now.

B: *Are you using the white light?*

HS: Yes, it's in her body. She should feel better now.

B: *Did you complete the healing?*

HS: Yes.

B: *Are you able to tell us the condition of the thyroid before the healing?*

HS: Hyperthyroid.

B: *So you were able to adjust it to normal operation and function?*

HS: Yes.

B: *Thank you.*

HS: We turned it down.

B: *Thank you! Would you help her to understand the reason for her cloudy vision, which began when she started her mediumship?*

HS: We're working on her. We're also looking at her third eye too. We're downloading in the back of her eye.

B: *Is this normal?*

HS: We're trying to adjust to make it normal.

B: *Are you working on it this moment?*

HS: Yes, just give us a moment.

B: *Yes.*

HS: We made some adjustments.

B: *Were you working on my left eye during this adjustment? I saw this brilliant star burst flash of light.*

HS: You? Yes, we are working on you too.

B: *Thank you.* [I remind myself the session is about the client. I stay focused on her issues.] *She has a concern in her knees.*

HS: Stop running.

B: *Stop physically running?*

HS: Not physically. Stop running. Stay. Stand. Don't run. You're here to do this. They haven't hurt because she decided to do this. She's not hurting anymore. She's not running anymore.

B: *So now she has perfect knee sensation?*

HS: Yes.

B: *She has an occasional constipation.*

HS: She needs to eat better.

B: *Recommendations?*

HS: More grains. It's okay.

B: *Any additional scanning?*

HS: We'll look. We're making a sweep. Things are good.

B: *Thank you.*

PARTING MESSAGE

HS: She's of the Divine. She's on her path. She is here to assist many. She brings love to many. She heals many hearts. Continue the work.

The following day I received this email message from Margaret: "Barbara, last night was my first full night of sleep!"

A month post session, Margaret shared that she's been listening to the recording as suggested. She said more and more insights are coming in each time she listens to it. She is now past self judgment. She's sleeping better, and the shoulder and neck discomforts are gone. Her bowels are better.

The reader may notice not every ailment requires a deep analysis. The client receives more information when they listen to their recording over and over. Plus, keep in mind, the Higher Self is working behind the scenes during the session. Let's speak truth here; they are working behind the scenes, all the time.

KNEE PAIN HEALED

I facilitated this QHHT® session for a thirty-six-year-old man who works with energy systems. Frank sustained a motorcycle accident in his mid-twenties and injured his right knee. He had to have surgery twice, once to repair the damage, and the second one to remove a bone spur. He's had insomnia for some time, and would like this to be addressed in his session.

He shares that he has no attachment to people, especially relationships with women. He is heterosexual. His nature is gentle, and I can feel the Divine Presence emanating from him. His aura is very calming and serene. He trusts and loves people and is focused on helping people. He perceives himself as a guide to anyone who needs and asks for help.

When they don't do the follow-through, then he no longer wants to be near them. He doesn't see himself as a guru or figure to "hold on to." He expects people to be honest, authentic, and have integrity.

Customer relations taken to the highest level is his job focus. People love him, trust him, and seek his advice and counsel.

PAST LIFE

At the beginning of the hypnosis, I note Frank's REM (rapid eye movement) and a small amount of tears down the side of his face. There is no outward emotional escalation, so I just keep monitoring him.

Frank reports that he doesn't have a body.

B: *All right. Do you get the sense you are awareness or consciousness?*

F: Yeah.

B: *Let's explore this.*

F: Okay.

B: *I wait for a response. What does it feel like?*

F: It feels like nothing, really. No responsibilities.

B: *Is there any surface?*

F: No.

B: *Is it like being in outer space?*

F: Could be. I don't notice any stars. Just darkness.

B: *Do you like being there?*

F: Yeah, it doesn't bother me.

B: *Like neutral?*

F: [Affirmative mumble] I don't see anything happening.

We are here for quite a while with Frank not offering any descriptions or feelings. Since nothing is happening after our exploration, I ask him to go to another important day…

B: *What do you see now?*

F: I'm just in the sky.

B: *What would you like see? Where would you like to go?*

F: I'd like to go to the forest and camp.

B: *Describe it to me.*

F: I'm at a campsite. My tent is set up.

B: *What does your tent look like?*

F: It's brown on the bottom and tan on top. I have like a small campfire that's been put out. And there's trees around.

B: *Is it day or night?*

F: Umm, it's like dusk.

B: *Your campfire is out already?*

F: It's smoldering.

B: *Look down at your feet and tell me what you see?*

F: I have some boots on.

B: *What color?*

F: Brown. The pants are tan. I have like a vest on, an over-vest with no sleeves.

B: *Is there anybody with you or are you all alone?*

F: I feel like I'm alone.

B: *Do you hear anything in the forest?*

F: No.

B: *No birds or wildlife at all?*

F: No.

B: *Does this place look familiar to you?*

F: No it doesn't. I feel welcomed and calm.

B: *Do you know how to communicate with nature?*

F: No.

B: *Are you able to talk with the trees?*

F: I can talk to the trees. I'm not sure I need to speak with my mouth. But just understanding.

B: *You can speak telepathically with the trees and hear their messages. Are they saying anything?*

F: They are not saying anything. It feels like I'm almost the tree. Very tall.

B: *In what way?*

F: In length. Kind of like I'm looking down at the camp.

B: *Tell me more.*

F: Kind of like looking out over the valley or the forest, and it's just peaceful.

B: *Do you get the sense you are with others?*

F: No, I don't feel anybody else is there. There are other trees.

B: *Do you feel any kinship with the other trees?*

F: Nope.

B: *Are you an old or a young tree?*

F: Middle-age, I guess.

B: *Are you a healthy tree?*

F: Very healthy.

B: *What kind of things do you learn from being a tree?*

F: Just being. It's not the same as a human and worry about the everyday problems and struggles. You can just be.

B: *Do you have leaves?*

F: Umm, I think on the top.

B: *What kind of a tree are you?*

F: I think I'm an older tree. I have some branches, all towards the top and it looks like it could be something all the way up top. I don't know if it's a nest or it could hold a nest. Like greenish.

B: *Do you ever have birds visit you?*

F: I feel… oh they do! But I don't see any at the moment.

B: *Do you have any memories of them coming?*

F: Umm, I think I do. Like an eagle comes and feeds its babies when they were there.

B: *Can you go to that time when you were with that mother eagle in her nest?*

F: Yes.

B: *Can you share with us the conversations you had?*

F: I don't know if we had conversations, but I'm looking at her fix the bedding of the nest. I don't have to talk. I know that she's doing everything she can to take care of the babies.

B: *How does it feel being the support for a nest?*

F: It feels great! To be able to be there and be strong and let the eagle know I'm there to take care of it.

B: *That's a wonderful responsibility to provide that support for life.*

Frank's hypnosis session progresses slowly. He doesn't offer spontaneous descriptions. Instead, I have to ask questions in order for him to give answers.

An hour goes by, so it is time to contact the Subconscious and get the answers to his questions.

HIGHER SELF

The life as a tree was chosen to let him know he's very strong and he does a good job of supporting his friends and family. The lesson learned is that he just has to be. He doesn't have to do anything outside of himself. He's just there. He's a support. He was shown the awareness in space because it was peaceful, without worries. That is why he was crying.

B: *Thank you so much. He would like to know is he a volunteer according to Dolores' definition?*

HS: I believe so. I can't say he's been in human form before.

B: *Has he ever incarnated in human form on Earth?*

HS: I don't believe so.

B: *What is his purpose in this lifetime? Why is he here?*

HS: To be. Just to the lives he comes into contact with, he's just to be. There's nothing special. To get them out of their ways. To be and kind of encourage them to do the things they want to do.

B: *Are these positive things?*

HS: Yes.

B: *Does he have innate skills or abilities he's not aware of?*

HS: To connect with people. He knows that.

B: *He would like to know what was his most recent past life. Could you show him this now and let him describe it?*

HS: I think I showed him that. I feel like the tree, as a past life.

B: *Could you share with us where that tree was located?*

HS: In a forest.

B: *On Earth?*

HS: Yes.

B: *Could you share with us where on Earth he was located as a tree?*

HS: It feels like a tree in the forest. It could be North America. The eagle coming to the tree, the eagle took care of its babies. It feels like it was his sister.

B: *They have a close relationship?*

HS: Yes, they do.

B: *Could you share with us what that relationship is about?*

HS: Because he's always there to support her. Emotionally, financially, and advice.

B: *He would like to know the root cause of his insomnia.*

HS: The difficulty and discomfort between him and his wife's family. He wrestles at night about this, and this keeps him awake. Once he releases his wife, and allows her to incorporate what he has taught her, this will be gone.

B: *What is the root cause of his right knee pain?*

HS: It's the tissue that connects the muscle to the bone.

B: *The ligament?*

HS: Yes.

B: *Would you go in there and heal it?*

HS: [there is about a minute of silence]

During this healing I see the room fill with white light.

HS: Done!

PARTING MESSAGE

HS: Always follow your heart. Don't be led astray.

Nine months later, Frank returned for another session for answers to new questions. He shared that his right knee was completely healed since the previous session. He no longer has insomnia. He and his wife are in the process of a divorce.

Frank's session story illustrated a different style of the hypnosis in which I invite the client to choose something they like to do. This is why I ask about a person's hobbies and interests in the interview. Using imagination, a person can transition very easily into a past life scene/movie, by focusing on what they love to engage in.

Here, we saw how Frank "went camping," admiring the trees and then becoming one. This is one way the Higher Self helps the client into a past life. It's comfortable, and an easy transition.

BREAST CANCER

I facilitated this session for a sixty-five-year-old retired woman who worked in the legal field. The parents never told Doris she was loved. Finally, before dying of pancreatic cancer, her father spoke his peace and said he loved her.

Doris didn't speak up for herself, she confided. Her health concerns included high cholesterol, breast cancer (left side), recent lumpectomy, and radiation (five days total). The growth was very small, without symptoms.

Doris had ringing in the ears that started when a nearby bomb exploded when she was young, and increased when she wore headphones at high volume during her military training. She wanted to know what diet would be best for her.

She had developed pancreatitis that resolved in one year; however, she reported a physical lump that her physician could feel. They were monitoring her; no treatment had been given so far.

PAST LIFE

Doris is in the Civil War era, as a young woman dressed in a beautiful Southern Belle gown. She is standing in a little town, at the court house, watching the soldiers go by.

At her home, she describes a one-story building made of brick with white-framed windows. She walks inside and sees a parlor, furniture, a dining room with many chairs, and a serving room for the food. I ask her to go to the kitchen. The kitchen is outside the house, in a separate building. As she enters, she sees a woman cooking a stew over the stove. The woman is one of her servants and is joyful to be employed.

She sees herself eating a meal alone at a big table. Her soldier husband is away at war. She misses him. There is no communication of any form with him. She feels lonely.

We move to another important day in that life…

Her husband comes home. He is a teacher of some form, and they have a child—a girl. In this scene the girl is a toddler.

When I ask what happens next, she finds herself in bed, ill with a flu virus that she cannot recover from. Her daughter is fourteen. Her husband, daughter, and the cook sit by her bedside. She slips out of her body without me even asking about the last day of that life. The body is removed from the house, a funeral takes place, and the body is buried.

I want to see what she will do next. I say nothing.

Drifting away… She continues to a place where there is white foggy area, then it clears. She sees beautiful green grass, a green that is very vibrant. Everything is beautiful.

She sees an androgynous humanoid being walking towards her. The being says, "Welcome back, we're glad you're here." Others come and welcome her. They take her to a large building where she walks upstairs and sees a grand room. They seat her at a table with an image screen imbedded in it. She watches the images.

After a while here, I ask what happens next. Her guides escort her to one of the healing rooms where she lays down on a piece of furniture or device that conforms to her shape, and she begins to rest.

We leave her there to rest and to heal…

HIGHER SELF

The Higher Self comes through strong and robust, answering all her questions in detail and completing a body scan. I ask about the various ailments in her body. They say they've been trying to get her to speak her truth all of these years. Since she wouldn't, they kept escalating the severity of the illnesses until she was given the breast cancer. Now, she's ready to listen.

This is the testimonial Doris wrote later to share on my website:

"I have to share with you a remembrance of healing as I awakened this morning—I saw some green light going over my whole breast area; I felt a definite tingling from that light, especially on the left breast. The tingling was proof enough of the continuing healing; 'seeing' the green light was just an added bonus! So, I was truly blessed to have witnessed my own healing as it continues from our session! I truly feel like a new woman!!!!! Life is wonderful! Thanks again, Barbara, for the beautiful healing QHHT® session."

Later, Doris would return for a second session to address some remnant fluid in her left breast and her knee discomfort.

SEVERE HEALING OF MIGRAINES AND TINNITUS

Early in my QHHT® practice, this was the most challenging session for me to facilitate. I'm including this session because it dramatically illustrates the power of the Higher Self and the beauty of the Quantum Healing Hypnosis Technique℠ in a client's self healing.

Clark came from the other side of the state to where I live in Wickenburg, Arizona. For those clients in the local hotels, I ask them to call me once they get settled; or I facilitate the session the following morning.

Clark is adamant about being cured today. He gets migraines, along with tinnitus (ringing in the ears). He receives multiple medical Botox injections all over his head every three months to manage his migraine headaches.

PAST LIFE

The entire time I speak the induction script, he snores. Coming up to the theta level of deep hypnosis, Clark finds himself as a cowboy, sitting on a cloud, wearing tennis shoes.

The scene changes. Clark now finds himself seeing colored domes, then in a sporting goods store looking at guns. He goes back to sleep, snoring loudly again. No matter what I say, he keeps going back to snoring.

I bring him out of hypnosis easily and ask him to take his magnesium oxide medicine for his headaches that he is prescribed to take throughout the day. I direct him to take a nap and return at two in the afternoon.

He says he had a great nap. I begin the regression. He seems to be settling in quite nicely. Suddenly, he opens his eyes and says, "Sorry Barb, this isn't working. I'm not even relaxing. I can't see anything. I'm just wasting your time."

I ask him if he would like to stop, and he says yes. I share with him that he did receive healing, he's just not aware of it yet.

When I speak with Clark the next day, he's sitting outdoors on a bench. He says he had the worst headache of his life, and now it is gone. His tinnitus of eighteen years is gone too! He is delighted to be free of the ringing in the ears.

One week later, Clark shares with me that the ringing in the ears still has not returned, which tickles him pink. That alone was worth the trip, he says.

I agree with Dolores Cannon that the client receives exactly what they need in accordance with their soul agreements and contracts. As Clark listens to his recording, he can continue to receive more healing. It's up to him. I have since learned it doesn't matter if my client goes to sleep during the relaxing induction into hypnosis. As soon as I start asking questions, the client is able to talk about their past life scene, and the Higher Self comes through and answers their questions, just like other clients who don't enter the delta brain wave level of sleep.

URINARY INCONTINENCE

I facilitated this session in a hotel room for a mother of two adult daughters. She came to me because one of her daughters received a QHHT® session from me, and it was transformative for her daughter.

Although an advanced spiritual person, Lois didn't meditate. She had no hobbies, but did love to travel by car.

Lois was born in a middle Eastern country. Both parents never told her they loved her. She doesn't remember her childhood. Lois' reason for a QHHT® session was curiosity. Her health concern was her low back discomfort of twenty-nine years from picking up her daughter.

During the interview, I shared with Lois that it's important not to compare her session with her daughter's or any other session material she had read about or seen on videos.

PAST LIFE

Halfway down into deep hypnosis, Lois sees the ocean. She then goes out over the sea as an air molecule. I turn on the recorder. The rest of the time is spent looking at colors and light, then nothing.

HIGHER SELF

I begin asking questions and hear Lois say in a defiant manner: "No, I don't have to tell you anything!"

This could be either the ego or an entity. I ask, "Who is talking with me?"

Lois responds: "No, I don't have to tell you!"

After attempting further conversation without dialogue with the HS, I methodically ask each of Lois' questions, with pauses of silence between them. I know the HS is present and listening.

Then I count Lois up and out, and she goes to the bathroom. When she returns, she refuses to go back into deep hypnosis. I honor her free will, and ask her to lay on the bed in order for me to follow the protocol to properly bring her back to the fully awake state.

She felt she was under hypnosis for fifteen minutes. When I tell her it was over an hour, she is shocked.

Lois remarks, "My session wasn't anything like my daughter's!"

I ask Dolores, "What is going on here?" Dolores replies, "Keep going, you're doing good. Watch what happens."

I remind Lois that each QHHT® is unique for each individual and prepare the recording for her to take home.

UNEXPECTED PHONE CALL TWELVE DAYS LATER

Lois calls me and says she has had bladder control problems in the form of urinary incontinence for the past twenty-five years, and, since the day of our session, she has had no problems with her bladder. She was used to changing her underwear ten times a day!

For the week after the session, she could feel a tightening sensation in her lower abdominal and pelvic muscles occurring throughout the day. Lois normally doesn't talk about this sensitive subject, but now, she is telling all her friends and her clients about her QHHT® session and what transpired after.

On the day she called, she said she suddenly has been receiving downloads of information from her Higher Self. Lois is very happy and so excited that she felt compelled to call and share her news. Lois didn't even mention about the bladder problem during the QHHT® session, but the HS hears everything. The HS knows everything. The HS takes care of it.

* * *

For some clients, the healing aspect of a QHHT® session is hampered by emotional attachments that developed from childhood and/or young adulthood trauma. We practitioners must then dive a little deeper into the blocks and barriers to help the client heal and free themselves of their self-imposed bondages and other shenanigans that have manifested in their body and energy fields.

Let's look at several session stories where the HS removes entities that block healing.

19
ENTITIES & EMOTIONAL ATTACHMENTS

I have clients with entities blocking them from living a purposeful and meaningful life with joy and passion. In these client sessions, I have found that some of those who have had traumatic childhood experiences filled with fear; hate; anger; guilt; physical, emotional, and mental pain; lack; etc., develop attachments that cause a barrier to form, preventing the Higher Self from engaging in conversation while the subject is under hypnosis. This could be due to thought forms of unworthiness, shame, and guilt, for example.

Giving away your power to another is also a possible cause of entity attachment. This next session story of unwanted anger gives us an example of both thought form and earthbound disincarnate spirit attachment, because the client had both.

Attachments can appear in the form of earthbound disincarnate spirits, caught in the spirit realm looking for consolation, comfort, or the same feelings they were caught up in prior to their crossing out of the physical plane. In his book, *Spirit Releasement Therapy*[33], William Baldwin, D.D.S., Ph.D., points out that the earthbound spirit is driven by the ego's needs, memories, desires, emotions, and appetites in an attempt to interact with people, objects, or substances. These souls are confused and have no idea how they are affecting the soul they are attached to.

Imagine a spirit or ghost that is stuck in a house or building, walking endlessly back and forth. Their mere existence can cause the house or building to feel cold, negative, and uncomfortable for sentient beings such as humans, animals, and plants. They are interfering with the well being of the structure—unless an agreement can be reached that benefits all concerned, such as a business offering ghost tours or a television show featuring hauntings.

---

33 *Spirit Releasement Therapy*, William J. Baldwin, 1995

An animal or human spirit from a previous life can attach to the client and interfere in the client's current lifetime. This is illustrated in the first session story below, giving us an example of a father figure who attached many lifetimes ago and was still interfering in the client's current life. The attachment caused havoc and unwanted behaviors that were disruptive to the family unit.

Entities can be removed prior to a QHHT® session through inner work with a trained healer, shaman, or therapist. There are various modalities that are very effective in entity removal. These techniques range from ancient verbal chants, energy adjustments, and simple tools for removal with the assistance of the Ascended Masters and Archangel Michael in particular.

When I incarnated, I brought a technique with me that removes entities within seconds. It would be remiss of me not to mention that anytime something or someone is removed from the human body and energy fields, the area must be filled with something, such as golden light, love, or whatever the Higher Self recommends. A person can become physically ill when the balance is not restored immediately.

Entities or emotional attachments are aspects that can emerge in the QHHT® session. The practitioner can explore the root cause of the attachment, and the Higher Self can address the situation. It's a matter of the practitioner asking the HS questions that will bring forward information, such as reasons for the entities, and then for the practitioner to facilitate the removal of the entities by the Higher Self.

THE OVERLAY OF DARKNESS

My first QHHT® client that exhibited entities was a woman who had a session with a female healer with a special healing device from South America. After the session, instead of feeling light and integrated, she felt her connection to God/Source was gone. She felt "dead" inside. Carol felt she had an "overlay" of darkness ever since that session with the Sedona, Arizona, healer and the device that was used.

Carol explained it was like someone was trying to hijack her spirit. This really bothered her. She was familiar with my work, so she contacted me for a QHHT® session.

Additionally, there were communication problems with her mother-in-law she also wanted to address. She asked for a surrogate healing for her husband's shoulder pain, and for the removal of the overlay.

Carol was my ninth QHHT® client.

PAST LIFE

Carol finds herself in 1800s England, standing barefoot before a house on a large estate. She sees a horse-drawn carriage next to her. She is a thirty-year-old healthy female, named Martha, wearing a dress with lots of layers, and a bonnet. Martha looks again at her feet and now sees she has black strapped shoes with a small heel. Her brown hair is fashioned in a bun. She's not carrying anything, nor does she wear any jewelry. She's single and doesn't have a family.

B: *What do you do for the majority of your time?*

C: Knit. I have a basket.

B: *What type of food do you eat?*

C: Fruit and scones.

B: *Does that carriage belong to you?*

C: No. It's like an estate.

B: *Do you get the sense that the people that live there are wealthy?*

C: Yes.

Martha feels she is a guest and doesn't want to go inside the building because the people don't want her there. They don't understand her. Since Martha doesn't go inside the building, nor doing anything but stand there, I think the best thing to do is to go forward. We leave that scene and move to an important day.

C: I can't see.

B: *Is there something covering your eyes?*

C: There's darkness.

Dolores' voice in my right ear suggests I move Martha backward in time. I move her back to the previous scene, standing there in front of the estate with the carriage.

As before, no action is occurring here. I move her forward to the last day of that life. She hears ringing, but cannot tell me what object is making the sound, nor from where it emanates. She's sick with tuberculosis, dying with two unknown people (a woman and a man) at her bedside.

Martha cries a little when she sees her dead body from the other side, so I give her emotional support.

She shares that she sheltered herself in that life because she didn't want to be like the other people. They had strong opinions about how they thought she should be. Martha feels the purpose of that life was about choosing to be herself.

HIGHER SELF

They showed her this life because it's about a relationship. Carol's current lifetime husband was in the carriage. There was another woman in the carriage, and that woman is in her life now, as her mother-in-law. The purpose of showing Carol this lifetime was for her to see the woman in the carriage rejecting Martha. The lesson for Martha was to be true to herself even while many people were trying to change her.

> HS: There's something around her. It's like a bag. She needs to go back to the Source. She has to believe that this force is not stronger than her. She's got fear, and this is not helping her.

When I ask the HS to remove her fear, they oblige.

> B: *How can she best tap into the guidance with you? She's having trouble.*

> HS: There is a thing around her. We're working on it.

The HS finds the throat, heart, and solar plexus chakras closed off.

> HS: The second chakra is being cleared. The first chakra has an issue with sexual abuse. She is carrying some shame and guilt that

it was her fault. This is being cleared now. She needs some help with the heart chakra. She needs love.

At this moment, the Higher Self takes over my body and expresses the mathematical (star) language through my vocal cords.

Referencing the overlay, the HS says that it's breaking up.

The HS asks me to focus on sending love from my heart into Carol's heart. I can palpably feel a four-inch wide tube of energy flowing at high volume and speed from my heart to hers. I've never experienced this before in my life!

The HS finds some issues in her solar plexus. When I ask how can we support her, the HS replies, "You're doing it." I watch Carol breathing very deeply, moving and raising the top of her body off the bed, head tilted back, eyes open and rolling upward, then closing. The HS announces, "Looks like we just expelled the darkness."

Now, Carol is breathing fast and heavily. Without touching her, I command Carol to relax, and tell her she's okay. She calms instantly.

Barbara: *Is the healing complete?*

HS: She just got disconnected. She's reconnecting. There were two entities that came out of her solar plexus. She felt it, and she's a little scared.

B: *Are you letting her know that everything is safe? That she is loved and we are glad that she is here?*

HS: Yes, there's something on her right shoulder.

The HS asks for my assistance. As before, they use my mathematical language, which ends with a deep forced exhalation. I feel and cognitively know there are more entities, so I ask.

HS: They like to hide. They move into her first chakra.

B: *Well, it's time for them to leave. They are no longer needed.*

Now, the HS scan Carol's body and find that the entities move into her legs. After one more clearing, the entities finally go. The HS confirm that her energy fields and body are all clear and balanced. Love is infused into her entire body. I inquire about Carol's reconnection to God Source. The HS confirm this. They add she is much stronger now. I convey our appreciation.

HS: And so do we.

The HS grant a surrogate healing for her husband. We send love to him while he is playing on the golf course at the time of this session. He later reports feeling warmth in his shoulder when we were sending him the healing.

PARTING MESSAGE

HS: She is very loved, and she is much stronger than she knows. She does have the strength of ten thousand lions. If she could love herself, as much as she loves others, then there wouldn't be any of this going on. We are always with her, giving her love.

Carol was ecstatic coming up and out of the deep hypnosis. She was glowing like a ten-thousand watt light bulb! She said she felt integrated and in the Oneness with God. In an email message the next day she reported,

"*I feel amazing, Barb! It feels good to be me again with no dark ties, just love and light. I feel like I have been birthed! It is amazing, and I am looking forward to creating.*"

In another email the following week:

"*I wanted to let you know that I have been getting stronger every day, and yesterday, I had quite the amazing day filled with God Light. I am currently listening to the session and I feel like I have a better understanding of what took place. That is the LAST time I give my power away. This is awesome Barbara!!*"

Carol reported that her throat chakra is wide open, and she's speaking her truth to her mother-in-law, with kind words.

Keep in mind, it's the Higher Self that does the healing, guiding, and removal of emotional attachments, not the practitioner.

UNWANTED ANGER

Renee wants to know why she has so much anger inside, and why she has very deep depression. She shares that she has a history of an extremely violent childhood and multiple suicide attempts later in life. The theme is father-daughter. The medication she was placed on gave her suicidal ideation, so she stopped taking it. She battles with raging anger and feels she's literally at the end of her rope.

When she meditates, she finds herself in a cave looking up at the white light outside the cave, but she can never leave the cave. When she begins her past life regression, it is no surprise where she finds herself.

PAST LIFE

Renee is in a cave staring out of the cave at the white light. A couple of people (she could not see their faces) pick her up and fly to the sky. I ask Renee to look at her feet. They are webbed with three to four talons.

She's an owl. The people let her go. She flies away and lands on a mountain top. We explore what it is like being an owl and seeing with this type of vision, as owls do. Subsequently moving forward, she has baby owls. Then, she sees her body on the ground. For some unknown reason, she fell down to the ground.

She felt the lessons learned in that lifetime is that life is precious and short. It happened fast. The purpose of that lifetime was to know that those baby birds were the most significant reason for her life as a mother owl.

B: *What happened to your soul after you died?*

M: I'm not sure.

As you can imagine from her history, her ego is very protective of her. After dialoguing with the ego, it obliges to allow the HS to come forward.

Barbara: *Why did you show her that lifetime as an owl?*

Higher Self: I wanted her to know the ancient time.

B: *How does that apply to her current life?*

HS: Don't get so caught up in it. Just one small portion of everything.

The HS identifies a form of interference. I ask the HS to please check Renee's energy fields for any entities or attachments.

HS: Laughing. Yes. There are other energies around.

B: *Okay, please describe them for me.*

HS: A man. A big man. He's trying to come through here.

B: *What is his name?*

HS: Fred.

B: *How did Fred die in his past life?*

HS: A heart attack.

B: *And what was the year?*

HS: 1476.

B: *How long has Fred been with her?*

HS: About five-hundred years.

B: *What was the vulnerability that caused Fred to be attracted to Renee?*

HS: He's a father-like figure. He has a crown on his head. [Renee is seeing him]

B: *What was Renee's vulnerability that attracted her to him?*

HS: To be controlled.

B: *Did they have a past life together?*

HS: Yes.

B: *What was that relationship?*

HS: Father.

B: *And what was she?*

HS: The daughter.

B: *What physical, emotional, or mental symptoms has this caused?*

HS: Not good.

B: *Not good. What does that mean?*

HS: I don't have positive feelings from him.

B: *Why hasn't Fred gone into the Light?*

HS: He's trying to stay here with me.

B: *Is he willing to go now?*

HS: Okay.

B: *I'm speaking to Fred directly now. Fred, can you look up and see the light?*

A powerful energetic explosion occurs, emanating from Renee's body in an outward trajectory in all directions, as she begins to contort her body, with a diabolical laugh, kicking off the blanket across the room. As the energy moves in a spherical outburst, it passes through my body.

For the moment, I am pure consciousness, not holding onto or attaching myself to the energy. And in this moment, I am able to interpret this experience as, "This is cool, another form of love."

Renee's legs and arms flail, violently pounding on the bed mattress. Her head moves side to side, and the laughter evolves into a screaming type, while I kept repeating in a loud voice, "All right! All right!"

More laughter ensues.

I state in a commanding voice, "Stop! Stop now!"

Fred: [With a fiendish laughing voice] I got through! I got through!

B: *Stop!*

Fred: [More laughing]

B: *Stop!*

I repeat Renee's name very loudly.

The laughter stops. I lower my voice and repeat Renee's name one more time. She gives two strong exhalations.

In a commanding voice I tell Renee to relax.

Her breathing slows down.

B: *Fred, it's time for you to go now. I'm asking Archangel Michael to escort Fred into the light. You must go now.*

Renee: [More diabolical laughing and hissing sounds, as she expels "him" through her lungs]

The SC are removing this energy, and Renee says she has shortness of breath.

B: *Renee, you are fine. You are fine. Let him go. Let him go. Breathe deep. Let him go. He's leaving. I can feel the energy leaving your body. Breathe, nice and deep. Let him go. He's leaving. Let him go.*

Renee is now breathing deep and fast as if she had just run a marathon.

B: *May I please speak to Renee's HS please?*

HS: Yes.

B: *How is she now?*

HS: Good.

B: *You're monitoring her body and her energy systems; would you please confirm Fred is gone?*

HS: Yes.

B: *He's gone. Thank you. Would you please go through her body and energy systems and make any adjustments you need to do, to bring her to that beautiful calm, relaxed state. Let her know that everything is fine. She's done good work. Let me know when you're done.*

I ask the Higher Self to remove all attachments, cords, and implants from Renee and to send healing white light to seal the area.

B: *Do you find any other attachments in her body or energy fields?*

HS: Yes.

B: *Please describe.*

HS: Something attached, pulling in here [pointing to the root chakra area] at the bottom.

B: *Are you able to describe it for me?*

HS: I need to release it.

B: *Are you able to do that now for her? I ask you do it gently, lovingly.*

HS: Yes. It's gone.

B: *Thank you. What was it about?*

HS: It was an entity attached.

B: *What was its purpose?*

HS: Feeding off of her.

B: *What was it receiving from her?*

HS: Draining her energy.

B: *Did the entity go into the Light?*

HS: Yes.

B: *As you go inside of her and look around. Do you see any other entities or attachments?*

HS: No.

B: *Now, we send love and respect to these entities and send them back home where they belong, with much love.*

Renee begins shivering. Her Higher Self asks me to cover her with the blanket, and I do. I also ask the HS to please stabilize her temperature and energy systems. Renee stops shivering immediately.

The Higher Self says that the root cause of her depression was the attachments and that assuredly, Fred will not be returning.

We give our love and respect to the concept of Fred, for the lessons he provided for her. We continue on with the session. The HS conducts all of the healing and answers her questions. They complete the surrogate healings.

Immediately after the hypnosis, while eating food, she comments that her reality no longer feels like a dream. She can now feel.

This is what her husband wrote to me the day after her session: *"I just wanted to say how grateful I am and can't express enough thanks for the positive change that has already occurred in my wife and all of us. You definitely have clients and friends for life, and I will be sending my family members to you also. I can't wait for my session."*

FOLLOW-UP TWO DAYS POST SESSION VIA PHONE

"I have a new life! My vibration is so high. I can feel love, give love, and receive love, for the first time in my life! All my depression and anxiety are completely gone!"

My big concern was what it felt like for Renee to listen to her recording with the "screaming Fred" part.

She replied: "Listening to the screaming entity leave my body brings me peace. I've been listening to my session recording over and over. The separation from the entity feels very positive and releasing. I am filled with great joy that the entity soul is now into the light and is at peace. My higher self is showing me downloads and downloads of what I'll be creating next."

Renee and her Higher Self did all the work. I was just a facilitator of the session.

MANY ENTITIES

I facilitated this session for a young divorced mother with two small children. After her parents divorced when she was four years of age, Tina's father married another woman who was very mean to her. Tina's many family members are drinkers who want to get drunk when they have family gatherings.

Except for a sister who she is close to at times, her family verbally abuses her at the gatherings. She caves in to their judgments and cravings. She understands she's giving her power away to them when she does this, as she feels awful about herself afterwards.

Tina shares she has a dark spot on her lungs according to her chest X-rays. After showing her a home planet made of pink gaseous material, and a primitive life on Earth, the Higher Self comes through very nicely.

I request a body scan. The Higher Self finds heaviness in the throat from not speaking and from repressing her ideas, along with heaviness in the lungs. The root cause is the dark. Taking the dark and trying to face it by becoming it and making her body dark with cigarette smoking and pollution. That's not facing it. That's what she was doing. "Instead of facing it, I became it."

B: *Dear Higher Self, does she have any emotional attachments in her lungs?*

HS: Yes.

B: *Can you tell me about these entities?*

HS: It's darkness that masquerades as fun. Like enjoying it that I was feeling earlier, of people and beings, like, they look like [laughing] gargoyles.

B: *Gargoyles?*

[Client is laughing.]

HS: Small dark beings. I just let them in.

B: *How many are there?*

HS: A lot. Maybe ten.

B: *Ten of them?*

HS: Now that I'm looking at them, there's a lot more.

B: *When had these first appeared? Was it this life or a past life?*

HS: This life.

B: *When in this life did they show up?*

HS: When she was a teenager at age fifteen.

B: *What was going on in her life at the time, when they showed up? What were the circumstances?*

HS: It was dark. At my dad's house. It was darkness. It's hard to deal with. So, I tried to become with it.

B: *Were they attracted to her or was she attracted to them?*

HS: Both, but only because they said they were so much fun. They're from my stepmom.

B: *How did they come from the stepmother?*

HS: She gave them. She sent them to me.

B: *Was this done on another level?*

HS: Yes, not conscious at all. She hated me.

B: *Dear Higher Self, are you able to remove this group at this time?*

HS: Not at once. It's overwhelming. It's deep. This might shock too much.

B: *All right. So, how gently do you want to do this for her?*

HS: In thirds.

B: *In thirds? Do you mean like three at a time?*

HS: Like a third of the group. I see a stadium of little tiny black beings and they have to be removed. Like a third of the stadium. A third of the whole amount of them at a time.

At this point I'm wondering if I will need to do more sessions with Tina. I'm looking at my watch and wondering how much time this will take, because a stadium full of these entities is probably between forty thousand to one-hundred thousand, more or less. And then, the Higher Self surprises me.

B: *All right. Dear Higher Self, are you able to do that now?*

HS: Yes.

B: *And how are you doing this?*

HS: It looks like a hose, but it's like icy cold light. It's like a medical procedure freezing something off. [laughing]

B: *Okay. Can you tell me more about these dark beings? Where they originated from?*

HS: They originated from the stepmom.

B: *And before that?*

HS: In her mind.

B: *And before that?*

HS: In the center of the Earth. I see the tunnel that I came out of. They go down there.

B: *They came from the center of the Earth?*

HS: Yah. Dark lava molten.

B: *And in that, are they considered God?*

HS: Yes.

B: *All right. Do they have the spark of God within them? The light of God within them?*

HS: Yes.

B: *Are you able to escort them to the place where they belong?*

HS: Yes.

B: *Are they beginning to see themselves as the Light?*

HS: They are! They know that they are for a reason, and they only come out to teach.

B: *They served a purpose for her?*

HS: Someone gave them to her. She [stepmom] gave them to me.

B: *Are they able to leave now and go into the Light?*

HS: Yes.

B: *Thank you so much. Are you able to make it so no others can gather in the area they left from within her?*

HS: Yes.

B: *How are you doing that?*

HS: We fill up the area with golden light.

B: *Can she see them leaving?*

HS: They're already gone.

B: *They're already gone. Thank you so much. I'd like to take this opportunity to give our love and gratitude for those that have left, that they had served a purpose for her, she's learned from it, and now she's that much more healed. The others that are still there, are they witnessing this transformation that just occurred?*

HS: They're happy. They're happy to see it. They are there to teach a lesson. And as I'm looking at them, I see more golden white light coming in, and they're leaving a little bit more. They're happy. They're not bad.

B: *So they can see this being done gently and lovingly for Tina? Is she able to handle this okay?*

HS: Yes.

B: *If you replace the area with the beautiful golden light, will she feel whole and at peace, stable, and centered?*

HS: Yeah, but they're protective. So, they are leaving.

B: *The golden light is protective too. Is that correct?*

HS: Yeah, but they were dysfunctional because they were attached. So now I see most of them gone.

B: *Very good.*

HS: I see the light spreading, and they're not fighting it.

B: *This gives them a chance to evolve too.*

HS: Yes. Yeah, they're all gone.

B: *They are all gone now? Very good. And you're filling in with the golden light?*

HS: Yes.

B: *Very nice. Thank you so much. I'd like to express our love and gratitude for all those have now left to the Light so they can continue on their journey and evolve. We thank them for the purpose they have served. We're very grateful for this transformation. Thank you dear*

White [I made a Freudian slip by saying the name of my Higher Self] *Higher Self. And how is she feeling?*

HS: She feels better. There's a little burning, but it's okay.

B: *Where is the burning sensation located?*

HS: In her lungs.

B: *What is the burning sensation about?*

HS: An adjustment.

B: *Are you able to put a cooling, comfortable sensation in there and dial down any discomfort?*

HS: Yes. Peppermint. [laughing]

B: *Peppermint.* [Now I'm laughing] *I love it!*

The HS and I are laughing together.

B: *How does she feel now?*

HS: Better.

B: *Thank you so much! You do such great work. You mentioned about her throat heaviness. What can you do to help that?*

HS: She has to speak. It's more energetic. It's energy balled up. It's stuck and it wants to come out. They only way out is to speak, instead of swallowing it.

B: *Is she running an old mind program that prevents her from speaking her truth and standing up for herself?*

HS: Yes.

B: *Are you able to remove that old mind program and download and install a new program where she can speak her truth and stand up for herself?*

HS: Done.

B: *Thank you so much. And anything else you feel would be appropriate and the best for her.*

After her session, Tina feels lighter and happier. She can feel more oxygen going into her lungs. The difference was tangible for her.

It was a serendipitous experience for me when Tina's Higher Self changed its determination about removing a fraction of the entities. All of the entities were removed in one session, in a matter of minutes.

ONE DAY LATER...

On the phone with me, Tina shared she feels peace. Things that bothered her before, don't anymore. She didn't even want coffee in the morning, and this surprised her. Her communication with her Higher Self is stronger now.

Later in the week, Tina wrote a message via email:

"A quick update: I have had an amazing week!! It was full of miscommunications and trials, yet I was able to face mostly all of it without losing my power. I truly saw that everything is in divine order and I cannot waste my energy with worry."

ENCOUNTERS WITH REPTILIANS

Maureen was a forty year-old divorced woman, born in the eastern USA, the middle child of parents who didn't get along. They divorced when she was three years old.

Maureen doesn't remember her childhood. When she was eight months old, she had double pneumonia and almost died. Maureen's mother physically abused her constantly. Her classmates bullied and tormented her. She hated school and didn't finish. Maureen was very claircognizant, and her other extra senses showed up prominently in her everyday life too.

She went abroad and met her current boyfriend. Maureen shared with me that she has reptilian beings trying to kill her at night when she sleeps. Her boyfriend, who is also clairsentient and knowledgeable about these beings, meets her in the astral planes and saves her all the time. He doesn't get much sleep because of this activity. She wanted these entities removed now in her session.

Maureen didn't understand why she had to sleep with the lights on at night. She wanted to know why and have this addressed. I was intrigued to learn more about this too.

PAST LIFE

Maureen: It's a reptilian community.

Barbara: *Are you one of them? Or do you have another sense of your beingness?*

M: No, I'm not one of them.

B: *Do you have the sense you have a body?*

M: No.

B: *Please describe what you are seeing.*

M: I see a city of reptilians. They are going about their lives like we humans do.

B: *Is it daytime or night?*

M: It's about one in the afternoon.

B: *What do the buildings look like?*

M: What I would envision the future would look like. The buildings are floating in the sky. There's no vehicles that drive; they fly.

B: *Do you notice any colors?*

M: Everything looks like silvery like; it's very sterile. Not a lot of colors. I feel that someone is looking for me. I feel frightened.

B: *All right. You will be able to look at this as an observer. You will not feel any discomfort whatsoever. Can you step out of your beingness and turn around and tell me what you see?*

She begins breathing deeply. I remind her that she will not have any physical symptoms, and that she can look at this as an observer.

M: I see myself as a very tall being. I'm male or of that energy. I don't really look human.

B: *Do you have any garments?*

M: No.

B: *Describe your body shape.*

M: Thin, tall, mostly light, no anatomy, no clothes.

B: *Does that mean you don't need to wear clothing?*

M: Yes.

B: *Do you have a head?(yes) A face?(no) Is that part of your vehicle that you're in?*

M: Yes.

B: *Okay, so are you wearing this for protection from the environment?*

M: No, for those who are looking for me.

B: *Do you know why they are looking for you?*

M: Yes, they want to kill me.

B: *Why would they want to do that?*

M: I have a message they don't want me to get out.

B: *Okay. Who's the message for?*

M: Humans.

B: *Are you in some type of space vehicle?*

M: It's like a protective pod. A light vehicle. It transports me everywhere.

B: *Is it—are you the only one in there?*

M: Yes, it's attuned to my energy.

B: *So, what do you do with the majority of your time?*

M: I negotiate.

B: *What do you negotiate?*

M: The slaves. [crying] The slaves that they hold. And children. [crying]

B: *You will be able to look at this as an observer. Where are the slaves located?*

M: Everywhere! [crying] They're everywhere!

B: *Throughout the universe?*

M: Yes.

B: *Are you really good at negotiating?*

M: Most of the time, I guess.

B: *Did you train for that?*

M: Yes.

B: *Where did you train for that?*

M: In another light system, far, far from here.

B: *How does the negotiating work? Do you have to go somewhere to negotiate?*

M: There's a council that meets. It's about eight to nine of us. It depends.

B: *Please describe the council for me.*

M: There's so many amazing wonderful light beings from so many different parts of so many cosmos. We're here to unify and end these reptilians' hold of these human slaves. This is what I specialize in.

B: *You have a very valuable position then.*

M: They hate me. They hunt me.

B: *Are you the only one they hunt? Are there others who do negotiations?*

M: No, they hunt others too, not just me.

B: *Okay. You're always protected though, aren't you?*

M: [Smirky laugh and affirmative whisper]

B: *Yes, otherwise you wouldn't still be around, huh? Very nice. Who does all the protection for you?*

She gives me the name of her current boyfriend who will have a session tomorrow.

B: *Very nice.*

WE GO TO ANOTHER IMPORTANT DAY…

M: The Federation meeting, there's a lot of activity, a lot of talking, a lot of flurry because something has changed, something's different. Not sure of what that is. Unexpected change. It's a shift. It's a good thing actually.

B: *So, people are feeling good about this?*

M: Yes.

B: *So, what is the flurry about?*

M: They weren't expecting it. They're preparing for—it was a meeting that was last minute. We all gathered abruptly.

B: *Okay, was this meeting at a particular place?*

M: Orion, the star system.

B: *Was this a physical place?*

M: No, it was like a giant coliseum and it's not up and down, we are all looking at each other in a circle.

B: *A large amount of people-beings?*

M: Oh, yes!

B: *Let's move forward in time when you are given the information about the change and what the preparations are for.*

M: It's coming.

B: *What information is that?*

M: She is coming.

B: *Who is she?*

M: Creator.

B: *Creator?*

M: She's making her way here.

B: *Okay. Tell me more about the Creator being.*

M: I can't. She doesn't want me to.

B: *Okay. Is there a reason why?*

M: It's not the time.

B: *Is that time coming soon?*

M: Yes.

WE GO TO ANOTHER IMPORTANT DAY...

M: I'm here in this life. It's my daughter being born.

B: *Very lovely.*

M: She's—we're talking with each other telepathically. She's ready. Asking if I'm ready. It's special, an important moment.

B: *Is she here to do something special on the planet?*

M: Yes.

B: *Did she tell you what that is?*

M: No. It's hers. She won't tell me.

HIGHER SELF

Barbara: *Why did you show her the reptilian colony observer lifetime?*

Higher Self: So she understands the question of her fears.

B: *Is this a parallel life or something else?*

HS: Very much so.

B: *And what is she learning from it?*

HS: Peace.

The purpose of that lifetime was to help her understand she sees the peace only if she sees the opposite of peace.

B: *So, she learns from the contrast?(yes) I've met ambassadors of the universe in these sessions. Is she considered an ambassador?*

HS: Yes.

B: *She shared with us she doesn't remember much of her childhood. Could you help us to understand why?*

HS: She doesn't want to remember them.

B: *Who is "them"?*

HS: The reptilians. They like to scare her to keep her away.

B: *Did she see them from time to time when she was a child?*

HS: Yes.

B: *Are all reptilians of this nature?*

HS: No.

B: *I've met them before.*

HS: [whispered] So many beautiful ones. Not these.

B: *There seems to be bad apples in everything, huh?*

HS: Yeah.

B: *To help us learn to love and forgive. So, what is your assessment of her childhood? Is this something that needs to be changed or is it in her best interest to let it be?*

HS: Her mother is a reptilian. They have karma. [See Chapter 5 for another perspective on reptilians.]

B: *Can we address that karma now so she can be done with it?*

HS: It's already done.

B: *She's already forgiven her mother?*

HS: Yes.

B: *So there's no more karma between them?*

HS: No. They would hide under her bed. She thought and knew there was something there waiting for her. She could sense their anger. That's why she sleeps with the lights on.

B: *So that's the root cause of why she sleeps with the lights on at night? Are they still bothering her?*

HS: Sometimes. But, her boyfriend stops them.

B: *Okay, but are you also taking care of them too because you're protecting her?*

HS: Yes.

B: *Yes, very good. Is there anything you can do that they won't be coming around and bothering her? It would be nice. It would make her boyfriend's job a little easier too.*

HS: [Laughing] Yes he needs the relief.

B: *Could you do something now? You're really good at this.*

HS: Yes.

B: *What are you doing?*

HS: I'm closing the portal.

B: *Very nice.*

HS: She forgets to do this sometimes. It's like leaving the light on. She forgets to turn the light off when she leaves the room.

B: *Okay, so you've closed the portal. They won't be bugging her anymore.*

HS: No.

B: *Are you able to go into her mind and change that program of fear, so she can sleep with the lights off?*

HS: Yes.

B: *Very nice. How are you doing that?*

HS: Changing the software.

B: *Very nice. Are you putting in new software?*

HS: Completely new software. Not even re-programming.

B: *Very good. Not even an upgrade. Brand new.*

HS: This is something that most people haven't experienced yet.

B: *Can you tell me about it? I'm very curious.*

HS: Something the Lyrans[34,35] have been working on, for the new consciousness of humans. As your vibration and frequencies increase, you will automatically receive these new software programs. All humans will receive them eventually.

B: *Is there a particular vibration level to be at?*

HS: We can't say yet.

B: *Is it five-hundred or above?*

HS: That's child's play.

B: *So, it's easy?*

HS: It's way beyond what the human mind can understand at this time.

B: *However, if it's our vibration that must be raised, is it love or above?*

HS: Oh, yes.

B: *Very nice.*

HS: No longer is five-hundred the measure. That has changed. It's an old science.

B: *Is it? So how is vibration being measured now?*

HS: By the way it always has been, by love. What you will feel and know and experience, if you're looking for it, and I think you're asking me it's like a base reference…

---

34 https://www.solarsystemquick.com/universe/lyra-constellation.htm
35 http://galacticconnection.com/the-lion-people-feline-humanoid-et-race/

B: *To help explain to other humans. Sometimes the concepts you speak of are not found in the human language.*

HS: Eagles make sounds that we can't hear. They hold a vibration that is so pure, as does the condor and very rare golden hawks, not sure if that's what you call them here. [We have red tail hawks here.] No, it's the golden ones. Their vibration is the base, the range that they hold is now the new base, and it's above ten thousand. It's the New Earth.

B: *She would like to know has she had other extraterrestrial experiences besides the reptilians?*

HS: Yes.

B: *Would you care to share with her at this time?*

HS: The blue avians.

B: *Are you showing them to her now?*

HS: Yes.

B: *She spoke about wanting to help human beings about to transition. Is this something she should pursue or not?*

HS: It will happen naturally in their chosen way. They will find her.

B: *It will happen naturally. When?*

HS: When she starts her sound healing.

B: *She had a dream of a long line of people waiting to hug each other, and she felt so much love. When she woke up she had tears in her eyes. What were you trying to communicate to her with that dream?*

HS: There's no reason to hide. They're waiting for you. It's time you know it's what has held you back to release that so you can bring forward the wisdom you already carry, to help these beings that are waiting for you.

PARTING MESSAGE

> HS: She is part feline. It's from her home planet. Yes, Maureen, you are Lyran. Yes, it no longer exists, and you know why. Yes, when you were a child, that was your family, making sure you were guiding yourself down your path. They are always with you. And yes, we felt your sadness for losing your home planet. We know. We know you're sad. But they have found other places. They are safe. And yes, you may not have a home planet to go to anymore, but you found a new one. You know where that is. And yes, when you see those eyes looking at you, that is she. That is your primary guide. She's ready to show herself to you. Are you ready? And it is so.
>
> Don't worry. Be happy. Hug, hug, hug. It always fills you. It's okay, keep doing it. Don't stop. They need it. They need it.

Once the emotional attachments are released and transmuted by the Higher Self, there is no reason a person cannot go forward on their Earth journey in the human form and realize their dreams and share their gifts they brought for humanity. Sound healing, embracing their empathic abilities amid the chaos and distractions of society, retaining one's power and connection with God Source, are examples of a client's outcome from a QHHT® session.

In his *New Regression Therapy*[36], Greg McHugh, CCHt, shares the importance of identifying the presenting issues and allowing the client's emotional release by feeling the emotions experienced in the past life or what occurred earlier in this current life. These are several key components of the deep hypnosis and its healing aspect.

When entities are released, the client feels lighter. My clients comment how much lighter they feel upon coming out of their deep trance theta level hypnosis.

---

[36] *The New Regression Therapy*, Greg McHugh, 2nd Edition, 2017

20

SURROGATE HEALING

The surrogate healing feature of the QHHT® session is an opportunity for healing to be done for someone not in the session. I say opportunity because it's not a guarantee. We ask permission of the Subconscious to heal whomever the client has asked on their behalf. As long as we are not interfering with the client's soul path or missions, contracts and agreements, then healing is done. If there is interference with the client's soul path or free will, healing is not done. We move on.

Surrogate healings are beneficial for people who are unable to receive a personal QHHT® session. Examples are children under age eighteen, elderly people who can't follow directions or play along, and mental illness that impairs the client's access to the Higher Self, such as schizophrenia.

It is not necessary for a client to tell the person who is receiving a surrogate healing about the healing, nor for permission. The client's Higher Self will ask the Higher Self of the recipient if healing is appropriate, and convey the permission to the QHHT® practitioner. I imagine if the client told the recipient about the surrogate healing, there could be added pressure in the client's conscious mind to perform. In reality, this is not the case. Healing is beyond our control. When we enter into a QHHT® session and further into the surrogate healing feature, we go in with no expectations, only with intention and appreciation.

In my QHHT® client sessions, we've had healing done for children, parents, spouses, co-worker, neighbors, siblings, grandparents, pets, cars, homes, and situations. When I ask my client in the telephone pre-talk to consider a surrogate healing, I tell them it is easy to come up with the names. If it takes a long time to search for a name, then it probably isn't necessary because the name is being subconsciously blocked.

I've observed the surrogate healing confirmation from the HS occur in zero seconds to about one to two minutes. I've also experienced the client's HS talk with me through my Higher Self during the session interview to tell me they are already addressing the concern of the recipient. Clients return home from their hotel session the next day and see the results. Here are some examples:

POTTY TRAINING ACCOMPLISHED

In this session, the client wanted his three-year-old daughter to be potty trained. He was tired of cleaning her diapers. When he returned home from his QHHT® session in a hotel, his daughter no longer needed to wear diapers. This was a significant improvement in his life!

POSITIVE CHANGE IN SITUATION AT HOME

A client shared with me that there was much negative energy in her son's home while she was there visiting. Her grandson had a girlfriend that was causing drama. When my client returned to her son's home the day following her session, the grandson had broken up with the girlfriend and announced his decision to move across country. My client felt a whole different vibration in the house. It was calmer and much more positive.

GOLFER HUSBAND'S SHOULDER PAIN

During the session, the HS granted a surrogate healing for a client's husband. We sent love to him while he was playing on the golf course. He later reported feeling a warm feeling in his shoulder at the time we were sending the healing to him.

HUSBAND'S HIP PAIN AND SMOKING

After this client's session, she reported her husband's leg was healed with the pain gone. It took a few days, but he just woke up one day and decided that the cigars he was smoking were actually giving him nicotine poisoning, and quit. No more pain and no limping.

21
LIVING MULTIPLE SIMULTANEOUS LIVES, PLUS ASCENSION TIMELINE REVEALED

Living multiple lives at the same time is not a new concept. Years ago, I had heard we are living at least six to seven lives at the same time. We call these parallel lives. Although we are meant to focus on the current life we are living, it is interesting to find out about at least one other life. When I was introduced to this concept, my first thought was that I hope my other lives are happy, prosperous, and healthy. I figure we are all connected anyway, and that what we focus and express is reflected back to us.

The following session was a treat and deep honor for me to facilitate, not just for the information that came forward, but also for the client and her amazing life journey. I can't divulge everything about her. I will share what people can relate to, and what others may find particularly interesting.

Our paths had crossed back in the mid-nineties when she participated in a nationally televised event on Pier 39 in San Francisco, California. When Melissa described the event, my jaw dropped in my mind as I realized that I was there as a spectator with my ex-husband, Hoyt.

It boggles the mind to think in a span of more than twenty-three years, two people would be in the same space twice, to connect and later create a friendship, meeting in another state in the country, under the circumstances of a deep level trance hypnosis session.

Like many, Melissa was born into a dysfunctional family. However, her situation was markedly abusive. A stepfather plotted to kill her younger brother, who was just a child. The stepfather went to jail.

Melissa escaped the home environment as a young teenager. She married another teenager and became pregnant. There was a complication during the birth of her son, causing Melissa to hemorrhage.

She went into full cardiac arrest from massive blood loss. She had a premonition that this would happen before it did. She met Jesus on the other side. It was a beautiful and profound experience for her. Melissa was shown everything. She was given a choice: stay, and the baby will die, or return and her baby will live. From her compassionate motherly decision, she was slammed back into her body. Her baby boy was resuscitated back to life and spent many weeks in neonatal intensive care. He made a full recovery.

Years later, from hard physical work, Melissa sustained a ruptured disc and fractured vertebra in her lower spine. Although she had surgery for the injury, for several years, she complained of continued alternating intermittent leg pain. Her doctors thought she was just seeking attention.

She met an angel of a man who connected her with a world-renowned neurosurgeon. He was flabbergasted upon viewing her lower spinal magnetic resonance imaging film that she was able to walk at all. The neurosurgeon conducted a twelve-hour surgery involving the spinal nerves and bones.

Melissa came out of the recovery phase in the most intense pain. It was so much, it sent her out of her mind. If you read the first chapter of my autobiography, where I describe the excruciating pain that causes one to grab equipment and supplies without restraint or control, screaming obscenities at everyone in earshot, you'll understand the degree of Melissa's suffering. In other words, the pain causes a person to go completely bonkers.

During her hospitalization in the neurological intensive care unit, Melissa had to be tied down with restraints to keep the life-sustaining equipment on and in her, for her benefit. She said a nurse stayed at her bedside, refused to leave her, and the nurse looked like me. The nurse asked her about her children, because Melissa could not remember she had two sons. As Melissa came into consciousness and realized she had children, the nurse kept talking with her, helping her to calm down and be still. She made a full recovery. Melissa feels the nurse who cared for her saved her life.

Three months prior to this session, a dear friend mentioned to Melissa that she had said out loud, "I wish I could meet that nurse who saved my life in critical care." When Melissa first saw me, she knew without a doubt I was that nurse. She was hesitant to tell me, because she didn't want to shock me. She waited until her session to reveal this story in the interview. We agreed it would be a valid question to ask her Higher Self for confirmation of the existence of a parallel life that I'm living in another city, if only for curiosity sake and further confirmation for her knowledge.

One more piece of information: Melissa is very intuitive, and extremely accurate with her psychic skills, to the point that those connected and in communication with the star beings from other places in the universe and planes of existence, respect and revere her. Her concerns for the QHHT® session included her low energy, liver issues, teeth grinding, pain in the neck and lower back, and confirmation of her life purpose.

PAST LIFE

> Melissa: I'm in a library. There's a book in my hand. It says *Immortality* on the cover of the book.
>
> Barbara: As you look around the library, tell me what you see.
>
> M: I see a wood ladder that slides and the library is very tall. I'm curious. I feel like I might be a boy.

The boy describes the library with carved wood furniture and tall back chairs. He sees carved lions on the chair. The tables are round and tall. The library has different levels. Some are old and some are modern. The chair has an Aladdin type lamp at the bottom. As he looks up he sees different levels, such as shiny wood on the next level. It looks heavy.

Part of the library has a mulberry scent. It smells like wood too. There are a lot of books everywhere with tall bookshelves. Some of the books are from the 1800s. The one in his hand is from 1885. It's very quiet in this library. He's the only one in the library.

One of the artworks on the wall behind the chair with the lion carvings is a lady with a white collar up to her ears. Her gray hair is in a doughnut. The face of the lady in the painting looks stern. Around her neck is a thing with a bow. As he touches the painting, he can tell it was done with a feather brush.

Looking down at his feet, he sees an old maroon-colored rug with a floral print, covering the whole floor. Describing his feet, he sees…

M: My feet are kind of dry. They are young. They don't have shoes on very much. The top of my feet are clean.

Describing his clothes…

M: My pants don't go all the way down to my feet. They go down to just past my knees, where my shins would be. I have a white poofy blouse. It pulls on over my head. The pants are fashioned… it could be elastic, and a plastic button. My hair is short brown, kind of curly. My eyes are green. I think I have a healthy body. I spend a lot of time in the trees. No ornamentation on me. I have a coin in my pocket. Looking at the coin, it has a very big angel on it. It might be a medallion. It's made out of a thick metal. Flipping the medallion over, there's a name and a date. It's very worn. There's a "d." It's brass. The angel is carrying a torch in one hand. I feel like it's a guardian angel of some sort from Heaven. I feel this was given to me from a great, maybe my great grandfather.

B: *You're looking at this book called* Immortality. *Is this book opened at this moment?*

M: No. There were two. One said, *Mortality* and the other said, *Immortality*. I had to go up the ladder to get it. I chose the *Immortality* one because I like the way it sounded better. I don't want to open it quite yet.

B: *What happens next?*

M: I go outside to sit in a tree. There are big strong trees. The branches are really awesome to climb in. I love climbing trees. It's easy to climb with bare feet. I don't like shoes.

B: *Do you communicate with the trees?*

M: Yes. They love me. They tell me they are all girls. All trees are girls. They will always protect me. I love to hide in trees. People can't find me. It's calming and peaceful to be in a tree. I don't want to be bothered.

B: *Did you leave the book in the library?*

M: No, I still have it.

B: *Can you go to the place where you live?*

M: [Big sigh] It's kind of run-down. It's a wooden cabin in a rural area. We have goats and animals. We're not well to do, so we don't get what other people get. We have a cow. The wood is made of cedar, big logs. There's a chimney. I see all kinds of railroad stuff, old lanterns, books, a lot of knitting. There's an old rocking chair.

B: *Can you see yourself eating a meal?*

M: My great grandmother is coming. She does the cooking. We eat a lot of beans and rice. We eat a lot from the garden. The forks have three tines. We drink water and sometimes goat's milk. My great grandfather is here. My great grandfather is very happy. My great grandmother is kind of stern and kind of grumpy. She's a very wise person. She knows things before they happen. She keeps a bowl of walnuts, and she knows if I get one.

B: *What happens when you get one?*

M: She tells me [laughing] she knows I got it.

B: *Do you help her get the walnuts out of the trees?*

M: Yes. I love to crack them.

We move forward in that life, to another important day.

M: An important day for me is the ascension. Lots is happening. I see a world coming up out of a world.

B: *How does it feel?*

M: Awesome! It's like, what took so freakin' long? Yep. I see very tall beings, very different. Well, they are family, you know. They are blue and white. Some are pink. Some are golden colors and beautiful. Very tranquil, like transparent. I see two worlds. One is very dark and bad. It's the old world. And its literally dead, there's nothing, no life, no green, things are dead. Fish, mud things are dead, wildlife is dead. The people have dirty teeth.

B: *Are there still people there?*

M: Yep.

B: *Are you just observing this?*

M: Yep.

B: *How are you observing this?*

M: Because I see it from the other planet.

B: *How are you seeing it from the other planet?*

M: Because I can see right through it. I can see right down upon it. It's not X-ray vision, but kind of like, I don't know how I see it. My feet are not even on the ground.

Looking at herself:

M: Wow! I'm really white light. Very goddess. Very glowing. Wow! Light, flowing golden beautiful gown. Like chiffon. Like a wedding dress, but not a wedding dress. It's a goddess dress. I don't know how to explain it. I have a lot of gems. I have a solid gold crown. Oh my goodness! There are gems, rubies and sapphires and emeralds and citrines. [whispered] Beautiful…

B: *As you are looking at the old Earth, what happens next?*

M: It's dead. It's gone.

B: *What happens next for you?*

M: I go home.

B: *Where is home?*

M: My home is on the thirteenth dimension. Everything is structured differently.

B: *Tell me more, I'd love to hear about it.*

M: Oh man, this is so beautiful! In the thirteenth dimension we have structures kind of like third dimension, but they're not solid. They are transparent, like glass, but they are not. It's literally made up of minerals. So we have amethyst structures. We have aquamarine structures. Aquamarine is my most favorite structure at my home. It is my most favorite. Each structure does a particular thing to your energy field. Aquamarine is my most favorite.

B: *What does the aquamarine do for your energy field?*

M: It's like experiencing bliss all of the time. Not just in the moment. It's like being the color aqua in the structure. Everything is translucent. People on the old Earth plug into a source or and outlet. We do the same thing. We plug into Source.

B: *Do you know exactly where to put those crystals?*

M: Oh, yeah!

B: *Is this something you learned?*

M: I just know.

B: *When you plug those crystals in, what happens?*

M: It charges them up. We use them for everything. Sometimes those crystals, they go back in time. Sometimes they will go down like a spiral into other dimensions, they need help, that need intelligence. Our intelligence is very very rare on the thirteenth dimension. They are very powerful. They are colorful. We have a lot of colors. Everything is a brilliant, brilliant, brilliant. So, we do things for other dimensions. We are here to help with the light and keep much light for the planet. Mmm, mmmm [affirmative sound]. We work for other planetary associations. Actually, they are not associations. They are federations. We get the crystals all ready and work with the Lemurians. We have laser wands too. Our laser wands are used in the modern day surgeries. Are you familiar with laser wands?

B: *Yes.*

M: You have to be very careful because if you are not the right person you could blow them up.

B: *What causes the crystal to blow up when it's not in alignment with the person using it?*

M: Too much light. It has to be a distributed octave. Like, too much power could go boom, sometimes the crystal has to come down to neutral. Neutral can be powerful enough. It all depends on… because we use crystals for planets too, and plant life, water, and everything that is light.

B: *Do you have the ability to communicate with other beings?*

M: Yes.

B: *Do you have a council that you speak with?*

M: Yes.

B: *Does the council help you do what you do?*

M: Absolutely. I speak with the council of the Great Central Sun out of ten thousand suns.

B: *Are you able to speak with them now?*

M: Sure.

B: *Were they the ones that sent you to Earth?*

M: Yes.

B: *Why?*

M: To help humanity. They tell me to assist humanity for this greatest transformation ever known to the human existence. I don't like it on Earth as much as I do in my other home. They show me things, and they tell me things. I know things before they are going to happen. I knew when the tsunami was going to happen. [This is the Fukushima, Japan, tsunami of March 2011.] I predicted the tsunami. I can predict particularly weather things natural, to our natives. I feel earthquakes in my body. The ley lines are in me. Chile runs through me. When there's going to be an earthquake, my belly will swell big like I'm nine months pregnant. I feel it. I just know. My body is accurate. I'm used to it now.

HIGH COUNCIL

B: *May I speak with Melissa's High Council from the Great Central Sun?*

HC: [Melissa nods her head in the affirmative]

B: *Why did you choose to bring forward the lifetime as a little boy in the library and climbing trees?*

There is a slight change in Melissa's voice to a voice of great power and presence.

HC: To learn dimensions in an earthly way and to be able to be with nature and to learn to listen to nature, not people. I have to learn vibrations. Everything is vibration.

B: *Is she applying that in her current lifetime?*

HC: Absolutely. She's crystalline. It's purple, like amethyst and peridot right now.

B: *What is her purpose in this lifetime?*

HC: To wake people up. To get people to understand that love is the only way. To help people ascend because the Earth is ascending with or without the human race. To help people raise their vibration. To master themselves.

B: *How is she doing that?*

HC: She has a radio show on YouTube; she has done a lot of people, she has met a lot of people. We have encouraged her to write a book, but we have not been successful. Melissa is solar seeded. She can think of things and heal things and never have to leave her house. She puts things into the collective consciousness and does a lot of work via that avenue.

B: *She's right on track with her mission?*

HC: Yes.

B: *Is there any mission she hasn't completed?*

HC: We would like her to be on a bigger platform. We continuously tell her she is not to be behind the scenes becoming a shrinking violet. She likes to work one-on-one with the people, but we want her to not have to work so hard. We want her to be able to speak to droves of people on a bigger platform. We have not been successful in getting her on that platform.

B: *Why is that?*

HC: She's afraid.

B: *What is she afraid of?*

HC: Her life.

B: *What about her life?*

HC: Melissa has spent many lifetimes being made an example of. She has been burned at the stake. She has been tortured. She has suffered. These are soul fractures. These are lifetimes that her soul never forgets and the fear. She has a tremendous amount of fear.

B: *Would it be possible at this time to go into her mind and brain and look at those fear programs and remove them?*

HC: You may try.

B: *You're really good at this. And replace it with a program of confidence, of love, self worth…*

HC: Self worth is the work that needs to be done. Confidence is there. There are things that happened that don't happen to normal people. That is what generates the fear. People follow her. She's had some serious encounters.

B: *Would you be able to change that at this time?*

HC: Sure. Would love to change it.

B: *What dimension is she vibrating at?*

HC: Well, you see, Melissa is vibrating at multi dimensions, all depending on what is her agenda for the moment in time. So, yes, I can vibrate to high dimensions, but there is a lot going on in fourth dimension and a lot of work being done in that while there is fifth dimensional frequency going on, that is not happening unwillfully. The grid is still third dimension. It is being dismantled as we speak.

B: *Is it possible she can always be protected?*

HC: Yes. We know that, but she doesn't.

B: *How can you address this for her? Now would be a wonderful time.*

HC: We try. It has been a challenge.

B: *What does she need to do to help open that up; to crack that nut, so to speak?*

HC: Not fear who she really is. We have been working on this dilemma. She IS the queen of the universe. She will not own it. She is the high priestess of this era in the now. She let people go before her, even when it was her time. She did not have the self worth. Just stand in the right of passage. There is a thing called negative ego. Our beloved suffers greatly of the negative ego. She is very humble.

B: *Was that from all the tribulation and suffering she had as a child?*

HC: Yes.

B: *Is it possible to let the ego know it loves and protects her as you do, the High Council? Is it possible for the ego to merge with you, as others have done, and that no one can harm her?*

HC: Lifetimes of harm has been done to the beloved that see, most people are born. And when they are born with nurture, they are nurtured through the pregnancy. This was not the case.

B: *Why did she choose this form of experience and all these lessons?*

HC: She signed a contract to heal the lineage. She signed a very, very complex contract. She signed a contract to heal the wounds of her mother, and the lineage of femininity, and not just in her lineage, but in femininity. She also signed a contract to heal the masculine energy.

B: *Has that been fulfilled?*

HC: Oh, she has worked lifetimes of work in one lifetime. We love her. The work that she has done is beyond human comprehension. Beyond.

Melissa is crying now.

HC: We had to get her here, and this is how she came. And everything matters in her existence, and now she came here and in her lineage bloodline. For she is the bloodline of Jesus. She is here to be the feminine representative of the Christ Consciousness. For it will be the Divine feminine that anchors peace. We had to bring the lineage of Sananda. It's just a modern day version, you see. So, for her, she just doesn't want to be ridiculed. She does not like nonsense and shenanigans at all. At all!

B: *So, going forward from today, what would you like her to do?*

HC: We would like for her to simply embrace who she is. That's all. And to continue to shine the light that she is.

B: *Are you able to do a body scan at this time?*

HC: Perhaps.

B: *As you go through her body, would you share with us what you find, the root cause of it and anything that needs to be removed, altered, dissolved, healed? And let me know when you are done.*

HC: There is lungs. Are you wanting an articulation?

B: *Yes, it's beneficial when she hears this. What are you finding in her lungs?*

HC: Despair.

B: *What is it about?*

HC: Her mother. Things a mother would never say to a child. Never. Never. We are very challenged in healing the heart. [With emotion] The heart needs to be strengthened. [Crying] I don't know if I can do this.

B: *What does she need?*

HC: [Crying] Love. Just love. To know that she's loved.

B: *Is she done suffering with this? Isn't it time?*

HC: Yes.

B: *How are you doing that?*

Melissa breathes deeply. I can feel the energy transmuting. I give her energetic and emotional support.

HC: They have to clear up programming.

B: *Would you please do this now?*

HC: We have to defragment, defragment, defragment.

B: *After the defragmentation is done, will you reprogram her so she remembers and feels she is loved beyond all measure? That she learned these lessons so that she would learn love? To love herself. That no one can diminish her light. We would like you to heal Melissa's heart at this time. Would you please do that for us?*

HC: [more deep breathing]

B: *Is she feeling it?*

HC: [Head nod in the affirmative, more deep breathing] Part of her healing is the cathartic cry that is healing the heart. It helps to heal. Melissa never wants to be a victim of her circumstances. This can be a challenge. She won't cry. She just keeps going. She needs to cry. Healing.

B: *Do you recommend she do some crying therapy after this session?*

HC: If she hasn't cried it out already. She has cried more today than we have seen in a long time.

B: *It's been very healing, what you've been doing with her today. We are very grateful for this.*

HC: We are, as she is.

B: *As you look into her lungs now. How do they look?*

HC: Definitely clearer. Not so much inflammation.

B: *While we are there, she mentioned she smokes cigarettes. Has that had any affect on her lungs at all?*

HC: Not so much the lungs. But we do perceive what is happening to her gums.

B: *Does she want to continue smoking cigarettes?*

HC: She does and she doesn't. This is complexity, you see. She enjoys it; yet, she doesn't. Ironically, she cannot stand the smell of cigarettes. But she loves to smoke. She is one of the most, mmmm, considerate smokers we've ever seen.

B: *You have the ability to maintain our health, no matter what we put into our bodies. Is this correct?*

HC: Yes.

B: *So, what would you like to do as far as her smoking cigarettes?*

HC: Well, we have brought this to her. She has a pyramid. She knows to put anything that needs to be cleared into the pyramid. But she gets complacent and she also gets busy sometimes. You see, for her, she needs to take time for herself. That's the biggest thing.

B: *Self nurturing. That's self love, isn't it?*

HC: Correct.

B: *What types of things would you like her to do, to nurture herself?*

HC: Nurturing herself is a challenge we have with her, and for her. We have tried to teach her to nurture herself. She will have a massage, but by the time she gets one, it's not enjoyable. Too much pain. So massage becomes painful. We suggest things such as pedicures, nurturing, and pampering of that nature. She does not feel worthy. She will only go if something is gifted to her in a certificate. She will not actually go out and get it for herself.

B: *Can you change that mind program right now?*

HC: Yes.

B: *Thank you. While you're doing that, may I continue to ask questions?*

HC: Yes.

B: *Is the location move another perfection of her creations?*

HC: Yes, we want to take her to a much larger scale. There are some things around the corner that we can't quite talk about now, because it is her surprise. We are waiting for the perfect opportunity in the solitary moment to reveal that.

B: *Is she on track with that location, good enough to know?*

HC: Yes.

B: *Thank you so much. As you go through her body, what else did you find?*

HC: Digestive and endocrine. Melissa is going to be the first human to go from density to light without dying. Does this make sense? We have never had this experience. People pass and they receive their light body. Do you understand?

B: *Yes.*

HC: The next dynamics happening, it will be dissolving the density. She is the very first person that will dissolve. Density, you see. The carbon body enter into light. For she has to do it first, so that the collective can come through. And it will not be as hard on them. During that process... are you familiar with the process of diamonds? and the pressure? and the heat? and the lava? and the molten? and the churning? That is what is needed to make a diamond out of carbon. She is a living, breathing, diamond crystal that looks like a human. She is the thirteenth crystal skull. She is of great intelligence. They think they found them. She is the conscious one. When they found the twelve skulls, they didn't think one would be conscious to activate the existing twelve skulls. To activate a much higher crystalline intelligence, which is all needed for the new Earth. While we have great compassion and great love for our beloved, we understand the contract she signed is to experience and be the sacrifice, if you will, so humanity can experience a light body. It took a lot of courage for her to sign such a big contract. Her contract is huge. It's actually beyond human comprehension, including yours. So, that is why she suffers, and we are always there to alleviate as much of the suffering as we possibly can.

B: *And the digestive system, are you making changes there?*

HC: Yes. These changes are happening. In particular in the product lines we are putting in her grasp, in order to access. She has been on only four glasses of the Vital Reds. She is not yet aware this product helps her. You see, she needs berries. Too much density is not good for her. Do you understand?

B: *Yes.*

HC: We have been trying to get her to understand. This has been a process. So we are working on helping her to make better, wiser decisions in her diet and her eating.

B: *Is there anything you'd like to share with her about her eating and diet?*

HC: She is on the right path and receiving the nutrients that her body and organs need through the product we put on her email. You see?

B: *Very good.*

HC: We put it right there for her. She responded appropriately, and she now has the product. She drank her fourth glass this morning, but it will take at least fourteen days for great relief.

B: *What about her endocrine system?*

HC: Well, this too is very complex. She has things that don't need medical attention. It's part of who she is, and it's part of her contract. Most importantly it's part of the process must go through as part of the contract, you see, as becoming, and going from carbon density to light.

B: *Does that include the discomfort from her surgical areas?*

HC: Correct. You see, this was put into her for her to be a conduit. She is a conduit to Heaven. To Earth. To Heaven. Not only is she a conduit, a messenger for us, she is for Mother Earth as well.

B: *Are you able to dial down that discomfort for her, especially when there's barometric and temperature changes?*

HC: Yes. We have been working on this. Remember, there have been things going on in your dimension that are very disturbing, if you will. There are a lot of chemicals on your planet. They are in your skies, your soil, your water, your air, they are everywhere. All of your resources have been contaminated. We contend with this. We are almost done with our ascension process. The ascension process will be complete in 2021.[37] So if our beloved can just hang in there, and continue to rest, rest, rest. She needs to know that is okay. She needs to rest. She is a conduit.

B: *And everything is being provided for. Is that correct?*

HC: Correct. Now, getting her to, hmmmm, believe that is a challenge on our part.

B: *Let's help her to remember that and to know it with all her heart, she's very important here. She must take care of herself, in order for everything to occur.*

HC: Correct.

B: *Because she's affecting everybody, because we're all connected.*

HC: Absolutely!

B: *How's her liver?*

HC: Her liver is better than what she realizes. You see, we have had to choreograph some things that have helped her. She suspects

---

37 This was the first time I heard an actual year for the ascension during a QHHT® session I facilitated. I have purposely refrained from reading material or viewing videos on the subject of the ascension. The year 2021 would be in sync with the number of souls who have already ascended, reflected in the number of Sacred Souls (90 percent or more) on planet Earth as of 2016, as shared in Chapter 16.

this, but as with anybody who is having the human experience, it's important to understand she doesn't have anybody else to go to but us, you see. She is the wisdom that people seek. She was stung by a scorpion September of 2016. This venom healed a lot of things in her body and a lot of viruses.

B: *Did it take care of the Hepatitis C?*

HC: Yes!

B: *Wonderful.*

HC: But, she does not know she's in remission. She knows it on one level, but our challenge with her is for her to know it on the human level. Much easier said than done. Particularly with this one.

B: *I know you're working behind the scenes with her, correct?*

HC: Absolutely. There's free will. You see, when she was younger, she was much easier to work with her, as a young, young child. As she grows older in her biological age, it becomes more difficult. She has to remember she is a super being in a human body. She must go through the human experience. This is the challenge for all involved in the mission and her mission. She knows it herself, but she doesn't want other people to know it. This is the comment behind the curtain shrinking violet. We have done everything. We know. It is a challenge for us. We brought you to her and her to you. We are also hoping you will also help in some of these matters. We speak to her all the time, you see? It is like your mother and father talking to you all the time. Then it becomes nagging, would you say? Have you had this experience?

B: *Yes, we sometimes have to be told over and over until it sinks into our thick skulls in the third dimension.*

HC: Hers is a crystal and has the hardness of seven. It's pretty hard.

B: *On the Moh's scale.*

HC: Yes! For her, we are like her parents. We're just nagging her. That is our dilemma.

B: *I know your job is to love and guide us. I know the amount of your love and compassion; we cannot even begin to fathom it.*

HC: Correct.

B: *We do appreciate all your efforts.*

HC: Thank you.

B: *You are most welcome. Does she still need to take that medicine for her liver?*

HC: We prefer she doesn't. She's not to get into anger. The liver is the seat of anger. With the proper nutrition and the proper energy, she will not need this treatment.

B: *What about her teeth grinding?*

HC: We have helped her and released some pressure points recently in the last forty-eight hours on her jaws and her face. This has been helpful to her. We have also provided instructions for things most recently… will also help to relieve this. The problem is she locks her jaws and channels her pain that way.

B: *How is the hardware in her body?*

HC: The hardware is a challenge for her because of the geographical location, which she resides in. She could very easily move somewhere else; however, we know this will not happen. We don't want her somewhere else. She belongs here. So, for her condition, it would be best for her to live somewhere such as Arizona. Somewhere different climate, but this is part of the contract, part of the sacrifice. We have been working on it. We have come a long ways; however, we are now working on her neck and shoulder pain. The top of the spine will compromise the bottom and the lower spine and vice versa. She is like an accordion, you see.

B: *Regarding the child with an ocular motor apraxia from the administration of vaccines.*

HC: We cannot get the parents of the platinum rays to fully comprehend and understand, as there is so much fear generated in your society, and schools and etc., etc. As far as your vaccinations. You see immunizations does not mean vaccination. This is very challenging. This is something we are contending with on a wave level. The children that are the platinum rays do not need any foreign objects or foreign medicine put in them. This can sometimes reverse their state of perfection and cause problems. This is what has happened to Matthew. If the parents do not listen to their wise mother, then he will continue to suffer consequences from their ignorance. We are working on all of these matters.[38]

B: *Regarding her dog who is present in this QHHT® session...*

HC: He is not a dog. He is an angel. He is there to protect her. He is there to keep the excess of toxic energies or vibrations that could potentially infiltrate her magnetic energy field off of her. This can cause his digestion system to be a little finicky.

B: *Is this what causes him to be hyperactive?*

HC: Yes.

B: *Is there anything he needs now? Anything that can be done to help him?*

HC: He needs energy. She needs to give him more baths. He cannot release energy when there's "feets" of snow. He needs Earth. In the summer, he will discharge energy into the Earth. He knows exactly what to do.

B: *Is he feeling better now, especially today?*

HC: Yes. He was very excited and loves the energy emanating from your being.

This sweet dog was rolling over and over when he came into the office for the session, acting giddy with delight as dogs do.

[Silence on my part.]

HC: Any further questions?

---

[38] This is the first session where the grandparent specifically asked about vaccinations.

B: *Yes, thank you. Any other issues as you go through her body that you'd like to bring to her consciousness?*

HC: Not at this time.

B: *Is your healing complete?*

HC: We are working. We cannot say her healing is complete complete, as her contract is a little different. We are working on it and we are working on it. Things are happening. We are preparing her for something extraordinary. This cannot be spoke of at this time.

B: *What will surprise Melissa the most about what was said here today?*

HC: That is a very excellent question. Probably that she doesn't have to quit smoking unless she truly wants to. That will be the most surprising to her. She feels she needs to quit or that we are pressuring her to quit. She feels a pressure to quit.

B: *When we agreed for her to have a session, what did you hope she'd receive the most from the session?*

HC: Confirmation and validation of her brilliance.

B: *Is there anything else you wish we would have asked about today?*

HC: Not at this time.

B: *What is the most important thing Melissa didn't know about herself that you would like to explain to her?*

HC: How highly she is revered to all the planets. How much she is loved and appreciated. We truly appreciate the work that she does. Not just for her family, but on a global scale. It's beyond her comprehension.

PARTING MESSAGE

HC: We can't wait for your surprise, beloved. Be well and be happy. Know that it's coming right around the corner. We promise you.

It's interesting to note that this other life I have is as a woman who is a critical care nurse. I'm retired from my career as a critical care nurse and now devote myself to the healing and intuitive work I offer people. The QHHT® modality I offer as a practitioner is icing on the cake for my life's work. I enjoy helping people help themselves.

22

DOLORES APPEARS

When Dolores appeared in my bedroom back in 2014, twenty-two days after her passing, she told me she would be with me during the sessions I facilitate for QHHT® clients. It wasn't a promise or guarantee, but rather, a statement of fact that I integrated as a private feature in my QHHT® practice.

If I need her during a session for consultation, she is there, and the information is downloaded into my mind within seconds. Although I heard her voice in my right ear in the beginning sessions, by the nineteenth session, she "sat back," so to speak, and let me facilitate without her input.

Since then, she will give guidance when needed, even when I'm unaware I need guidance. I'm forever grateful for her infinite knowledge and the wisdom she imparts from time to time. Dolores often comments about the session while I'm driving home. Her comments are always positive and constructive.

The following compilation of Dolores' presence is offered as confirmation that she indeed is with QHHT® practitioners all over the world.

DOLORES SPEAKS

At the one hour and forty-minute mark in the session interview for the client I wrote about in Chapter 17: The Eternal Question, I heard a loud tone in my right ear. Then, Dolores said this,

"We have a lot to do here, Barbara. Let's wrap this up."

The client heard the tone coming out of my ear while she sat on the other sofa!

Seasoned QHHT® practitioners who worked with Dolores confirmed this is how she talked. I like Dolores' style: Let's cut to the chase and get down to business. Her style parallels mine.

Many of my clients can hear Dolores' voice from my vocal cords as I read the induction script she wrote for the purpose of relaxing the client into the deep level of trance hypnosis. They find it comforting and reassuring that our beloved Dolores is present.

FEELING DOLORES' PRESENCE

People who are extremely clairsentient like Amanda in the "Clink-clink" session story of Chapter 14, can feel unseen things and spirits. When I arrived at Amanda's apartment, she gasped and stepped back, unsteady on her feet.

I asked her, "What is it?"

She replied, "Dolores is with you!"

With a smile I added, "Yes she is!"

CLIENT SEES DOLORES THE NIGHT BEFORE HER SESSION

During a de-briefing after the session, a client shared her experience of seeing Dolores in her bedroom. When she saw my notebook with Dolores' photo on the front, she said, "That's the woman who was sitting on my bed last night!"

When she expressed her experience, I received chills of confirmation in my body that it was indeed our beloved Dolores.

I WALKED WITH DOLORES

In the session of the creator being who "Got the Giggles" in Chapter 13, when I began his session, he shared confirmation of Dolores' presence. His session was facilitated at a local hotel. When I got out of my vehicle and walked across the parking lot to the lobby, I sensed Dolores was walking beside me. I had not felt this before. I slowed my pace down to keep with hers, as if she were still in her earthly body.

When my client and I began his interview, I acknowledged Dolores' presence in the room.

He replied, "Yes, she walked with you across the parking lot."

I hadn't shared this experience with him until he said those words.

I SAW DOLORES

In this session, while I was speaking with the client's Higher Self, I looked to my left and saw Dolores sitting in the stuffed chair at the foot of the bed, plain as day! For me, she looked just like she did in her videos and photos. Remember, I didn't meet her when she was alive in this incarnation.

Feeling a little bit surprised, I watched Dolores cock her head to the side, with her eyes pointed in the direction of my client, as if saying, "Get back to your client."

DOLORES SITS ON THE BED

My clairvoyant life coach client in Chapter 14: ET Past Life, didn't want to alarm me, so he waited until we walked out to my car to tell me he saw Dolores sitting on the end of the bed while he was laying there, waiting for me to come out of the bathroom before the start of the hypnosis.

PHOTOS OF DOLORES' SIGNS

A whimsical form of communication from Dolores are the road signs I've seen close to my QHHT® client homes. Here are a couple:

Dolores is known for her love of cardinals

We're on the right path with Dolores' QHHT®

23
BEYOND QUANTUM HEALING

Just as the Reiki modality is a launching point or gateway to the healing gifts we brought with us into this human incarnation, Quantum Healing Hypnosis Technique^{SM} is becoming the launching point for practitioners who are creating their own modalities, separate from QHHT®. These practitioners are no longer calling their hypnosis technique QHHT® and thus, people who are seeking a different form of healing, specifically are guided to these practitioners.

There are practitioners who specialize in entity removal, removing old and unhealthy habits, contact with extraterrestrials, etc. Likewise, there are QHHT® practitioners who are not ready to explore the concept of extraterrestrials or entities. The client must follow their inner guidance in selecting the perfect healing practitioner for themselves, just as much as selecting a medical doctor that fits their needs for health and wellness goals.

For myself, I'm a generalist. Meaning, I will address any subject, any concept. It goes along with my last ten years as an emergency room nurse, specializing also in critical care, I was drawn specifically to work in the ER in order to interface with all the branches of medicine, such as pediatrics, OB-GYN, trauma, non-critical concerns, initial drug overdose management, community medicine, riding with the fire department paramedics, etc.

We were never meant to stop at one plateau on our journey. Boldly, we go further, one step at a time, trusting and knowing all is well. All is in Divine order, no matter how it presents in our reality. Once we open our healing gifts, we are obligated to engage, share, offer, or allow. We were sent here to dear Mother Earth to be of assistance in the ascension and the healing of the planet. Through our service to humanity, our missions are accomplished.

Julia Cannon has continued the legacy her mother began, through the offering of QHHT® classes around the world, and in publishing her mother's unfinished books. In that legacy is the intention that the technique is not to be changed. Some seek QHHT® practitioners because they want the modality be facilitated just like Dolores did it. Others seek QHHT® trained practitioners because they have a particular expertise and/or healing gift that they resonate with.

Practitioners can facilitate the hypnosis session as pure QHHT®, or they facilitate hypnosis sessions as conventional hypnosis. Trained hypnotherapists are creating cutting-edge new techniques in hypnotherapy. They are flexible and open to their client's needs, with full open disclosure prior to facilitation of the hypnosis. Clients can find QHHT® practitioners on the official website[39] by searching through the levels of practitioners, viewing the professional profile and contacting the practitioner directly.

Additionally, the official website offers background historical information about Dolores Cannon and QHHT®. Interested readers can check out blog articles too. QHHT® practitioners have a special portal to the support forum where they can ask questions and share session stories confidentially.

After many years working side by side with Dolores, QHHT® Practitioner Candace Craw-Goldman created the Quantum Healers and Beyond Quantum Healing platforms. She is the one who created the original worldwide support forum for QHHT® practitioners to share session stories in a confidential manner for educational purposes, with the blessing of Dolores Cannon. The Quantum Healers[40] global directory allows clients to find practitioners not only certified in QHHT®, but also other modalities. By entering a ZIP Code or location, with one computer click, a person can find a list of practitioners in their local area, view the professional profile, and contact the practitioner directly.

Although Dolores created a beautiful modality that works even for new practitioners coming out of the Level 1 course, I wonder about those who have a healing gift modality that is innate. In other words, they have no control over the healing occurring just by being in the presence of the client. I am one of those. In my autobiography,

---

39 https://www.qhhtofficial.com/

40 https://www.quantumhealers.com/

I describe the mathematical star language playing in my mind 24/7. I have no control over it because I came into this incarnation to freely heal. I'm able to push it back so I can converse with people and do my everyday activities without interference. I'm also able to bring the mathematical star language forward and speak it. When I facilitate a QHHT® session, that healing is occurring without my say so. It is not me doing the healing. It's the Higher Self in conjunction with the other person's Higher Self. I can't stop it, nor prevent it from manifesting healing in the client.

Another point I've been wondering about for some time, is how the QHHT® modality will be kept pure when more and more gifted souls incarnate onto the planet Earth, bringing with them innate modalities such as mine and greater ones. How can we keep the world the same, without evolution of humans? I don't think we can. Do we want to limit the natural progression of healing? I don't think so.

I believe that some day we will no longer need Western medicine because injuries and illness will not be required for our lessons. What about when we humans are existing in 5D all the time? I also add it is my opinion that QHHT® is based in Creator Source. QHHT® is a highly evolved modality when applied as intended, from the heart and compassion of the practitioner.

The following dialogue is from a QHHT® session when I was under hypnosis with fellow practitioner, Virginia. In it is an example of the star mathematical language from and through my Higher Self:

> Virginia: *Thank you. I would like to know about the metal in my leg. I'm wondering if it's affecting the chi flowing through my body. And I'm wondering if there's any specific remedy should take place. Should I have surgery to remove the metal? Can the metal be dissolved metaphysically or should it be left alone?*
>
> HS: [Silence. Big sigh] It can be left alone, but we would like to do an adjustment for you.
>
> V: *Please do.*
>
> HS: We are doing our assessment at this moment. [Silence] The chi is flowing. How would you like the metal to be gone? How would you like to have a normal knee?

V: *I would like that very much.*

HS: All right. This will have to be done in stages, my dear. So, we will begin now. And we would like you to have a session with Barbara. Would you be willing my dear?

V: *Yes.*

HS: Alright. [Silence. Big sigh. Mathematical language is spoken, then tones at the end of each "sentence." Big sigh, breath work.] First stage is done.

V: *How long should I wait for the next phase with Barbara?*

HS: You have an opportunity at the end of this course. This week.

ANOTHER MESSAGE FROM DOLORES

During a session, I ask to speak with Dolores about QHHT®, through QHHT® practitioner Virginia's Subconscious.

>Barbara: *I'd like to ask for permission for the HS to recede and for Dolores to come forward. Is this possible?*
>
>Dolores: I'm here.

Virginia's voice turns soft and her facial expression softens. Dolores' voice is louder than Virginia's HS voice, even though Virginia's HS voice is strong and clear, and has good volume.

>Barbara: *Hi, Dolores! Do you have a message for us? I know you've been observing us.*
>
>Dolores: I'm going to suggest that you not limit yourself. I'm going to suggest that you recognize yourselves as powerful as you really are. I'm very proud of the learning that you are doing. It's very comforting for me to see the learning continue, and the technique to be perpetuated and expanded. The larger and the greater that we can make this technique more beneficial to all of those on the Earth, for the enlightened souls on the Earth will be. The coming times will be difficult and more traumatic, and the more connected we are, to the larger picture, the better the situation will be for those, the more pleasant the situation will be. And the changes that are

necessary for the transition will be better facilitated. [The] work is critically important. It is not the only modality that is important, but it is a technique that is important. Do not limit your belief or your power. Do you follow me?

B: *Yes!*

D: And Barbara, as I told you, on Monday, relax, have fun, experiment, grow. How do children grow? By playing. How do they learn? By playing. You are my children. Play. Grow. Learn. It is so sad to see a child sit at a desk, spelling words over and over again. Boring, repetitious, work; not play. Make this play. Make this life, not work. I need to put a boundary on this, though. And understand that orthodoxy. Please understand this word. Go look it up in the dictionary; it's important. Remember, it took me forty-five plus years to learn what I learned. So, changes without experimentation and validation, they might be fun, they might be play, but the orthodoxy should still be respected.

B: *Yes, thank you. You mentioned in one of my sessions and in my QHHT® session with Virginia, you learned from me. Can you share with me? I'm curious.*

D: The way you manipulate energy, Barbara, is masterful. If you could see you, the control and command that you have of energy is masterful, and this is why you were selected for the portal work. This work requires very advanced energy manipulation. This is impressive. From where I am today, I'm learning from you, how to do this!

PARTING MESSAGE FROM DOLORES

D: Expand, do not limit yourself in your practice. Think big!

Every one of my clients gives me inspiration. Their life stories are truly a testament to the master they are. Just like in my legal nurse consultant career, tackling the most complex and convoluted medical cases, I am given the challenging QHHT® clients who come with blockages, entities, emotional trauma experiences, diseases, and conditions that are considered incurable or untreatable.

Dolores knew I was writing a book about my QHHT® client sessions and my experiences being the facilitator of these sessions. She orchestrated the perfect client coming to me at the perfect moment, as I learned and tested the verbiage of my questioning and curiosity. Dolores knows the meaning of a vibrational match, and she indeed delivers.

CONCLUSION

The first two years of providing QHHT® sessions for clients was located in the Greater Phoenix, Arizona, area. My life circumstances changed, enabling me to move my location in the late fall of 2016. I joined Virginia's QHHT® office as an independent contractor in a small town in Colorado. I completed my Higher Self missions there and returned to the Phoenix area the following spring.

The session stories I shared in this book are from the first three years as a QHHT® practitioner. There are more to be told. In this sacred service, I am finding each person's life story is a beautiful symphony filled with the drama of the human condition and the subtle melodies of love lived and lost. It is a deep honor to be a witness to the amazing transformation of people who have struggled within their lessons and still have garnered the strength and courage to meet themselves, in order to dive deep into their healing. Quantum Healing Hypnosis Technique℠ is well worth the trip of amazing discoveries about oneself. To have someone at your side, traveling with you across space and time, to get to the root cause of your illness and turmoil, and ultimately release them, is a gift you give yourself, that keeps on giving. The icing on the cake is that it doesn't matter how the session is experienced. The client receives exactly what they need.

Virginia, you're right. QHHT® is the tangible evidence that proves people heal themselves. Thank you!

ABOUT THE AUTHOR

Barbara Becker is a certified hypnotherapist, author, retired critical care and emergency room nurse, angel communicator and trance channel. She speaks a mathematical star energy language that heals. She facilitates Quantum Healing Hypnosis Technique[SM] sessions in the Greater Phoenix Arizona area. Her clients come from all over North America, and Hawaii. She has been interviewed on Internet television and radio shows. Please visit her website at www.BarbaraBeckerHealing.com.

www.ingramcontent.com/pod-product-compliance
Lightning Source LLC
Chambersburg PA
CBHW050615300426
44112CB00012B/1515